Imperialism, Labour and the New Woman

Olive Schreiner's social theory

Liz Stanley

sociologypress

Published by:
sociologypress
Room 003, 32 Old Elvet, Durham DH1 3HN, UK
http://www.sociologypress.co.uk

sociologypress is supported by the British Sociological Association. It furthers
the Association's aim of promoting the discipline of sociology and disseminating
sociological knowledge.

British Library Cataloguing in Publication Data
A CIP catalogue record for this book is available from the British Library

ISBN 1 903457 04 1

Printed and bound by York Publishing Services, 64 Hallfield Road, Layerthorpe, York
YO31 7ZQ enqs@yps-publishing.co.uk

Contents

Acknowledgements

When writing a book has spanned three continents and half a dozen major archives, and its production has traded on the goodwill and knowledge of many others working 'in the field', there are inevitably debts of gratitude to be acknowledged. I am very pleased to be able to do this here.

The initial funding to carry out archive work, first in the USA, then in South Africa, was provided by the British Academy. I am particularly pleased to publicly acknowledge the Academy's early assistance for my Schreiner research, as without it neither this book nor a number of related publications would have been written. More recently, the UK's Economic and Social Research Council (ESRC) has funded an extended period of work on Schreiner's letters through a Research Fellowship, and I would also like to gratefully acknowledge its support here.

This manuscript was first contemplated while I was the Faculty of Arts Senior Research Fellow at the University of Auckland, New Zealand, during 1998. I am grateful to the University of Auckland for this opportunity for an extended period of thinking, reading and writing, and to the Women's Studies Centre and its head, Maureen Molloy, for hosting me. After returning from Auckland, I then rewrote the manuscript substantially, having done that terrible thing, changed my mind; and I am grateful to colleagues and friends for putting up with a great deal of distraction and 'elsewhereness' while I did so. The final work on the manuscript was carried out during 2000, while I held the Hugh Le May Fellowship at Rhodes University, South Africa. I would like to thank Rhodes University for awarding me the Fellowship and also the Sociology Department and its head, Fred Hendricks, for hosting me. I am particularly grateful to Jan and Este Coetzee for their kindness, help and friendship, and to Denise Wisch for making my life in the department run so well.

I am extremely grateful to all the archives I have worked in, including for permissions to publish material that has appeared in chapters and journal articles over the years: in South Africa, the Cory Library, Rhodes University, Grahamstown; the National English Literary Museum, Grahamstown; the Manuscripts and Archives Department of the University of Cape Town Library; the South African Library, Cape Town; and the Cullen Library (Historical Papers) at the University of Witwatersrand, Johannesburg; in the USA, the Harry Ransome Humanities Research Center, University of Texas, Austin; and in the UK, Sheffield City Archives, and the University of London.

There are personal debts of gratitude I would like to acknowledge and also to give thanks for advice and help gratefully received. My thanks to: Arai Noriko, Joyce Avrech Berkman, Lucy Bland, Leila Carnill, Jan Coetzee, Alison Donnell, Rosemary Du Plessis, Debbie Epstein, Michael Erben, Betty Govinden, Lesley Hart at UCT, Steve Hicks, Renee Hoagland, Alison Laurie, Ronit Lentin, Jackie Loos at SAL, Magda Michelsens, Maureen Molloy, Colin Murray, Karen Phillips from Sage Publications, Michele Pickover from Wits, Pauline Polkey, Vicki Robinson, Monty Roodt, Sara Scott, Charlotte Sing, Dale Spender, Ann Torlesse at NELM, Volker Wedekind, and Heather Worth. My love and thanks to Heather for interesting ideas, good dinners, excellent wine, much laughter and the great gift of friendship; if new technology is worth the candle, it will bring the UK and New Zealand closer together. Joyce Berkman and Volker Wedekind read and commented in depth on the manuscript; I am very grateful to them both and have done my best to use all of their suggestions. I am of course responsible for the errors and infelicities that this book may contain; but then, I am largely responsible for whatever strengths it has as well. I hope the first are outweighed by the second and that reading it is half as interesting as writing it has been.

Sue Wise has put up with living with Olive Schreiner for a good few years now. She will know that, once Ms Schreiner goes off to the publisher for the last time, then an equally expensive and time-consuming other woman will make her entrance in our lives, so she is doubtless pleased that my work on Schreiner is to continue for a while yet, even though her erstwhile friend Emily Hobhouse (with 27,000 dead women and children) has joined her. Thank you dearest Sue, including for the last nearly thirty years of love, lust and a good many excellent dinners as well. A public goodbye goes to the furry St Thomas Aquinas (deceased), otherwise known as Our Sweet Tom. I hope his brothers Alfred Schutz and Precious Mackenzie and his sister Jessye Norman will at some point forgive my various gallivantings round the world.

This book is in memory of Pauline Polkey, who was generous and good fun, and who cared a good deal about getting 'women's lives into print'. She is much missed.

A Note on Referencing

Details of the main archive sources used are provided in the Appendix on 'Schreiner Writings and Archive Collections'. The main abbreviations are as follows:

Cory: Cory Library, Rhodes University, Grahamstown, South Africa

NELM: National English Literary Museum, Grahamstown, South Africa

SAL: South African Library, Cape Town, South Africa

UCT: University of Cape Town, South Africa

Wits Findlay: Findlay Family Papers, Historical Papers, University of Witswatersrand, Johannesburg, South Africa

London Pearson: Karl Pearson Collection, University of London, UK

Sheffield Carpenter: Edward Carpenter Collection, Sheffield City Archives, UK

HRC: Humanities Research Center, University of Texas at Austin, USA

There are endnotes to each chapter. In these, references to Olive Schreiner's own publications take the form of an abbreviated title (and page numbers where relevant); details about the particular editions used will be found in the Appendix on 'Schreiner Writings and Archive Collections'. Cronwright-Schreiner's *The Letters of Olive Schreiner* is referred to in endnotes as *The Letters*, while other references in the endnotes follow the Harvard style. Full publishing information is provided in the 'References and annotated bibliography' at the end of the book.

Where Olive Schreiner's published writings are referred to using a short form, the abbreviations are:

An African Farm: The Story of An African Farm

Dream Life: Dream Life and Real Life

Trooper Peter: Trooper Peter Halket of Mashonaland

An English South African's View: An English South African's View of the Situation

W&L: Woman and Labour

Thoughts: Thoughts on South Africa

Stories: Stories, Dreams and Allegories

FMTM: From Man to Man

The Dawn: The Dawn of Civilisation

Around 5,000 Schreiner letters are archived and are crucial to present-day scholarship. References in the text to Schreiner unpublished letters take the form of: author to recipient, date, archive location. I also provide a published source wherever possible for the convenience of readers who want to read whole letters. Thus, for example, 'OS to Betty Molteno, 22 May 1896, UCT Schreiner, Rive 1988 p. 277' indicates this letter from Olive Schreiner to Betty Molteno is located in the University of Cape Town Schreiner collection and is also published in Richard Rive's edition of the published letters.

Epigraph

Human life may be painted according to two methods. There is the stage method. According to that each character is duly marshalled at first, and ticketed; we know with an immutable certainty that at the right crises each one will reappear and act his part, and, when the curtain falls, all will stand before it bowing. There is a sense of satisfaction in this, and of completeness. But there is another method – the method of the life we all lead. Here nothing can be prophesied. There is a strange coming and going of feet. Men appear, act and re-act upon each other, and pass away. When the crisis comes the man who would fit it does not return. When the curtain falls no one is ready. When the footlights are brightest they are blown out; and what the name of the play is no one knows. If there sits a spectator who knows, he sits so high that the players in the gaslight cannot hear his breathing. Life may be painted according to either method; but the methods are different. The canons of criticism that bear upon the one cut cruelly upon the other.
(from the "Preface", *The Story of An African Farm*, 2nd edition on)

Chapter 1

Enter Olive Schreiner

The Woman Who Fits the Crisis

The Victorian writer and theorist Olive Schreiner was the quintessential feminist, as well as a woman of power, persuasion and fiery magnetism and much worldly fame, both for her own generation and also that which followed. Born in 1855 in the Cape Colony of what later became South Africa, while living in England in her late twenties Schreiner published a best-selling and extremely influential novel, *The Story of An African Farm*. By her mid-thirties this was followed by first one highly successful collection of allegorical stories with a feminist and socialist message, *Dreams*, and then another, *Dream Life and Real Life*. During her forties and living in South Africa again, Schreiner published a number of politically interventionist pamphlets and essays, such as *The Political Situation*, *An English South African's View of the Situation* and *Closer Union*, and a string of equally contentious newspaper and journal articles (some also published in the posthumous collection *Thoughts on South Africa*), as well as the controversial, indeed at the time highly scandalous, anti-imperialist allegorical novella *Trooper Peter Halket of Mashonaland*. Then in her fifties Olive Schreiner published one of the most influential works of feminist theory of its day, *Woman and Labour*.

In addition to her published writings, Olive Schreiner wrote many thousands of letters, some in correspondences that lasted thirty or forty years, sent to her family members, close friends and a wide circle of 'like-minded' people. Many of her correspondents were, or became, influential public figures; and it is clear from their memoirs and autobiographies that Schreiner's letters and friendship were a source of great influence. As well as these private letters, she also published a large number of public letters, including on prostitution, 'race' matters, the South African War, the use of the 'Taal' or Afrikaans in South Africa, trades union issues, discrimination against Jews, and conscientious objection during the 1914–1918 War. Like her other publications, these reached very wide audiences in the USA as well as Britain and South Africa and were widely published in translation in many other countries too.

Starting with her estranged husband, who was also her first biographer, it has been claimed that Schreiner wrote little. This claim is contentious, but the high sales and the influential nature of what she published are certain. An experimental writer across a variety of writing genres, Olive Schreiner's trademark was to combine different forms of writing in anti-realist texts that, regardless of whether these were 'fictional' or 'factual' in character, were supremely concerned with ideas. Schreiner was always insistent that it was her ideas and writings that mattered, and her as an individual not at all. Her contemporaries were variously admiring, intrigued, stimulated, provoked and sometimes appalled and outraged by her writing, and some regarded her as one of the most important social commentators of her age. She saw her ideas as bound together by an ethics that combined feminism and socialism and extended to writing itself. In this book, Schreiner is viewed as a social theorist of a particularly interesting kind, for a number of reasons including that her work encompassed writing itself, was concerned with the local and grounded, and was responsive to the particularities of events and circumstances. It also refused being confined to 'fit (theoretical) work for women' and her analytic attention was engaged by labour, value, 'race', class, capital and capitalism, imperialism, and the nature of nation-states, quite as much as by domestic divisions of labour, relations between women and men, motherhood, and feminism as a social movement.

Olive Schreiner was keenly interested in and immersed within the intellectual and political events of her time, starting when she arrived in Britain from the Cape Colony in 1881, continuing after she returned to South Africa in late 1889, and also when she lived in Britain again between 1913 and 1920. But Schreiner was also a contemplative, someone who spent much time alone living in a very spartan way.[1] Wherever she lived, she had a 'walking up and down' place, where she paced and told herself stories as she had done since a young child; and as they developed into written form, these stories crossed different genres, including the novel, the allegory,[2] the short story, the polemic, the essay, and the theoretical treatise.

Schreiner was concerned with 'the method of life', as the quotation from her "Preface" to An African Farm (used as the epigraph to this book) phrases it, that is, with how social life should be represented. For her, it was the 'strange coming and going of feet' in a world in which 'nothing can be prophesied' which characterised social life and which therefore required 'the method of life' as an aesthetic and also an ethic for writing about it. Life certainly has a pattern – a play, footlights, curtains, people; but this is a broken fragmented pattern – there is no name to the play, the lights are unexpectedly extinguished, there is the unaccountable absence of key players, and the curtain falls in mid-action. Similar depictions of social life recur in Schreiner's writings, and 'the method of life' encapsulates three important aspects of her approach.

First, she rejected, on ethical as well as aesthetic grounds, purportedly realist ways of writing and she attempted to construct an alternative. Second, she insisted on the priority of life over art, seeing writing as an intervention for ethical, political or other purposes and not an end in itself. And third, she wanted to convey the unpredictability of life's events, their often perplexing quality, and to develop an ethically appropriate representational response. Analytically speaking, Schreiner's work was concerned with capitalism and imperialism, class and socialism, 'the woman question' and 'the native question' and the relation of both to 'the labour question', as well as with aggression and war, and the relationship of life to death in a world characterised more often by cruelty and exploitation than by mutuality and egalitarianism. Both her ethics and her aesthetics influenced her understanding of these issues, her ideas about the relationship between writing and life, and her experiments within and across genre conventions.

Comments about Olive Schreiner abound in the letters, diaries and memoirs of British friends and acquaintances such as Eleanor Marx, Havelock Ellis, Amy Levy, Edith Nesbit, Alice Corthorn, Isabella Ford, Kate Salt, Mary Brown,

Herbert Spencer, Oscar Wilde, William Gladstone, W.B. Yeats, W.T. Stead, Edward Carpenter, Karl Pearson, Margaret Harkness, Henrietta Müller, Beatrice Webb and Elisabeth Cobb. They do so in those of South African political contemporaries such as Mohandas K. Gandhi, Cecil Rhodes, John X. Merriman, James Rose Innes and Jan Smuts; and in those of friends such as Betty Molteno and Alice Greene, Mary Sauer and Anna Purcell. They also appear in those of members of the succeeding feminist generation in Britain, including Constance Lytton, Adela Riviers Smith, Frederick and Emmeline Pethick-Lawrence, Sylvia Pankhurst, Rebecca West and Vera Brittain. For all these people, Schreiner was a presence to be reckoned with, a person of enormous magnetism to attract but sometimes to repel, and to whom respect or at least recognition was due even when closeness or admiration was not.

Mary Brown, a close friend who became a liberal feminist, Poor Law Guardian and active in the Cooperative Movement in Britain, described their first meeting in South Africa:

> I shall never forget my first impressions ... Backwards and forwards on the long front step she walked rapidly with her small hands clenched behind her back ... She was talking to herself, and though she looked before her, she was quite oblivious of her surroundings ... I asked Mrs Hemming what she was doing, and she replied: 'She is like that sometimes. Even when she was a child she would walk about, talking to herself.' ... I felt as if I had seen something uncanny ... she seemed to hold me with a sort of subtle power.[3]

Olive Renier, the adopted daughter of Schreiner's particularly close friend Alice Corthorn, wrote about the impact of Schreiner's death in 1920 on Corthorn and her circle, conveying something of Schreiner's compelling character: "... for my mother and the host of Olive Schreiner's friends, it meant the end of a great turbulent force in their lives ... this woman whom they so passionately loved".[4]

This 'turbulence' was connected to Schreiner's expression of strong conviction and emotion. For example, Joan Hodgson, a much younger acquaintance, asked Schreiner's advice in 1914 about whether she should support the British war effort or not. In reply, Schreiner:

> was overwhelming; my little arguments never so much as got themselves marshalled, let alone suffered defeat. 'Rivers in flood' is the simile that presents itself ... She sat on a hard sofa, with her feet tucked up under her ... and denounced like a prophet of Israel ... I never came up against that side of her again, and yet at the time awe put friendship quite out of court.[5]

And even at her sunniest there was the same intensity, but now engaging and amusing, which caught up other people in Schreiner's mood. A self-aware woman, she sometimes used this quite deliberately. Her husband Samuel 'Cron' Cronwright, for instance, described an occasion when she did so on his behalf:

> in England ... two or three of her closest women friends being present ... she was asked what sort of man was it that she contemplated marrying ... Olive staggered them by saying: 'He's a man who can knock eight

other men down with his fists one after the other!' And she said this with every sign of joy and admiration ... Her friends were inexpressibly shocked and were absolutely staggered when Olive began to dance around the room ... throwing her arms up, punching the air ... They gazed ... and then with cries of 'Oh Olive! Olive!' went off into uncontrollable shrieks of laughter, and, while they held their sides and rocked with laughter, with the tears running down their cheeks, Olive bounded about the room.[6]

Schreiner's friend, the socialist and homosexual rights campaigner Edward Carpenter, invoked a related aspect of her personality:

Beneath the mobile and almost merry-seeming exterior of Olive Schreiner there ran a vein of intense determination ... crossed and countered by an ineradicable pessimism ... her ... books realize and force the reader to realize almost too keenly the pain and evil of the world.[7]

This is an interesting remark applied *to An African Farm* (Mary Brown had also recoiled from Schreiner's insistent gaze upon 'pain and evil' in this novel), although Carpenter was actually aiming at her pacifism and their disagreement about British militarism during the 1914–1918 War – an erstwhile pacifist, he had backtracked on his principles and found it irksome when Schreiner reminded him of his earlier moral and political teachings.

Schreiner's ethical stand impressed many other people, none the less. After her death in 1920, the South African politician John X. Merriman wrote to Schreiner's husband Cronwright that: "Above all I admire the contempt she felt for the worship of the golden calf, the divinity whom we, for our sins, have sent up as the idol in our midst here in South Africa".[8] Merriman opposed women's rights, and in his diary in 1891 he wrote that Schreiner was "a very clever woman who would be happier if she believed in what the rest of her sex believe", while in a 1900 entry he noted that his wife Agnes had heard Schreiner hold transfixed 1,300 people at a women's peace meeting against the South African War,[9] but he felt that she was "illogical, appealing to feeling rather than reason".[10] And of course Schreiner's person, views and writings did not appeal to everyone. For instance, in London of the 1880s, some women acquaintances, including Elisabeth Cobb and Beatrice Potter (later Webb), found her too 'wild', loud and unrestrained, although it was the same cheerful refusal to stay within the conventions of bourgeois ladyhood that attracted others to her.[11] Moreover, disentangling personal remarks from disagreement about principles can be difficult. Thus Oscar Wilde developed a literary aesthetics very different from Olive Schreiner's and, although apparently commenting to the poet W.B. Yeats on Schreiner's naiveté, he was also dismissing her aesthetics when he wrote that: "Olive Schreiner ... is staying in the East End because that is the only place where people do not wear masks upon their faces, but I have told her that I live in the West End because nothing in life interests me but the mask".[12]

But some men reacted much more positively to Schreiner's character, aesthetics and politics. Thus regarding Schreiner's speech at the same Cape Town peace meeting in 1900 that had fuelled Merriman's dismissal, the radical journalist and pro-women's suffrage campaigner Henry Nevinson (who, unlike Merriman, had actually been present) provided an admiring account of Schreiner's magnetic force of character and he observed that "when she began to speak she was ... transfigured into flame ... I have heard much indignant eloquence, but never such a molten torrent of white hot rage. When it suddenly ceased the large audience ... could hardly gasp"; he also commented "if Mrs Schreiner had ordered them to storm Government House, they would have thrown themselves on the bayonets".[13] And Mohandas K. Gandhi, who lived and worked in South Africa from 1893 to 1913, appreciatively noted that Schreiner lived with a black woman servant and treated her as an equal, sharing household tasks with her; and he commented that Schreiner was "a friend of the Indians equally with the Natives of South Africa. She knew no distinction between white and black races".[14]

Olive Schreiner's work profoundly impacted on people's lives quite as much as her presence. The feminist prison reform and birth control campaigner Constance Lytton, for instance, described how recounting Schreiner's feminist allegory "Three dreams in a desert" had affected a group of suffragettes in Holloway prison:

> The Freedom League prisoners were soon to be released. The Sabbath day ... evening hours sometimes produced an atmosphere almost of amiability ... We were to gather round the fire, and to tell yarns, stories or poems ... Mrs Lawrence ... then repeated Olive Schreiner's 'Three Dreams in a Desert' ... this 'Dream' seemed scarcely an allegory. The words hit out a bare literal description of the pilgrimage of women. It fell on our ears more like an ABC railway guide ... than a figurative parable ... We dispersed and went back to our hard beds ... content.[15]

Even in more ordinary circumstances, Schreiner's writing could have life-changing impact. The writer and pacifist Vera Brittain, for example, described what a turning point reading one of Schreiner's books had been for her:

> To Olive Schreiner's Woman and Labour – that 'Bible of the Woman's Movement' which sounded to the world of 1911 as insistent and inspiring as a trumpet-call summoning the faithful to a vital crusade – was due my final acceptance of feminism ... I can still tingle with the excitement of the passage which reinforced me ... in my determination to go to college and at least prepare for a type of life more independent than that of a Buxton young lady: 'We take all labour for our province!'[16]

A similar response to W&L also moved D.L. Hobman, later to be one of Schreiner's biographers, to become a feminist:

> No other book, before and since, has ever had so sudden or so lasting an influence on me as this one; and I have since heard from some of my contemporaries that the effect on them in their own youth was equally startling.[17]

It is difficult now to appreciate the narrow intolerant confines of the Cape Colony, Natal and the neighbouring Boer Republics of the Transvaal and the

Orange Free State in the 1870s, and so the impact on people of the unworldly and shabby young woman who startlingly flouted convention by her freethinking and plain-speaking ways. Or indeed of the world-famous woman in the 1890s who, though probably 'no better than she might be', had returned, to analyse and criticise and find politics in white South Africa morally wanting. An important aspect of Schreiner's sharp drawing-in of moral breath here concerned her critique of imperial and South African politics in relation to 'race' matters. Although in our time Schreiner has been criticised for her ideas about 'race', it is important to remember that the 1990s and early 2000s are not the same as the 1890s and early 1900s, and that it is really not sensible to dismiss Schreiner's writings because these might seem wanting according to political standards operating now, a hundred years after she wrote them. Some of these criticisms in fact judge Schreiner for views and ideas held by characters in her novels, rather than being contained in archival material that tell us about Olive Schreiner herself. There are of course enormous problems in assuming that Schreiner's characters 'are' her and that her opinions and beliefs can be confidently read off from theirs, not least because her archived letters make clear she often intended these as deeply ironic statements within a piece of writing and not as her own views at all.

Also Schreiner's ideas about 'race' changed considerably from the 1870s to 1920, moving from liberal patronage to determined opposition to racism and segregation. Schreiner herself remarked that her ideas changed through her increasing personal knowledge of black people; it also occurred because of dramatic upheavals in South Africa over this period that changed the meaning of 'race' itself. What remained constant was Schreiner's public commitment to full democracy on the same terms for all people, women as well as men, black people as well as white, and her life-long opposition to and analytically sharp critique of capitalism and imperialism.

Olive Schreiner wanted to construct feminist and socialist politics and ethics which saw ideas as powerful sources of change in the world while fully recognising the importance of material factors, and which also rejected seeing biology as deterministic. Her analytical approach, together with her innovative approach to writing, makes Schreiner's work of much present-day relevance, across the social sciences and humanities, but also for those 'common readers', to use Virginia Woolf's phrase, who are concerned with analytical ideas. Her work addresses important issues for people now – it isn't simply of historical significance. This is because Schreiner was an experimental writer whose work, both fictional and factual, was concerned with the intellectual issues lying behind what are now called 'modernism' and 'postmodernism', but which clearly pre-date both 'isms'. She was very much a 'woman of her time' regarding the issues which engaged her, as a 'New Woman' who was a feminist, socialist and freethinking opponent of imperialism, deeply concerned with the sexual exploitation of women and the dehumanising of labour, who saw 'the labour question' and 'race' as inextricably intertwined in South Africa, and who came to see 'the woman question' as central to the dynamics of 'race' as well.

Olive Schreiner as a writer and social theorist, and also as an emblematic figure, played a fascinating and important part in the development of western feminist ideas, with her work being influential from the 1880s through to the

1930s. She was also a major intellectual presence for other circles and collectivities of people, in South Africa, Britain, North America, Japan, Russia and elsewhere,[18] as well as for many individual people who came across her work and felt their ideas and lives changed by it. A lesson that Schreiner learnt early in her life is that ideas know no frontiers, an important aspect of their ability to encourage change in the world. The sense of ethical purpose she invested in her writing, and her sadness and frustration later in her life that serious ill-health – asthma and a congenital heart problem – prevented her from completing a number of the writing projects she had engaged on, are closely connected to this.

As well as Olive Schreiner's undoubted personal and intellectual influence on feminist politics of her day and that following, she was also an active behind-the-scenes presence in South African political life during what was a temporally short, but politically crucial, period of time from 1890 to 1913. This is rarely mentioned, let alone discussed, in present-day historiography concerning Anglo-Boer politics, the South African War of 1899–1902, the Union of the formerly separate states (the Boer Republics of the Orange Free State and the South African Republic, usually known as the Transvaal; and the British colonies of Natal and the Cape Colony) in 1910, and then the subsequent development of the foundational apparatus of the apartheid state in the 1913 Natives Land Act. But here the archive papers of South African white male liberal (relatively) politicians of the day, such as her brother Will Schreiner, Jacobus Sauer, James Rose Innes, John X. Merriman, and the considerably less liberal younger politician Jan Smuts, provide the grounds for a rather different assessment.

These private documents were written contemporaneously, rather than retrospectively with the wish to carefully construct public accounts, and they do not expunge Schreiner's activities and influence. This was not because these men believed women should play a prominent role in political life (Merriman, for instance, insisted that women should have no place in 'public' life or the professions), nor was it because they experienced Schreiner as anything other than 'difficult' on questions of gender and 'race', and nor was it because they accepted her political views and her refusal to 'know her place' and leave politics to men. It was rather because of their often grudging awareness that she was an astute commentator who could reach a large international audience; and they tried to make use of this when it suited them, and resist it when it did not. But the awareness was real enough. Schreiner's brother Will had been Cecil Rhodes' Attorney General, then became Prime Minister of the Cape Colony for a brief tumultuous period between August 1898 and June 1900, and later he became South African High Commissioner in London. However, Ruth Farringdon wrote that, when Will Schreiner's ashes were re-interred in South Africa in 1922:

> There was a ceremony at the re-interment at which General Smuts spoke eulogistically of him and his more widely famous sister, Olive Schreiner. Later, speaking to me of this occasion, he said, 'She was a very great woman; a very great woman. She was a greater woman than her brother was a man; but of course I could not say that'.[19]

Just how prescient Schreiner's political thinking could be is indicated by her developing ideas about imperialism and racism in South Africa. Her open opposition from 1891 on to Cecil Rhodes' abuses of political patronage as the Prime Minister of the Cape, as well as his role in imperialist expansionism through his control of the 'British South Africa Company' chartered by the British government, occurred well before other liberals and radicals realised how corrupt and ruthless, as well as magnetic and compelling, Rhodes was. The impact of mining, land use changes and the proletarianisation of black labour threatened the pastoral Boer and African farming ways of life, and also led Schreiner to critique expansionist policies because of their impact upon the then independent black states of southern Africa.[20] From the early 1900s on, she supported the proponents of Indian 'passive resistance' against institutionalised racist policies in South Africa. Gandhi, working in South Africa as a lawyer defending Indian civil and labour rights and highly involved in Indian political organisations there, saw her ideas as an important influence on passive resistance; and certainly passive resistance accorded with Schreiner's pacifism and also influenced her approach to feminist activism.[21]

After the South African War ended, Schreiner and her brother Will became determined opponents of the Union of South Africa proposed by a National Convention composed by representatives from the four white settler states. Instead, she supported federalism as more likely to encourage liberalism as an oppositional political force and bring with it a measure of respect for black political and civil rights.[22] Similarly, Schreiner's insistence that South African trades unions should be (but were not) inclusive of all workers was connected with her growing conviction of the paramount importance of 'race' and racism in South African political and economic life.

This conviction underpinned her dealings with South Africa's new political leaders post-1910. She had no compunction, for instance, in telling Smuts exactly what the key issue was that he had to deal with when he became Prime Minister after Louis Botha's sudden death in 1919 – and, what's more, to deal with well:

> I wish I knew you were taking as broad and sane a view on our native problem as you took on many European points when you were there. The next few years are going to determine the whole future of South Africa in 30 or 40 years time. As we sow so shall we reap ... Jan dear, you are having your last throw: throw it right this time. You are such a wonderfully brilliant and gifted man; and there are sometimes things which a simple child might see which you don't. You see clear close at hand – but you don't see far enough'.[23]

As later events were amply to prove, Smuts indeed failed to 'see far enough', as she had predicted but hoped otherwise.

Schreiner's opposition to the 1913 Natives Land Act[24] was matched by her concern that the relatively liberal 'English' element in the South African government was being swamped by the authoritarianism and racism of its 'Boer' component. But her analysis of the development of institutionalised racism in South Africa had started much earlier, with the 1894 Glen Grey Act passed by the Rhodes administration in the Cape Colony; and she saw the 'new' policies of 1913 as the codification of a 'separate and unequal' approach embryonically put in place twenty years earlier and with Rhodes as its propagator.

The Method of the Life We All Lead

My introduction to Olive Schreiner came about one wet Manchester night in December 1982, following a Society for Research in Higher Education (SRHE) conference on gender issues in educational research. The feminist writer Dale Spender encouraged various of the women who had gathered in the bar to write about particular 'women of ideas' she wanted to include in a book she was editing; and when her gaze turned on me, she suggested I should contemplate the chapter on Olive Schreiner, for she was sure I'd be interested in her. The rest is, as they say, (my) history. I went quickly from only a vague awareness of Olive Schreiner (she was a novelist, wasn't she, but what on earth had she written and why was she important?), to being an interested reader of Schreiner's published works and then of biographies and memoirs of her, of the people who were her friends and acquaintances, and these people's own writings as well. The result appeared in 1983 as a chapter in Spender's edited collection, *Feminist Theorists*.

In writing this chapter, I was surprised to discover that Olive Schreiner had achieved international fame immediately following publication of *An African Farm* in 1883, and that she had been a major public figure of her time. I was dismayed that such an internationally well-known woman could so thoroughly sink from public trace and feminist esteem. I wanted to know whether publishing in a number of different writing genres might have dissipated her intellectual energy and contributed to her 'vanishing'. I was interested in the fact that Schreiner and her work didn't fit the usual classifications: Does she 'belong' to South African or British historiography or does she come under the sign of literary scholarship instead? How should social scientists read her fictions? And literary scholars her political writings? Is she a social theorist and if so of what kind? I was also puzzled that she and her work were seen so critically by some of the commentators I read – were they floored by her 'genre-busting', outraged by their readings of her character, or was there something else going on?

As I investigated further, including the key primary source of Schreiner's letters, I realised that the 'vanishing' and 'failure' had started with the deliberate misrepresentation and coy bowdlerisation engaged in by her estranged husband, Samuel 'Cron' Cronwright (he became Cronwright-Schreiner on marriage, she stayed Schreiner). His biography of Schreiner, his edited collection of her letters, and his introductions to posthumously published works by her, all ruthlessly present Schreiner as neurotically damaged and childish, a damaged genius. These have none the less had considerable influence, and for many years have been referenced as though straightforward sources of incontrovertible factual information.

Alongside this, a large strand in Schreiner scholarship has been dominated by literary scholars, who (by and large and with some honourable exceptions) have focused on her fictional writing as 'texts' divorced from the contexts in which they were written and read, and also divorced from Schreiner's more overtly political writings on capital, labour, sex, 'race', imperialism and the nature of nation-states. The emphasis in this work has been on re-reading a literary text (or sections of it), and generalising from this to 'the author' and 'the past' but without researching either at first-hand. Another baleful influence comes from biographically based work on protagonists who were friends or acquaintances of hers, pronouncing what are seen to be 'facts' about Schreiner but taken from chance remarks or mere gossip.

The legacy of all this is that re-reading Schreiner now takes place in a context in which her writings are sometimes found wanting against highly 'presentist' ideas which recycle often erroneous secondary sources 'as fact', typically combined with 'ad feminam' negative or slighting judgements of her as a person. But what relationship, I found myself wondering in the later 1980s, does the result bear to the woman as shown in archival sources and in her writing considered as a whole, as an 'oeuvre'? I was considerably intrigued by the disjuncture between 'the sources' and 'the secondary literature'.

My interest in Olive Schreiner, then, was stimulated, not slaked, by my contribution to the *Feminist Theorists* collection. I became interested in developing the ideas now known as 'feminist auto/biography',[25] including the way that very different views of the woman and work can be pieced together from contemporary, as well as present-day, sources. An essay on this, 'Feminism and friendship', traced the overlapping networks of feminists Schreiner had been immersed within, doing so as an antidote to the relegation of these to brief asides in accounts which see Schreiner as male-identified or even almost anti-woman. A related essay, 'Why did Olive Schreiner vanish, leaving behind only her asthmatic personality?', analysed Cronwright Schreiner's 'widower's biography' of his wife, apparently all reverence but actually a hatchet-job on her character and writings, in response to the curious way that otherwise sceptical commentators, including Ruth First and Ann Scott in their 1980 proto-feminist biography of Schreiner, treated it as effectively primary source material.

Through researching all the major archive sources, including the unpublished letters, I subsequently became fascinated by the very different views of Olive Schreiner gained from archive materials and from secondary sources. I also developed a stronger interest in the form, as well as the content, of Schreiner's writings and with re-reading these in relation to the contexts of their production. This re-reading of Schreiner's work overall significantly changed my understanding of what kind of analysis Schreiner was engaged upon and how it developed over time: I came to see her as a social theorist of a particularly interesting kind, and as someone who made an important analytical contribution. At the same time, I remained very aware that Schreiner was also a white woman of her day, someone who was a member of both the colonial society of the Cape and the imperial one of Britain, as well as being a feminist and socialist who offered a critique of capitalism and imperialism. Consequently, for some present-day readers a justification for my interest in a 'white liberal' from South Africa is needed.

During the period leading up to 1910 and the Union of South Africa, the activities of Rhodes, the British imperial government, the machinations of Milner as High Commissioner in Southern Africa and Chamberlain as Colonial Secretary, of Kruger as President of the Transvaal, and of the Afrikaner Bond within the Cape Colony, have all been subject to detailed historical inquiry. The relative silences surrounding the responses of the African peoples of southern Africa and also the Indian resistance movement there during this consequential period are, then, all the more notable as a consequence. And also relatively silenced in present-day re-assessment are the activities of white liberals and radicals, including the feminists and others active in its peace movement during the South African War of 1899–1902 and in opposing the development of the segregationist state thereafter.

Schreiner, back in South Africa between late 1889 and late 1913, actively encouraged the development of organised 'progressive liberalism' in public life as necessary for any radical politics to develop. Later she was an important presence in the peace movement during the war of 1899–1902, insisting on the iniquities of the war both within South Africa and also to an international audience. She was also part of the 'hands on' feminist response to the British-established 'concentration camps' in which some twenty-seven thousand Boer women and children died.[26] Subsequently Schreiner opposed union and supported federalism as more conducive to political freedom, particularly regarding 'race' matters; and then, as the Union became more overtly racist in its politics, so she vehemently opposed the 1913 Natives Land Act, other segregationist legislation and also anti-trades unionist policies. Schreiner's life and political involvements, then, point up the complexities of this period and that it was not peopled by clearly differentiated and easily recognisable goodies and baddies.

Schreiner's writings and their analysis of imperialism and 'race' were matched by her refusal in her letters to friends and political acquaintances to turn away from the fact that 'imperialism' meant genocide and sexual terrorism, as well as the expropriation of land and the displacement of peoples. With hindsight, it has become clear how accurate she was in predicting where these things would lead South Africa in the future, not least in pinpointing the brutalising effects of segregation and apartheid on oppressors as well as oppressed and the implicatedness of all whites in the perpetuation of what became the apartheid state. I am also fascinated by the fact that Schreiner's critique of capitalism and imperialism went hand in hand with the effective elision of colonialism – that is, of South Africa as a 'settler society' for whites – from her analytic gaze and the effects of this on her analytical approach overall.

Olive Schreiner is, then, interesting and important in her own right as an influential and prescient social analyst of those times and events. Few – I would say no – feminist theorists now have produced work which influences so many people of highly diverse kinds world-wide; and the radical edge to her work remained sharp, as did her passionate commitment to helping to change the world. And in addition, Schreiner's work and her life provide an important starting point for unravelling more of the history of white liberal and radical resistance to racism and apartheid in South Africa as well.

Events in South Africa around and after the 1994 free election do not, cannot, change the previous three centuries and more of exploitation, expropriation, terrorism and oppression. While Olive Schreiner would, I am certain, be joyful about recent changes, I am also sure she would insist on the continued need to look forward, to 'see far enough', and to do so from a clear-sighted understanding of the past and the ways it informs the present and so the future. As part of this, it remains important not to treat 'imperialism' and 'racism' as unchanging monoliths, but rather to recognise their complexities, and also the fact that awkwardly resistant voices such as Schreiner's were raised within and from the beginning. This is another factor in my interest in her work, because the changing configuration of imperialism and colonialism in southern Africa forms the backcloth to Schreiner's writings, her political involvements and her life. She would I think have recognised strong continuities, rather than stark separations, between her own oppositional analysis and politics and the new political developments in South Africa. The long years of apartheid, which had their origins in the segregationist policies of the 1890s and also the 1913 Land Act, have now been succeeded by new developments and intellectual debates that actually hark back to many of the things that were central to Schreiner's life and work, including what should be the form of the South African state and its system of government.

Olive Schreiner remains a fascinating presence within the political and literary scene of the 1880s through to the 1920s. There is her energy and 'aliveness', so that, even a hundred years after, something of the extraordinary insightfulness, humour and power of the woman, the magnetism that so engaged or repelled her contemporaries, can still be sensed in her archived letters, in her published writings, and in the comments in the letters, diaries, autobiographies and memoirs of her contemporaries. And this level of interpretational complexity and disagreement continues, about Olive Schreiner's character, behaviours, writings, and also about her as a person. Intriguingly, people still take up radically different positions about Olive Schreiner: they are for her or against her; they admire or disapprove of her; they see her as a radical in sexual and racial politics or as a woman-despising racist; they dismiss her work as old-fashioned and irrelevant or see it as crucial to contemporary feminism and socialism. Such a sharpness of response more often characterises how we think about the living – and often annoying – people who are our contemporaries. It is certainly testimony to the 'aliveness' of Schreiner's work that the ideas of a woman long dead can have this effect on people of four or five generations after hers.

My own interest in 'the life' of Olive Schreiner goes hand in hand with a greater interest in 'the context' in which she lived, and with both of these supporting my major concern, which is 'the work' that she produced. For many people, biography overtakes contexts and works, and certainly claims are still being made to have discovered increasingly minute portions of Schreiner's life and relationships, with often an emphasis on putative discoveries concerning the sexual dynamics of her life. These or any other claims to have found the real Olive Schreiner are particularly problematic given her insistent protests at 'biographising', her criticism that focusing on 'the life' trivialises the ideas that someone promotes, and her clear rejection of there being any 'essential meaning' to social life.

My view is that Olive Schreiner was right and that 'what matters' is her work, which should be read by locating it in the social and political contexts that gave rise to it and which are complex, intriguing and extremely interesting in their own right. Schreiner was a high modernist before modernism was named or had become a movement, and one who rejected not only realism but also the moral neutrality of the modernists. She was a 'new woman' who wrote 'New Woman' novels, but did so well before the genre was conceived and rejected the very idea of the 'New Woman'. She was a fin de siècle writer immersed within symbolism, but doing so in the 1870s and 1880s and by drawing upon Christian allegory. She was a decadent, but one who was in deadly moral earnest. And she was a revolutionary who was also conventional and moralistic. What this demonstrates, of course, is that these 'opposites' cheerfully co-existed, thereby pointing up that using binary categories to demarcate periods of time and types of people is too simplistic, rather than saying anything distinctive about Schreiner herself, for many of her friends, comrades and acquaintances were equally 'out of place' in such terms.[27]

The symbolist, decadent, 'New Woman', fin de siècle concerns, and the ethical and moral ideas, that run through Schreiner's writings are as important to understanding her and her work as is her feminism, socialism and freethinking. She gained a strong sense of herself while positioned between ostensibly clashing intellectual and political discourses: of anti-realism and high positivism, of materialism and symbolism, of conservatism and feminism, and of anti-imperialism and colonialism. Relatedly, she sought to establish a workable 'ethics of living' in the face of her perception of the random unpredictability of life, and to a large extent succeeded.[28] A complicated woman living in interesting times.

Olive Schreiner's work, then, still matters. To be able to 'see far enough' as a young, uneducated white woman living on the border of the Eastern Cape in the 1870s, so as not only to struggle and survive but also to achieve international acclaim, was no small achievement. To have produced ideas then that still have relevance and importance now: this is to have achieved something quite distinctive.

What Follows

In Chapter 2, 'A life in Context', I sketch out some of the key events and relationships in Olive Schreiner's life, as the backcloth to the chapters that follow. In doing so, I look at the context of Schreiner's feminist and other intellectual and political convictions and networks, rather than focusing on 'personal events' in her life as such.

Chapter 3, 'Olive Schreiner's Writings', is the central chapter of the book and provides an overview of Schreiner's unpublished letters and her published writings, focusing on the key analytical and theoretical ideas that she developed. Schreiner's analytical ideas were extensive and in a number of ways innovative, while important aspects of them interestingly developed over time. This should not be ironed out by over-generalised summaries of her work, and so I discuss her writings in the approximate chronological order they were written in order to point up the shifts and changes.

In Chapter 4, 'Interpretations', I discuss a number of influential accounts of Schreiner's work published from the 1920s on. These are Cronwright-Schreiner's interpretation of Olive Schreiner as an 'unfulfilled genius', together with Marion Friedmann's view of her 'damaged childhood'; Ruth First and Ann Scott on Schreiner's 'asthmatic personality'; Karel Schoeman's perception of an 'emotional flaw' which led her to be unable to detach herself from events and persons; Nadine Gordimer's view that Schreiner inhabited 'the prison-house of colonialism'; 'social Darwinism' as the leitmotif of Schreiner's thinking in the work of Carol Barash and in the earlier work of Carolyn Burdett; Joyce Avrech Berkman's interpretation of Schreiner's 'healing imagination'; and Anne

McClintock's view of Schreiner as 'distinguished by a paradox'. The chapter concludes with my own position, which sees Olive Schreiner as 'a woman of her time'.

In Chapter 5, 'When the Curtain Falls ... Olive Schreiner's Social Theory Reconsidered', I consider some of the questions and issues raised in the rest of the book. The chapter begins by outlining what Olive Schreiner's 'feminist theory' adds up to as a body of social theory. It sketches out some responses to criticisms of Schreiner's work as essentialist, maternalist, social Darwinist and so on, and it also considers why she 'vanished' as a significant writer and producer of ideas. In doing this, I provide an overview of Schreiner's key ideas and also some of the fault-lines in her thinking.

Although later chapters build on earlier ones, I have endeavoured to be mindful of the complex ways in which readers read, so that each of the chapters deals with a separate topic and can be read on its own. Inevitably this means there are some small overlaps, although I have tried to ensure these are not too intrusive for a reader who 'starts at the beginning and finishes at the end'. Throughout the book I draw upon, or draw my distance from, the work of other Schreiner scholars, although it is only in Chapter 4 that I do this in a very explicit way. This is because I use the 'References and Annotated Bibliography' as an extension of arguments in the composing chapters, by providing brief annotations of the main references on Schreiner and/or her writings, and of some other interesting work as well.

Notes

1   In an unpublished memoir from around 1925, Emily Hobhouse commented that 'Olive thought deeply – for days together I have found her wrapt in silence. At such periods she would not respond. On these occasions she withdrew into herself...' (Van Reenen 1984 p.188). Perhaps an over-statement, it none the less pinpoints the importance of silence and 'withdrawal' for Schreiner.

2   An allegory is a short story using abstract metaphorical categories of persons ('Man', 'Woman'), places and symbols to convey a moral or ethical message. Schreiner wrote short allegories, in longer novella form, and as constituent elements within 'other' genres, including her novels and political essays. See Chrisman 1990, 1993.

3   'Mrs Hemming' was Schreiner's older sister Alice. See Brown 1937 pp.184-5.

4   Olive Renier (1955) 'A South African Rebel' in *The Listener*, quoted in Clayton 1983 p.52.

5   Cronwright-Schreiner 1924a p. 371.

6   Cronwright-Schreiner 1924a p. 257.

7   Carpenter 1916 p. 229.

8   John X. Merriman to Cronwright-Schreiner, 20 December 1920, UCT Schreiner, Clayton 1983 p. 24.

9   Often referred to as the Anglo-Boer War, or in Britain sometimes just the Boer War, the return to using 'South African War' (as it was often known at the time) recognises that more than these two protagonists were involved. Tens of thousands of black as well as white women and children died in the British concentration camps; black male servants were involved as support (and more) for their Boer commando employers, but more often voluntarily fought in large numbers as soldiers on the British side (although this was usually disavowed in 'official' communications).

10   Lewson 1960, vol 2, p. 29; vol 3, pp. 89-90.

11   The emotionally needy seemed particularly drawn to her strength and ebullience –
      including Bryan Donkin, hysterical because she would not marry him; Edith Nesbit, for
      comfort about her philandering husband Hubert Bland; and the poet Amy Levy in the
      deep depression leading to her suicide in 1889 (Briggs 1987; Beckman 2000).

12   See Wilde 1950a, 1950b; Yeats 1955 p. 165.

13   Nevinson 1924 p. 282.

14   Gandhi 1968 p. 361.

15   Lytton 1914 pp. 156–8.

16   Brittain 1933 p. 41.

17   Hobman 1955 p. vii.

18   *Dreams*, for example, was published in at least twenty-two editions and, like *An African
      Farm*, *Dreams*, *Dream Life*, *Trooper Peter* and *W&L*, was translated into a very wide
      range of languages. Her political essays and pamphlets, which might be supposed to
      have primarily South African appeal, were also translated widely. For instance, most of
      her work was translated into Russian within a short time of being first published and the
      Russian influence of her work is discussed by Davidson & Filatova 1993, 1998 pp.190–3;
      and its less straightforward influence in Japan is discussed in Arai 1998.

19   Ruth Farringdon 1942 'A Very Great Woman' *University Forward* (University Labour
      Federation, Cambridge) vol. 7 no. 4 March 1942, SAL Schreiner 12.2.4.

20   See Nasson 1981, Parsons 1998.

21   As Schreiner explained to Adela Villiers Smith on 27 August 1912, she was a 'non-force-
      using *passive resister*' (*The Letters* pp. 315–8, her emphasis), but she refused to
      condemn the militant suffragettes, for 'I cannot possibly be so unjust as to make one
      rule for one set of persons and another for another. I have a horrible idea that many
      people condemn the militants because they are women'.

22   See Molteno 1896 for an early argument in favour of federation; and Thompson 1960 for
      a useful discussion of the debates and activities leading up to Union in South Africa.

23   Olive Schreiner to Jan Smuts, 28 October 1919, Central Archives Depot Pretoria, copy in
      SAL Schreiner, Clayton 1983 p. 131–2.

24   The 1913 Natives Land Act was the major legislation enabling the expropriation of land
      and other rights from black people; and it underpinned the 1950s and 1960s construction
      of the apartheid system.

25   An epistemologically orientated concern with the shifting boundaries between self and
      other, past and present, writing and reading, fact and fiction, and an analytical attention
      to the presence of these within the oral, visual and written texts that are 'biographies'
      and 'autobiographies'. See Stanley 1992 for a detailed discussion.

26   In spite of later self-justificatory propaganda by the Afrikaner-dominated apartheid state,
      these had little in common with the concentration camps of the Nazi state: the deaths
      that occurred came from British military stupidity rather than active malevolence, and
      were due to epidemics of measles and typhoid followed by enteritis and pneumonia.
      There is now an awareness that there were many black concentration camps and
      probably even more deaths in these; see Warwick 1983; Nasson 1991, 1999a, 1999b.
      Feminists and other whites were denied access to the black camps and most of the
      white ones as well. For the subsequent nationalist 'memorialising' of deaths in the
      camps, see Stanley 2000c, 2000d, 2001c.

27   Maccoby 1938, 1953; Porter 1968; Maynard 1993.

28   The drunken drugged death of Willie Bertram, the 'original' of 'Waldo's Stranger', the
     character who tells the allegorical 'Hunter's Story' in Schreiner's *The Story of An African
     Farm*, is a salutary reminder of what the literal as well as existential loneliness of
     freethinking in the colonial context of southern Africa in the 1860s and 1870s could bring
     people to. See Schoeman 1989, p. 206.

Chapter 2
A Life in Context

Introduction

There are quite a number of biographical accounts of Olive Schreiner, some published before the major reinterpretations of her life and writings of the last twenty years, and these contain at times radically different views of what kind of woman Olive Schreiner was, as well as of the meaning and value of her writings. There are also numerous discussions of Schreiner's work, some of which contain brief sketches of her life, and these too often offer very different views of her. Summaries of both appear in the annotated bibliography to this book.

Readers wanting a research-based overview may well find that Ruth First and Ann Scott's *Olive Schreiner*, published in 1980, is still the most informative in its mixture of biographical detail, original research and discussion of ideas. Although still influential, twenty years on it is inevitable that in some important respects their work has been superseded. This is in part because of the increasing sophistication of present-day feminist analysis compared with their at points rather sledge-hammer amalgam of marxism and psychoanalysis. It is also because of increased awareness of the importance of the archival sources to Schreiner scholarship, substantially due to the work of Richard Rive, not least in his collection of Schreiner letters,[1] followed by the publication of Karel Schoeman's very rich primary research-based accounts of two periods in Schreiner's life, 1855 to 1881, and 1899 to 1902.[2] However, some of the earlier biographies contain interesting material about Schreiner's life, and also interpretational slants on her writing not found in later work. Consequently dipping into a variety of sources is rewarding; while, for those readers interested in the whys and wherefores of the different interpretations of Schreiner's ideas and writings, this will be essential.

A caution, however, to start with. Some secondary sources treat the relationship between Schreiner's life and her writing by assuming almost a one-to-one relationship between episodes and characters in her fictional writings, and people and events in her own life, with the effect of portraying her as an 'autobiographical writer' (still 'the fate' of many women writers, of course).[3] For instance, Otto in *The Story of An African Farm* has been treated as a literal 'portrait' of Schreiner's father Gottlob; Rebekah's statements about marriage, prostitution, men and women in *From Man to Man* have been interpreted as a direct expression of Schreiner's own beliefs; and "The Child's Day", the Prelude to this novel, is seen as a literal memoir of her early childhood. However, these are actually disputable attributions; and there are three particular problems about reading 'the life' from 'the works' I want briefly to flag.

Firstly, for Olive Schreiner as other writers of fiction, the act of writing is transformative. While the autobiographical may form a basis for fiction writing, nevertheless the unfolding requirements of plot, narrative and characterisation within the writing process shift and change the factual into the fictional. The one cannot be simply read from the other, in Schreiner's case not least because of her frequently expressed criticisms of 'realist' novels and her experiments with non-realist forms of writing, even though some 'Schreiner biocriticism' blithely proceeds as if they can.[4]

Secondly, attempts to identify Schreiner with one of the key protagonists in her novels (typically Waldo or Lyndall in *An African Farm* or Rebekah in *FMTM*) founder once her statements about what would now be termed a split or fragmented authorial presence or 'voice' within her work are confronted. Schreiner actually identified with most of her characters, 'the bad' as well as 'the good'. For instance, regarding *FMTM*, she wrote to Havelock Ellis that "Rebekah is me. I don't know which is which any more; but Bertie is me, & Drummond is me, & all is me, only not Veronica & Mrs Drummond (except a little!). Sometimes I really don't know whether I am I; or I am one of the others".[5] More generally, she commented to Mary Brown that during concentrated periods of writing, "sometimes I forget I'm Olive Schreiner at all and wish anyone would tell me *which* of the characters I am".[6]

Thirdly, Schreiner clearly stated her disagreement with views expressed by characters, even favourite ones, in letters which emphasised that she had positioned characters and 'points of view' for ironic purposes but critics read these in ways she ruefully thought almost wilfully misrepresented what she had written. This flat-footed approach to reading Schreiner's work still continues, bedevilled by assumptions about plot, narrative, characterisation and 'the author' that pre-date modernist, let alone postmodernist, rethinking of these.

What now follows looks at the broad development of Olive Schreiner's ideas in relation to her political and aesthetic commitments and inter-personal relationships. Also some of the changes in her thinking over time are outlined and related to the contexts in which her writings were published and her letters written, to provide the basis of my more substantial discussion of her work in Chapter 3.

Freethinking, Ethics and Relationships

In 1838 Gottlob Schreiner (1814–1876), originally from south Germany, and Rebecca Lyndall Schreiner (1818–1903), from England, arrived in the British-governed Cape Colony in southern Africa to join the London Missionary Society presence there, transferring to the Wesleyan Missionary Society in 1842.[7] Their children were:

Catherine (Katie) 1838–1898, m. John Findlay
Frederick (Fred) 1840–1901, m. Emma Chapman
Albert 1843 d. infancy
Theophilis (Theo) 1844–1920
Alice 1845–1884, m. Robert Hemming
Oliver 1848–1854
Henrietta (Ettie or Het) 1850–1912, m. John Stakesby Lewis
Emile 1852 d. infancy
Olive Emily[8] Albertina 1855–1920, m. Samuel 'Cron' Cronwright

William (Will) 1857–1919, m. Frances (Fan) Reitz
Cameron 1859? d. infancy
Helen (Ellie) 1862–1865

Olive Schreiner was born on 24 March 1855 at the Wittebergen Wesleyan Mission Station, near the then eastern frontier of the British-governed Cape Colony. One of the consequential events of her life occurred early in 1865, when her much loved youngest sister Ellie died; throughout her life, Schreiner emphasised this as a major turning point or epiphany in her thinking about religion, life and death. Later the same year, the Wesleyan Missionary Society dismissed Gottlob Schreiner for violating its prohibition on 'trading with the natives'[9] and the family's financial position became more than precarious as they moved from Healdtown to Hertzog and Gottlob turned unsuccessfully to trading, then 'smousing' or hawking. As a consequence, in 1867 the twelve year old Olive Schreiner was sent to join her older siblings Theo and Ettie in Cradock, where Theo was headmaster of a school;[10] thereafter she never lived with her parents again for any extended period.

In 1871 Schreiner went to stay with her cousin Emmie Hope and aunt Elizabeth Rolland in Hermon, a mission station in what was then Basutoland. While there, a late night unexpected knock on the door heralded another epiphanous event in Schreiner's life: the arrival of Willie Bertram, the son of another missionary who was working as a magistrate's clerk in the Cape Colony legal system. In the small inward looking and frequently evangelical white communities of the Cape, Bertram was unusual in speaking openly about his 'freethinking', his questioning of the ideas and beliefs of Christianity. A conversation took place between him and Schreiner the next morning, a conversation she later commented she had only half-understood at the time but which profoundly influenced her. When Bertram left, he lent her Herbert Spencer's *First Principles*, and Schreiner wrote to Havelock Ellis that "I always think that when Christianity burst on the dark Roman world it was what that book was to me. I was in such complete, blank atheism. I did not even believe in my own nature, in any right or wrong or certainty".[11] She later explained its impact on her to a South African friend, Betty Molteno: "When I was sixteen and doubted *everything*, his *First Principles* showed me the unity of existence; but it was an intellectual aid, which I myself had to transmute into spiritual bread".[12]

Olive Schreiner's introduction to Spencer's work was such a turning point for her because it demonstrated that consciously constructed human frameworks of understanding, such as socialism and feminism, could provide an alternative to Christianity on which to ground principles, although she rapidly rejected the mechanistic determinism of Spencer's approach. Perhaps more importantly, her meeting with Bertram and its confirmation of her freethinking conveyed to Schreiner the enormous power of ideas, which could speedily traverse the specificities of time and place, to influence people unknown to the author in unpredictable but powerful ways.

After a period of being parcelled around between her older siblings, other relatives and family connections, in 1872 Schreiner joined Theo, Will and Ettie at the New Rush (later Kimberley) diamond fields. There she started to write down the story-telling she had engaged in from being a small child. Then in 1873, visiting her sister Alice Hemming in Fraserburg, Schreiner was introduced to Alice's friends Dr John and Mary Solomon Brown, initiating a friendship that was to be important for her in a number of ways. The Browns supported, indeed perhaps helped formulate, Schreiner's medical ambitions;[13] after they went to Britain they gave her financial and other support, including in starting nursing training when she went to England in 1881. She later repaid this by supporting her friend Alice Corthorn's successful training as a doctor, assuming a financial responsibility as well as creating a mutually loving friendship.[14] Through Mary Brown's family connections, Schreiner later met the cousins Adela Villiers (later Smith) and Constance Lytton when they were visiting their uncle (the then-Governor of the Cape Colony) Sir Henry Loch and his wife Elizabeth in 1892; both women became life-long friends who shared many of Schreiner's ethical and feminist convictions. Perhaps most importantly, the Browns supported Schreiner's move from South Africa to England in 1881 and encouraged her writing;[15] also, after her arrival in England, Mary Brown was one point of contact between Schreiner and like-minded socialist and feminist women.[16]

Following extended visits to relatives and family connections when she helped look after their children, Schreiner sought independence through employment as a governess with a succession of Boer farming families, including in Colesburg, Ganna Hoek, Ratel Hoek and Lelie Kloof, from 1874 until the spring of 1881. At Klein Ganna Hoek she worked for the Cawoods, and Elrilda Cawood became a lifelong friend after first having an 'almost idolatrous' love for her and then just as passionately rejecting Schreiner for her freethinking.[17] Through her governessing experiences, Schreiner came to rethink her earlier prejudices about 'the Boers' and to appreciate even while she criticised. This change in her ideas about 'race', she emphasised regarding first Boer and then black South Africans, was due to 'increased knowledge' – to first-hand personal knowledge of the peoples concerned.

Her reaction to the death of her sister Ellie underpinned Schreiner's development from ethical Christianity to freethinking and an accompanying insistence on the 'universal unity' of life and death. 'Freethinking' – the active rejection of fundamental features of canonical forms of Christianity and an accompanying search for alternative ethical foundations – in a sense characterised only one generation, those people who were the first publicly to state 'I cannot believe'. These 'freethinking' men and women took social, emotional, political but also existential risks that are now almost unimaginable. Indeed, these were already difficult to comprehend for the generation that followed Schreiner's, and her young acquaintance of the 1914–1918 War years, Joan Hodgson, wrote to Cronwright-Schreiner that "What I most remember was the mixture of wicked joy and aesthetic appreciation she put into the recitation of denunciatory passages from the Bible... There was a bitterness about her freethinking, I thought, which was not known to my generation; her battle had been hard and lonely and long, one guessed. We found our feet because of the pioneering that had been done".[18]

Often treated in narrow terms as a departure from Christian beliefs, in Schreiner's case freethinking indicates a much wider cast of mind – literally, 'free thinking', thinking against the grain. She frequently articulated her free thinking to often outraged or bewildered friends and acquaintances who had more conventional ideas; but it was her need for free speaking more than free thinking which made her seem odd, different, in the narrow conforming white society of the Cape Colony. The ethical position Schreiner constructed had, as she later noted,[19] something in common with Buddhism, but with the difference that it propelled her into the fray of social and political life rather than removed her from it. By the later 1870s, it had led not only to what Edward Carpenter called her 'ineradicable pessimism',[20] but also to her understanding death as a return to a universal whole, to 'life' in a wider and deeper sense than that of any single individual. And while not extraordinary now, it has to be remembered that she came to these views from the midst of a fundamentalist Christian society seemingly cut off from the winds of intellectual, religious and political change blowing in Europe.[21]

When she "discovered" the "Sermon on the Mount" in the New Testament of the Bible as a child, Schreiner immediately perceived it as providing a guide for living as a Christian, although her very 'Old Testament' parents were horrified at any such suggestion.[22] As her ideas developed, Schreiner increasingly saw ethical precepts as crucial to guide behaviour in the face of the unpredictability of life. The phrase 'a striving and a striving and an ending in nothing' from *An African Farm*[23] is one Schreiner frequently used to summarise her view of social life – but in order to emphasise the need for ethically proper conduct, to make life as good as it could be. Her perception of ethics as a guide to 'practical living' in the face of the illnesses, disappointments and cruelties of life is an intriguing aspect of her work, a central concern in her thinking, including her particular 'take' on aesthetics.

The defining importance of this ethical quest for Schreiner and many other freethinkers of her generation needs to be recognised. It underpinned their political concerns and involvements, the way they lived their lives, the causes they were committed to, how they understood the way the world was – and how it ought to be. This has to be taken on board in thinking about her work, for Schreiner's ethical convictions were not the atheistic equivalent of 'Sunday observance' for token Christians, but were enveloping and informed her views on life, politics, writing and the way she conducted her friendships and other relationships.

Some commentators on Schreiner's life have seen her relationship with her parents as outweighing all other influences. Here Schreiner's father Gottlob is viewed as gullible, simple and saint-like, just like his fictional representation as old Otto in *An African Farm* and in spite of the clear reservations authorially expressed in it about Otto's incompetent powerlessness to protect the children who rely upon him. And Schreiner's mother Rebecca is seen as a savage disciplinarian, with both parents united in imposing on their children a cruelly disabling, because emotionally denuded, version of Wesleyan Protestantism. The results are presumed to be Olive Schreiner's asthma, interpreted as the neurotic product of childhood miseries, and also her supposed 'failure' as a writer to transcend the scars of her upbringing.[24]

Against this, Schreiner's experience of parenting was in fact characterised by its removed absences, with her being left largely to amuse, instruct and discipline herself, rather than by any harshly intrusive mothering or lovingly involved fathering. Her parenting in adolescence came from her older siblings Theo and Ettie, and certainly they brought the zeal of a harsh evangelicalism to this, to Schreiner's misery and then great anger. But it should not be forgotten that both sets of 'parents' were remarkably accepting of Schreiner's determined independence, her movements across great distances of South Africa from one visit or governessing job to another, and her constant desire for education. The result is that she – and the siblings (Theo, Ettie and Will) closest to her – grew up eccentric, opinionated and fiercely resenting any external checks. The probably infrequent instances of Rebecca Schreiner's maternal injustices, including a number of beatings, certainly rankled a good deal with all her children. However, these are likely to have had less of a long-term emotional effect on Schreiner than some commentators have assumed.[25]

Schreiner's letters suggest that in adulthood she conducted her family relationships through simple expressions of loving and caring, removing from them the features of living and growing relationships, although her relationship with her younger brother Will was an exception to this family pattern because it became a real friendship. Thus in the period immediately before the South African War of 1899–1902, Schreiner resolutely communicated with her 'little Mother' around childlike expressions of affection, because anything else would reveal the enormous political and ethical chasm between her own anti-imperialist pacifism and the rest of her family's fervent support for Cecil Rhodes;[26] and she also tried to stop Ettie and Theo stirring up dissent with their mother about this. And she and Will disagreed, then continued in the family pattern until later events brought a change of mind about Rhodes and also about 'race' for him. It is possible that the surface amiability of her adult family relations merely masked a whirlpool of primal emotion, rather than political disagreements and differences of taste and opinion. None the less the historical record strongly indicates the political as the site of adult differences between Schreiner and her family, rather than the fallout of childhood trauma.[27]

Olive Schreiner's frequent withdrawal from conflict with people she was close to was, however, a strongly marked characteristic, running counter to her general openness and willingness to speak about things most people found unspeakable. As a child, for instance, she would bite her hand or retreat under her bed to knock her head against the wall rather than openly express anger; and as an adult she removed herself, physically as well as emotionally, from any relationship that a 'rival' wanted to compete about.[28] Undoubtedly this had deep roots, probably related to the 'Christian training' of self-denial and self-abnegation promulgated in Schreiner's missionary home, although later she reworked it as part of her pacifism, while her rejection of the evils of competition was very strongly linked to her anti-capitalism.

There were three epiphanous 'moments' that Schreiner mythologised as the source of her ethical thinking, then. The death of her sister led to her strong conviction that Ellie remained close in a fundamental sense, and this underpinned Schreiner's perception of the underlying unity of life and death and the natural world. Her interpretation of the 'Sermon on the Mount' and realisation of Christian hypocrisy led to her conviction of the ethical duty to put beliefs into practice. And she became aware that a systematic framework for understanding the world could come from meta-narratives other than, indeed oppositional to, Christianity. The result was that for Schreiner ethics could be prised free from organised religion, to provide meaning for individual and collective behaviour in the face of the lack of any essential meaning to life, and to ground the conduct of all kinds of relationships.

Obviously Olive Schreiner was not alone in her concern with evolving a practical ethics formulated within a freethinking and feminist/socialist frame. Of her circle in England in the 1880s, for instance, Karl Pearson and Edward Carpenter wrote extended statements of ethics, and many discussions of the London-based Men and Women's Club that Schreiner was a member of in the middle 1880s were concerned with ethical questions. Schreiner's ideas, however, were distinctive in being articulated around 'writing, as such', through what I noted in Chapter 1 as her experiments with form and structure around the idea of 'the method of life'; and they also conjoined 'the personal' (relationships, friendships, marriage and sex) with 'the structural' (capitalism, imperialism, labour and war).

The New Women and the Not So New Men

While in her late teens in the early 1870s, Schreiner was already immersed in writing what became three novels, *The Story of An African Farm* (published in 1883), *Undine* and *From Man to Man* (both published posthumously, in 1929 and 1926 respectively). In a sense, telling stories *was* Olive Schreiner, fulfilling in fictionalised form an activity her brothers and sisters remembered her engaging in from being a very young child: walking up and down, up and down, talking to herself and largely oblivious of her surroundings and other people.[29] But although 'telling stories' expressed an aspect of her deepest sense of self, Schreiner also needed to be involved in attempting to change the society around her. She left the Cape for Britain in 1881, and when her attempts at nursing and then midwifery training ended in severe chest infections and asthma attacks, she concluded that "scribbling will be my only work in life".[30] It is also likely that, when faced with it, writing was the only kind of life she really wanted and her asthma enabled the unconventional, independent-minded and argumentative Schreiner to withdraw from the highly regimented contexts of nursing and midwifery without too much loss of face.

Olive Schreiner's much older brother Fred had left South Africa to attend school and then college in England before she was born. He stayed in England to set up and run his own (very successful) preparatory school, New College, in Eastbourne; but he remained in close touch with his siblings by letter, offering advice, financial and also emotional support to them. By the time Schreiner went to England in 1881 and met him for the first time, Fred had become 'the Dadda' to his youngest siblings and a continued source of loving support in Schreiner's life, in spite of a period of estrangement when *An African Farm* was first published and respectable bourgeois Fred reacted badly to its controversial reputation.[31] His school magazine, *The New College Magazine*, also provided her with her first publications, with four of her allegorical stories appearing in it.[32] Still closely in touch with the Browns, and after first staying with Fred and his family, Schreiner then pursued nursing training at the Edinburgh Royal

Infirmary in Scotland in May 1881, later in 1881 at the Women's Hospital in Endell Street, London, and then in March 1882 attended lectures at the London School of Medicine. This was combined with unsuccessfully submitting the manuscript of *An African Farm* to a number of publishers before it was published by Chapman and Hall in London in 1883.

Olive Schreiner wanted to change the world, not just comment on it. From her encounter with Spencer's work and then the socialist literature she read after arriving in England and meeting Eleanor (and Karl) Marx, she realised that writing could itself be a political act, a form of social intervention capable of bringing about change. The immediate enormous popular as well as critical success of *An African Farm*, and the large number of testimonials to its influence she received from readers, also made her aware of this concerning her own writing, showing her that she possessed skills and aptitudes as effective, indeed more so, in promoting change than medicine. But this was also a 'precious bane' in her life thereafter.

Many matters close to Schreiner's heart had been written about in *An African Farm*; when she saw copies in bookshops, as she wrote to her friend Havelock Ellis, "It was like a knife in my heart... I get to loathe it when I think of how many people have read it... I can't bear to desecrate the thing I love by showing it to others in a form they can't understand".[33] Meeting people who had read the book made Schreiner feel proud it touched so many people's lives, but also vulnerable to their criticisms. It made her public property for the rest of her life, an international 'public persona' about whom people felt able to pass judgement, based on their mis/readings of this book, or simply gossip other people relayed about it or her. This made her feel vulnerable when meeting people, for experience told her that they might disapprove of her as a consequence of their prior disapproval of what many saw as an immoral book. However, a number of Schreiner's close friendships as well as a large number of passing acquaintanceships and requests for information and help followed its publication.

Olive Schreiner and Eleanor Marx (1855–1898) had already become friends by the time *An African Farm* was published. Eleanor was the youngest daughter of Karl and Jenny Marx, the daughter closest to her father as well as to his friend and collaborator Friedrich Engels. It is likely that she met Schreiner either in Eastbourne in June 1881 or in Ventnor in the Isle of Wight between December 1881 and January 1882, staying in both places with her very ill father at the same time that Schreiner was there because of her asthma.[34] As Schreiner's 'mental champagne' (as she described Eleanor Marx to Ellis), Eleanor Marx was a political and intellectual equal, someone she could debate ideas with, who was independent-minded and politically challenging and provided grist for the mill of Schreiner's own trajectories of thought. The friendship became complicated by Marx's common-law marriage in 1884 with the already married fellow socialist Edward Aveling, because of Schreiner's (and many other people's) reservations about, indeed strong antipathy for, him. Nevertheless it continued, including through regular exchanges of letters, after Schreiner's return to Africa at the end of 1888.

Following Eleanor Marx's suicide in 1898,[35] Aveling destroyed Olive Schreiner's letters to her, as well as Marx's diary. Then in 1921 and 1924,

Cronwright burned a large number of letters, including from Eleanor Marx, to Olive Schreiner.[36] With both 'ends' of their correspondence destroyed, only very broad outlines of their friendship are possible, although it was clearly very important to both. In analytical terms, it enabled Schreiner to place her developing ideas within a socialist frame concerned with divisions of labour in society, and to locate gender and 'race' inequalities within a labour theory of value – as *Woman and Labour* insists, 'we take all labour for our province'. And with (and also perhaps because of) Olive Schreiner, Eleanor Marx became involved in some of the key feminist political debates and campaigns of the time. Both actively opposed the Contagious Diseases Acts which gave the state the power to 'regulate' prostitutes but left their male clients unhampered; and both supported the massive 1885 Hyde Park demonstration in favour of raising the age of sexual consent for girls, in the wake of editor W.T. Stead's "Maiden tribute of modern Babylon" revelations in the *Pall Mall Gazette*.[37] In addition, both were members of the feminist circle interested in Ibsen's work which supported the initial translation and public readings of his play, originally known as "Nora" and later as "The Doll's House" (this circle included its first translator Frances Lord, also Ellen Terry, Dollie Radford and Edith Lees as well as Marx and Schreiner).

Olive Schreiner's friendship with Alice Corthorn (1859–1935) is as hard to comment upon as that with Eleanor Marx: establishing even its broad lines, let alone the detail, is difficult, because archival evidence is just not available.[38] However, secondary sources suggest that, noticing Corthorn hard at work reading in the British Museum and then meeting her at the post-box outside, Schreiner had engaged her in conversation and found she was a governess but wanted to become a doctor. A more single-minded person in this respect than Schreiner herself, Corthorn persevered through many difficulties to realise her ambition. Schreiner helped her financially, but clearly more than this was involved, for their relationship became a life-long close friendship.[39] Alice Corthorn qualified as a doctor in 1895, went to India in 1898 to work for the Plague Commission and returned in 1902, to enter private practice, with many of the London feminists of the time among her patients.[40] She named her adopted daughter after Schreiner, and later she was one of Schreiner's most consistent sources of loving friendship and support during the period Schreiner was living in England between 1913 and 1920.

Havelock Ellis (1859–1939), in later life best known as a 'sex reformer', wrote a critically complimentary letter to Schreiner about *An African Farm* in February 1884.[41] He had earlier taught at a school in the outback of Australia, an experience that enabled him to share something of Schreiner's experiences of governessing and also her passionate feelings about the karoo in South Africa.[42] In addition, Ellis was training as a doctor through financial support given him by the widow and sister of James Hinton, whose philosophy he wrote about and whose writings he edited as a consequence, at just the point Schreiner surrendered her own medical ambitions.[43] Ellis never practised medicine but instead pursued a literary career and combined this with the 'study of sex psychology', the title of an influential and contentious series of books he later published.[44]

Schreiner and Ellis met in May 1884, and the relationship soon became engrossing for both. Ellis, surprisingly in view of his marked lifelong reluctance to 'engage' politically, was Schreiner's first point of contact with the Progressive Association (of which he was a founding member) and thence the Fellowship of the New Life,[45] the meetings and lectures of which were linked with the Association, as were its related activities, from country walks to the founding of a shared cooperative household.[46] Schreiner and Eleanor Marx had been among the eight women at the founding meeting of the women's branch of the Social Democratic Federation chaired by Helen Taylor, step-daughter of John Stuart Mill;[47] and Schreiner's first letter to Ellis in February 1884, in reply to his, shows that her socialist convictions pre-dated meeting him.[48]

In 1885 Ellis sent Olive Schreiner a copy of his draft article "The red spectre in England", a description of the Hyde Park age of consent demonstration. This article, rejected by the *Temple Bar* journal and never published,[49] comments about the 'names' present – but does not even mention the cause of the demonstration and is written in a very detached way. Schreiner severely criticised it, seeing its approach as indicative of Ellis's wider emotional disengagement and lack of clear principle.[50] By this stage, her relationship with Ellis had moved from centrality in Schreiner's life, to being experienced as an emotional trap she was constrained by, and from which she effected her escape by removing herself emotionally and geographically from his reach. She also took considerable pains to re-establish the relationship as one of comradeship, successfully so in that the friendship continued, albeit in an emotionally more distanced way, including after her return to South Africa and both of their marriages. However, Ellis' resentment about her emotional retreat and her support for causes and people he disapproved of, and Schreiner's feelings about his combination of emotional disengagement and manipulativeness, continued to impact on their friendship.

From early in their relationship, indeed in the midst of their closest emotional involvement during 1884, the fact that Ellis was 'a man' was a political issue for Schreiner. Thus she wrote to him, during a period when she was concertedly reading and thinking about prostitution, "In that you are my-self I love you & am near to you; in that you are a man, I am afraid of you & shrink from you".[51] Ellis paid lip-service to Schreiner's feminist analysis of the role of men in producing 'the woman question' but (what changes?) thought he should be the exception to her feelings about men in general. Schreiner soon rejected Ellis's attempts to immerse her in his emotional needs. He in turn could not accept her need for independence and self-directedness any more than her refusal to be responsible for his emotional life, while she saw these as important aspects of 'the problem of men' at an interpersonal level.

What Ellis later, post-1914, came to characterise as Olive Schreiner being 'difficult' was for her simply facing up to real issues and disagreements, and in this later period these concerned war and pacifism and Ellis's support for British militarism. Schreiner started by confronting the disagreement between them, but she then resumed a surface amiability for the sake of continuing affection and because she did not wish to hurt him (what I earlier noted as a pattern in her family and close relationships). Ellis' sometimes ruthless emotional disengagements went much wider than his friendship with Schreiner;[52] and something of his later feelings can be discerned from his cooperation with Cronwright-Schreiner's *The Life* and *The Letters*, and his archly dismissive portrayal of Schreiner in his autobiography, *My Life*.

Edward Carpenter (1844–1929) was a member of the Fellowship of the New Life, attended its meetings on visits to London, and met Olive Schreiner in 1884 or 1885 through the social networks surrounding the Fellowship.[53] Carpenter had been a clergyman, and his move into freethinking in the early 1870s came through struggling to express his attraction to working class men and his related questioning of the class basis of Church and state. He became a university extension lecturer and then attempted to live 'the new life' on a small-holding at Millthorpe, just outside of Sheffield in the north of England. When Schreiner and he first met, Carpenter was beginning to be known in socialist and feminist circles for his long Whitmanesque prose poem, 'Towards Democracy', while his later publications were wide-ranging, influential and included work on religion, ethics, 'equal marriage' and 'same-sex love'. For Carpenter, the life of the mind and the spirit was as important as that of the body, and he combined writing and lecturing about relationships, spiritual matters and socialist politics with market-gardening and sandal-making.

Carpenter wanted to be open about his feelings for other men, indeed to encourage greater openness about feelings and relationships more generally. He encouraged Ellis' collaboration with John Addington Symonds in their planned study of 'Greek love' and then, after Symonds's death in 1893, helped Ellis with *Inversion*, the first-published volume in Ellis's 'Studies in Sex Psychology', as well as himself writing increasingly openly about same-sex love.[54] Schreiner's relationship with Carpenter was a friendly and loving one, and she knew about Carpenter's emotional draw to 'working men' and the various entanglements and unhappiness he experienced up to 1898, when he started living with George Merrill. These difficulties constituted a bond, rather than a bar, between them, for over a similar period Schreiner had experienced her own relationship problems. Also she and Carpenter shared the conviction that emotional love, sexual feeling and intellectual attraction should be combined.

The friendship between Carpenter and Schreiner was based in part on their shared background: both were children of ministers, rejected Christianity and became freethinkers, and held similar convictions about socialism and ethics. Olive Schreiner was notoriously unconventional, going hatless and gloveless, travelling and socialising on her own and being very 'free' in her ways, and this is likely to have accorded with Carpenter's wish for greater openness about feelings and behaviour. From their earlier letters, he had clearly spoken as well as written to her about his involvement with the married George Adams, and also Schreiner to him concerning the circumstances in which she left England for Europe, which I discuss later. They communicated for more than thirty years about politics and religion, the ebbs and flows of their lives, writing, and the work each was doing.

This is not to suggest their friendship was problem-free for Schreiner, but she was more easily able to express her reservations to Carpenter himself because, unlike Ellis, he did not immediately retreat emotionally or punish her as a consequence.[55]

Her reservations were similar to those she had attempted to explain to Ellis and concerned her perception of the highly gendered intellectual, political, emotional, and sometimes also sexual, exclusion of her and other women from the 'male world of loving friendship' constructed by heterosexual male friends such as Pearson and Ellis as well as by homosexual ones such as Carpenter. Their friendship too experienced new strains during the 1914–1918 War, when Schreiner remained firmly pacifist, while, to her considerable surprise as well as disturbance, Carpenter appeared to her to condemn German but to be more accepting of British militarism.[56]

Olive Schreiner's friendships with Ellis and with Carpenter were of lifelong importance to her, compared with a more 'in passing' relationship with Arthur Symons (1865–1945). Symons is now best known as the editor of the *Savoy Review* (a flagship of symbolist writing in the later 1890s) and author of *The Symbolist Movement in Literature*,[57] as well as being involved with Beardsley, Verlaine and other symbolist and decadent poets, writers and artists. Symons was a rather unlikely close friend of Havelock Ellis, and his connection with Schreiner stemmed from this. Symons was interested in the links between Schreiner's writing and the symbolist and decadent work of the 1880s, particularly Schreiner's allegorical 'dreams', then being published in leading magazines and journals. Symons experienced their first meeting in June 1889 as momentous; their conversation, at least as recorded soon after by him, focused on her allegories – "she thinks of them as the very essence of art: all art is a symbol, and these are pure symbols themselves – the only artistic expression of the passion of abstract ideas, which are to her the keenest, the deepest in her nature".[58] Symons helped Ellis to arrange the publication of Schreiner's *Dreams* in 1890 after her return to Africa, so his feelings about her allegorical writing were genuinely held.[59]

Schreiner's allegories were certainly concerned with 'abstract ideas' and 'pure symbols', but they were also concerned with making an ethical and emotional impact on the reader. She became increasingly engaged by allegory as a form, as she attempted to craft a way of engaging with analytical and political ideas while retaining emotion as the mainspring of analysis and politics. This development in her work occurred alongside (to put it no stronger) her initially warm admiration for Karl Pearson's analytical mind coupled with her increasingly critical response to the 'frozen rationality' she saw characterising his approach. Pearson (1857–1936), a polymath mathematician, social theorist and later a eugenicist, was a major, indeed dominating, intellectual presence in the circles he moved in. While his 'frozen rationality' prompted a strong critical reaction from Schreiner, Pearson also provided her with the intellectual grit of independent and sometimes conflicting ideas and opinions. Schreiner responded to Pearson as an equal, someone who could be made fun of, treated as human, fallible and capable of lightness and laughter,[60] responses which Pearson seems to have found unexpected, attractive and intriguing, but also difficult to handle and, eventually, to be retreated from.

Schreiner's attendance at Progressive Association and New Life meetings, her involvement in the women's branch of the Social Democratic Federation, in opposing the Contagious Diseases Acts, and supporting the 1885 Hyde Park demonstration, were certainly only the tip of her political involvements.

Prostitution became a major issue in radical circles, including the Men and Women's Club.[61] Schreiner attended its meetings from July 1885, only a short time before Stead's articles appeared in the *Pall Mall Gazette*,[62] indeed while debates about the club's name were still taking place. The Club had been founded to discuss the interconnections between morality and sexuality; papers were given and minutes were kept; and letters exchanged between Pearson as its guiding presence and other members. However, Schreiner, like a number of the women involved, became increasingly dissatisfied with the approach taken by the men and some of the women, which focused, as with Pearson's opening paper, on women's problems and apparent limitations and ignored the source of these in 'the problem of men'.[63] One indication of this was the mooted club name, the 'Wollstonecraft', which Schreiner objected to because it elided the role of men in producing the condition of women.

The mutual attraction between Olive Schreiner and Karl Pearson was intellectual and also perhaps involved what she referred to (and denied the existence of) as 'sex love'. The relationship involved complex feelings on Schreiner's part, and on Pearson's too, including because she increasingly drew her intellectual and political distance from his ideas and work. Later the complex relationships between Schreiner, Pearson, Bryan Donkin (Schreiner's and Marx's doctor, also an unwelcome insistent suitor of Schreiner) and Elisabeth Cobb (Schreiner's friend, a Men and Women's Club member and great admirer of Pearson) broke down around gossip spread by Cobb and others in her circle. Schreiner was extremely angry about Cobb's gossip that Havelock Ellis had had sexual relationships with two of their women acquaintances[64] because of the maliciousness involved. She also felt betrayed by someone she thought was a friend and this was a component in ending what had become the mutually problematic relationship with Pearson, for Elisabeth Cobb had also acted as an assiduous conduit of mis/information between Schreiner and Pearson.[65]

Schreiner's letters to Pearson are archived in his papers, while only one letter (a draft he kept) from Pearson to her apparently still exists. The effect of the historical accident of what has survived is to spotlight Schreiner's part in their relationship, while Pearson's equally fascinated response to her has largely escaped attention.[66] The resulting emphasis has been on whether Schreiner felt 'sex love' for Pearson and this in my view trivialises her critical response to his intellectual approach, her ideas about why this felt so unsatisfactory even while 'rationally' his argument might seem superior, and the impact of this on her search for ways of writing which were both analytical and also emotionally engaged.

The relationship reached an impasse when Schreiner had an emotional breakdown and left England for Italy in mid-December 1886, with Pearson's 'rejection' typically seen as the cause. However, there is a silence surrounding Pearson and his behaviour, for the tacit assumption is that Pearson neither initiated nor participated in any emotional or 'sex love' between them. Also the activities of other people in their social circle remain in the shadows. These include Bryan Donkin's hysterical pursuit of Schreiner after she refused to marry him; the malicious gossip of fascinated friends; other women's interest in Pearson; Schreiner's conviction that Elisabeth Cobb had betrayed important standards of friendship; Cobb's very tangled feelings for Schreiner as well as for Pearson;

and Schreiner's feelings of guilt about avoiding many demands that needy friends and acquaintances made on her emotions and her purse.

The intellectual and political objections that a number of women members of the Men and Women's Club, as well as Schreiner, had to Pearson's analysis of 'the woman question', are important and also connected with these events. The apparently dispassionate discussions and arguments of male members of the Men and Women's Club cloaked a misogynist response that these 'new women' experienced from their male counterparts, and Schreiner mocked the men's pretensions in letters to Pearson. Also, whatever conclusions might be reached about the relationship, emotional and intellectual, between Olive Schreiner and Karl Pearson, it is important to keep in perspective its scope and impact on her life. It lasted over an approximately two-year period, with its reverberations felt by Schreiner for another year or so; but thereafter, in the remaining thirty years of her life, in neither her letters nor her other writing is there much discernible personal influence. The impersonal influences are, however, clear. Thus Schreiner gave titles to some of her work that echo Pearson's writings on 'the woman question', and the contents of these take on and rebut Pearson's key assumptions and arguments.[67] Its greatest long-term impact was I think her determination not to separate emotion from analysis, her insistence that emotion and feeling could be and indeed should be integrated with reason and logic; as she commented to Carpenter, "Edward, it isn't really the intellect and nature that are at war, it's the personal and impersonal".[68]

Schreiner removed herself from these complications by going to Europe in mid-December 1886. For two years she lived mainly in Italy, although she made a number of return visits to England, before leaving for South Africa in October 1889. It seems from her letters of this period that Schreiner was in search of solitude and a withdrawal from the high level of sociability and emotionality of her time in England. She characterised this, writing to Pearson after his marriage, as a time when human suffering had eaten into her feelings and energies, when she had been at the beck and call of every woman in need and 'simply bleeding to death'; and she emphasised to Ellis that "One must hold the balance perfectly even between knowledge and service of our fellows".[69] While living in Italy she started to write again, editing work already written, and also putting on paper what seems to have been a large number of allegories (the basic form she wrote in, as I shall argue in Chapter 3).

Moving between sociability and her immersion in the particularities of events and relationships, and solitude, writing and her engagement by the general and abstract, was more widely characteristic of the way Schreiner lived, for each seems to have been necessary for her at different points in time. Throughout her life, from living on upcountry Boer farms in her youth, to being a middle-aged woman living in war-time England, she moved between a keenly enjoying sociability, and an extreme solitude of place and person. Schreiner's need for solitude and an impersonal way of life is under-acknowledged as part of her makeup as a writer, and was a kind of emptying of the everyday from her mind so as to enable it to function on a different and more creative level.[70] People close to Schreiner tended to see these things as in competition, rather than supporting each other. Her niece, 'Dot' Schreiner, for instance, wrote that: "A person of great vitality herself, who spent much time in friendly intercourse, she might have written a larger number of books if she had led a more cloistered existence, but their quality must have suffered, since she was always deeply interested in the neighbours and the life around her".[71] What she was probably unaware of were the long periods of imposed loneliness, as well as freely chosen solitude, in the life of her favourite aunt: ill-health, the constraints imposed by martial law during the South African War, and her husband's work, kept her in Kimberley, Johannesburg, Hanover and later De Aar, hundreds of miles away from most of her family and friends in Cape Town and Port Elizabeth.

South Africa: Turning With a Keen Relish to the External World

Arriving in Africa in late 1889 and looking back on her years in England, Schreiner characterised her state of mind when living there as 'bleeding to death'. She had felt guilty about her own good fortune, especially given the constant demands for emotional and financial support made on her. Relatedly, she felt responsible for solving every social problem and in particular what she saw as the immensely consequential evil of prostitution. She explained her 'draw' to Pearson by noting that his apparently harsh insistence that she was wasting her gifts in such 'social work' had provoked her by asking 'is it moral?', and saved her from herself by encouraging her to change her life.[72] 'Europe' was a transitional time and place for Schreiner, and her return to Africa represented a choice she was making about how to live, and also how to be, as a person. To Ellis, she commented that in returning to Africa she had turned "with such a keen kind of relish to the external world", and to him and to Pearson she noted that the earlier period of being buried in 'abstract thought' had immersed her too much in herself, so that tiny things hurt her disproportionately and thereby incapacitated her.[73]

Schreiner's powerful response to the South African landscape was connected to this. There was its scale, beauty and sheer grandeur, with the karoo quintessentially representing these characteristics for her; but she also closely identified with an 'Africa' of her mind which made her feel strong, free and self-contained, which attracted and exhilarated her, and which she loved passionately.[74] Earlier in her life, then after her return to Africa, Schreiner experienced a number of what can be seen as mystical experiences – overwhelmingly powerful sensations of oneness with the universe experienced through a loosening of the boundaries between her and the external world – which occurred in connection with the African landscape.[75]

As Schreiner discussed in essays written in the early 1890s, the Boers felt passionately, even obsessively, about their rights over and possession of 'ons land', seen as a literally empty land they had competed for against black Africans also migrating there, and had paid for it with their blood.[76] Schreiner's Africa was a more personal, more symbolic, one, mapping onto the allegorical landscapes of her allegories, and also intimately connected with how she was, or rather how she wanted to be. At the same time, her Africa was also an everyday one that was peopled and historicised by her. Its white population encapsulated the narrow-minded inward-looking Philistinism, and immersion in personalities and destructive personal gossip, that Schreiner had escaped from as a young woman; and after her return she felt the same utter separation between herself and white other people.[77]

Within a few weeks of returning, Schreiner's mother became very ill and was thought to be dying; a hasty trip some hundreds of miles from Cape Town for a prolonged stay in Grahamstown, where her mother lived, left Schreiner extremely ill from asthma.[78] By March 1890, she was living high up on the karoo in Matjiesfontein, around 200 miles from Cape Town, and feeling in better health than she had since leaving Lelie Kloof for England in 1881.[79] It was in Matjiesfontein at this time that she met Betty Molteno (1852–1927), an educationalist and pacifist who became her closest friend, and Molteno's partner Alice Greene, also an educationalist.[80] Schreiner had quickly engaged herself in the political life of the Colony 'on the ground'. Intellectually, her return to South Africa was a watershed, as her move to England in 1881 had been. She determinedly set out to 'know about' South Africa, producing a series of linked investigatory essays concerned with the four settler states and their peoples, as an auto-ethnographic insider variant on the 'travel literature' written by outsiders to 'exotic locations'. Most were published contemporaneously in journals and magazines in the UK and the USA; they were also reworked for a book on two occasions, although changing political events prevented its publication, and were finally published posthumously as *Thoughts on South Africa*.[81]

Schreiner had heard much about Cecil Rhodes from friends such as the newspaper editor W.T. Stead and also members of her family, not least the energy, power and driven purpose that attracted people to him. She met Rhodes in November 1890 in Matjiesfontein and for a short time admired him a good deal.[82] Her public change of mind about Rhodes, from attraction and support to revulsion and open opposition, began in 1891 around the so-called 'Strop' or Master and Servant Bill introduced in the Cape Parliament and her growing awareness of the ruthlessness of Rhodes' imperialist ambitions and disregard of any ethical propriety in his desire to create cheap docile labour.

Will Schreiner was Rhodes' legal adviser from 1889 and the formation of the De Beers diamond cartel that Rhodes controlled. Rhodes then became Prime Minister of the Cape Colony in 1890, and Will became his Attorney General in 1893. Will was also a fervent supporter of 'the imperial dream' Rhodes seemed to embody, with the rest of the Schreiner family apart from Olive, indeed most of the English people in the Cape Colony as well as a high proportion of its Boer population too, sharing these feelings.[83] Will Schreiner questioned Rhodes' morality and motives only reluctantly in the aftermath of the Jameson Raid, which occurred over Christmas 1896 and New Year 1897.[84] Thereafter he worked politically with members of the Afrikaner Bond[85] and opposed the anti-Boer move in imperialist ambitions that the Raid signified. For many other English-speaking South Africans, Rhodes' recall to London to appear before a parliamentary Committee of Inquiry in March 1897 was seen as quite unwarranted. Also Olive Schreiner's swingeing criticisms of the genocidal activities in Mashonaland of the Chartered Company controlled by Rhodes, in her allegorical novella *Trooper Peter Halket of Mashonaland* (published the same week that Rhodes appeared before the Inquiry and an instant bestseller), was seen as scandalously unfair.

Rhodes' pursuit of Olive Schreiner, his attempts to cajole her even when she pointedly refused to speak to him and openly condemned his politics, together with his close relationships with other members of her family, led many people to assume there was some kind of romantic interest between them.[86] But as 'Dot' Schreiner commented:

> ... my aunt, always a political Cassandra of much prophetic insight ... even before the Jameson Raid ... had become suspicious of Rhodes's Imperialist policy ... 'Can't you see, Old Man,' she wrote to [Will], 'what is coming?' But my father loved and trusted Rhodes ... My aunt had ... broken with Rhodes ... and this makes it the more annoying to have it ignorantly said – and still repeated – that she was in love with him. She admired his intellect and his vitality, but did not take long to condemn his Imperialism and the ruthless warpath he had chosen to tread.[87]

The bitter controversies and disagreements that erupted within the Schreiner family, as well as the Cape population generally, continued through the lead-up to the South African War, for profound differences about the British imperial presence in Southern Africa, capitalism versus pastoralism, and questions of 'race' and racism, were involved here. Olive Schreiner's championing of the Boers in her South African essays stood for profound political and ethical differences between her and many other people in the Cape Colony. Through her essays, she began to piece together her critique of finance capitalism, its destruction of pastoralism, and its amoral search for land, minerals, cheap labour and profit, as the undesirable mainspring of irrevocable change in Africa.

Marriage, Politics and 'Race'

In early 1894 Olive Schreiner married Samuel Cronwright, known to his family and friends as 'Cron', who came from a family of English-speaking settlers.[88] She had met Cronwright, who managed an ostrich farm at Krantz Plaats, a farm adjoining that of her friends the Cawoods at Ganna Hoek, in mid-December 1892.[89] Schreiner oscillated between considerable attraction to and great doubts about him. She returned to England for a visit in early 1893, to maintain her visibility as a highly publishable author, but also to put some perspective on the relationship. She found deciding whether or not to marry Cronwright difficult and she hesitated for a considerable period, because of doubts about his character, about whether she was 'the marrying kind', because of her analysis of marriage in general, and because of another woman in his life.[90]

At some point, however, it seems to have been agreed by letter that she would marry him. When Schreiner told her English friends what kind of man Cronwright was, most were astonished at her choice. She was strongly attracted by his physical 'manliness', while the hopes and aspirations she invested in him coexisted with a very down-to-earth estimate of his strengths and weaknesses. Thus a few days before their marriage in February 1894, Schreiner wrote to her brother Will in very measured terms that "The worship which it has all my life been my dream that marriage should enable me to GIVE will I know not be mine; but marriage will give me I believe something to love abidingly and naturally and that I have needed greatly; I feel satisfied it is right".[91] She was even more forthright to Cronwright himself:

> My one fear is, not that you will ever sink your note and run with others from cowardice but from ambition and the desire to gain a field for expanding your powers. Your time of danger will come when you see that by temporizing you will gain what may seem on the surface a larger power for good. I think it is well to resolve in one's early youth that no good ever shall be good to one which is bought at the smallest price of one's intellectual integrity ... [92]

Ambition, temporising and a loss of intellectual integrity, together with a mulishness that led him to ride rough-shod over circumstances and people, later became pronounced features of Cronwright's character. However, for a time the marriage went well, although there were disappointments on both sides. For Cronwright these probably began sooner, for within a short time Schreiner's asthma led them to leave his much-loved farm and move to Kimberley;[93] then, in spite of his careful manufacture of what he thought were exactly the right circumstances for writing (absolute quiet, no other activity, sharpened pens and piles of paper, and an anticipatory Cronwright watching over her shoulder), Schreiner's promised 'big book', the novel which was to earn a lot of money, was not forthcoming. There were disappointments on her side too. In spite of her very strong feelings about unscrupulous political manoeuvrings, she realised that Cronwright had gone behind her back to make (unsuccessfully) political overtures to Transvaal politicians he knew she would disapprove of. Then in late 1897, while they were living in Johannesburg, his hasty public complaint about being excluded from the voting register produced a libel action from one of Rhodes's henchmen, Cornwall, which Cronwright humiliatingly (and expensively) lost.[94] His actions, indeed his general approach, were tantamount to political suicide.

But earlier, following their initial meeting, Schreiner described Cronwright to Edward Carpenter as being "something like Waldo, but fiercer and stronger".[95] Perhaps such an identification was almost inevitable. Waldo, a protagonist in *An African Farm*, represented a side of her own character, and a 'Waldo-ish' man could act in South African public life in ways that Schreiner, as a woman, was excluded from, in spite of her keen political interests and well-developed tactical sense concerning practical politics.[96] Indeed, Cronwright shared many if not all of her political convictions and concerns during this period, including her encouragement of 'progressive' political organisation along the lines of the Afrikaner Bond.

At the time of her marriage Olive Schreiner, with other women, had no publicly acknowledged role in formal and white politics in the Cape Colony, Natal or the Boer Republics. Among the women most visible in political life in the 1890s were Harriet Colenso, daughter of the subversive Bishop Colenso, involved in campaigning against racial injustices in Natal; Marie Koupmans de Wet, a Boer grandee in Cape Town who hosted a political salon attended by the political elite, and who during the South African War helped organise relief for Boer women and children in British concentration camps; and Schreiner's older sister Ettie Stakesby Lewis, who led a highly visible temperance campaign which pinpointed alcohol as a weapon whites deliberately used against black people in creating debt and expropriating land. White women at that time came no closer to public politics than as 'social workers', behind the scenes organisers, or hidden sources of influence over men, as with these three women. Schreiner's position in relation to these conventional 'women's spheres' of influence on the one hand, and on the other to the self-interested localism characterising the political life of public men, was thus highly anomalous. She was a female player but one who moved on an international public stage; she fitted within neither, belonged to neither.

Olive Schreiner's letters to Will Schreiner, James Rose Innes, Jessie Rose Innes, Betty Molteno, Mary Sauer, John X. Merriman, and later Jan Smuts, show her to have been an astute political commentator with an eye for spotting shifts and developments in contemporary political life; and during even the last few months of her life she assiduously read a wide range of newspapers and periodicals and kept up her remaining political contacts.[97] After her late 1889 return, she quickly became convinced of the need for an organised liberal movement in the four settler states cutting across existing political and 'race' divisions, which would promote full adult suffrage and encourage the development of democracy more generally. She also thought someone was needed to lead this progressive grouping, to bring together different sets of people and become an important political presence while remaining out of high office and out of the public eye.[98]

Schreiner seems initially to have conceived this role for Cronwright, as it were on her behalf; and she wrote papers for him to read at public meetings, provided him with introductions, offered suggestions as to more and less sensible paths to follow. The externalities were fulfilled, including an extended anti-war lecture tour in Britain in 1900 which Cronwright undertook because, for health reasons, she declined the invitation made to her by the economist and journalist John Hobson on behalf of the South African Conciliation Committee. This brought him into contact with many of the key figures of socialism and the more radical end of Liberalism.[99] After the South African War, Cronwright flirted with accepting John Tengo Jabavu's suggestion he should stand for the Cape Parliament for the predominantly black district of Tembuland, but he was eventually elected for Colesberg in the north-eastern Cape in 1903. However, Cronwright lacked Schreiner's political sensibility and also her marked ability to get on well with people even while disagreeing with them. From contemporary comments, he seems to have been arrogant and domineering to his perceived inferiors, and combined resentment and obsequiousness towards those more powerful, while his views were inflexibility held. But at the same time, he was also steadfast over this period on 'race' matters, concerning freethinking, and in defending the civil and legal rights of members of the Boer communities during the South African War.

After a very difficult labour and the use of chloroform, Olive Schreiner gave birth to an apparently healthy baby girl on 30 April 1895. The baby was dead when the nurse woke the next morning, with Schreiner always feeling strongly that if her daughter – who seems not to have been given a name – had received proper nursing care over night she would have lived. Afterwards Schreiner had at least three increasingly serious miscarriages. Their daughter's death greatly affected them, both being moved to tears for years afterwards at chance mentions of it. The child was buried in a lead coffin, so that she could be later re-interred with her mother; Neta, Schreiner's dearly loved dog and "the best friend I've ever had",[100] was similarly buried in 1904, and child and dog were both re-interred with Schreiner after her death.[101]

Ideas about motherhood, much thought about both before and after her daughter's death, form an interesting component in Olive Schreiner's thought. However, she was more concerned with 'social motherhood' than with literal or biological motherhood, as I discuss in Chapter 3. The most dramatic example of this in her fictional writing involves the transvestite transformation of Gregory Rose in *An African Farm* from a stupidly egotistical boy to the selflessly-loving carer of the dying Lyndall.[102] It is also a theme in a number of Schreiner's dreams and allegories, as well as being discussed theoretically in *Woman and Labour* regarding the relationship of men to society and to war.

By the time the South African War started in 1899, there were strains in the Schreiners' marriage at a personal level, mixed more positively with large remaining areas of political agreement between them. By the time of Cronwright's return to South Africa from his anti-war lecture tour late in 1900, a sea-change seems to have occurred, brought about by a number of factors, some known, some not. In the late 1890s, Cronwright's widowed mother presumed she and her unmarried daughters would live with her eldest son and his wife. Difficulties occurred with Cronwright as well as his mother by Olive Schreiner's outright refusal to countenance this, as something that would destroy all opportunity for her to write. Also although Schreiner greatly disliked Johannesburg (she felt ill in its climate for most of the time), Cronwright liked living there and was determined to stay.[103] In addition, in the late 1890s Schreiner wrote to Betty Molteno that 'something' had happened, affecting all of her life and pre-occupying her mind, but about which she could neither write nor speak.[104]

The change in their relationship also seems to have been linked to Cronwright's growing sense of self-importance. By the time he returned from England, he had decided on a life independent of her in Johannesburg (she was living in Hanover).[105] Olive Schreiner visited him in Cape Town at his mother's, telling Will and her sister-in-law Fan that unless she did so she might not see him for months, perhaps years. During the remainder of the South African War they lived largely apart. They continued living apart for much of each year afterwards as well, although with a base first in Hanover and then De Aar, ostensibly because of the opposing pulls of her asthma and heart condition versus his growing para-legal business, but it would seem with resentments and increasing emotional distance on both sides. Cronwright left the Cape Parliament after Union in 1910 and devoted himself to business, golf, his car and a social life organised around local dances. At the same time, Olive Schreiner became an increasingly radical commentator on South Africa's move rightwards on questions of labour and 'race', and also largely housebound because of her heart problems.

In 1913, the difficulties erupted around two apparently unlinked but major differences between them. The first was her conviction, and his denial, that he was engaged in a clandestine relationship with Isaline Philpot, an acquaintance from her years in Britain.[106] The second involved their very different responses to the increasingly segregationist national state in South Africa, he immersed in his social life and she in political despair, including concerning the passing of the Natives Land Act in 1913. The rift seems to have been at some level acknowledged, and with sadness at least on Schreiner's part, writing to him, "Dear loved one, I'm glad you like my writings. I wish I could more often show you myself that which you could as well love".[107] Cronwright denied having any kind of involvement with Isaline Philpot, and insisted that Schreiner's suspicion that Philpot gossiped about her was merely imagination, in fact madness. His ultimatum was that, if she ever mentioned her suspicions again, he would have nothing further to do with her.[108] They also responded very differently to political developments and the rise of white nationalism in South Africa post-Union. Schreiner's analysis increasingly linked her feminism with her critique of capital, racism and the state, while after 1910 (when he left the Cape Parliament on its dissolution) Cronwright increasingly retreated from politics.

Their growing political distance had in fact become a gulf, something revealed around the policy of the Cape Women's Enfranchisement League, of which Schreiner was a vice-president. Cronwright-Schreiner considerably misrepresents her resignation from the League, presenting this as the product of her 'wild' and incomprehensible objection to the amalgamation of branches.[109] But the facts are that, starting in 1908 or 1909 with splits in some branches, the League abandoned universal suffrage and adopted a franchise policy which excluded non-white women; and as a direct consequence Schreiner, a life-long supporter of universal suffrage, resigned from the League, insistently writing on one of its suffrage leaflets 'The women of the Cape Colony, all women of the Cape Colony'.[110] Moreover, the change in the League's policy was the tip of the iceberg of political changes then happening with regard to questions of 'race'. In particular, following a succession of retrogressive measures, during 1913 the Natives Land Act was guided into law by the erstwhile liberal Jacobus Sauer, thereby codifying a number of legal provisions with regard to 'race' concerning land-holding, residency and labour. It was an important feature later in the construction of the apartheid state, being used to change land ownership and its control, both immediately after being passed, and then to massive consequence in the 1950s and 1960s.

Schreiner's support for women's suffrage was always as part of full adult suffrage, and this in turn was linked to her commitment to democracy within the framework of a feminist and socialist analysis of capitalism, 'the labour question' and 'the problem of men' as well as women. When she returned to South Africa, she began to work out an analysis of 'race' and its connections with labour and capital. This appears in part in the essays published in *Thoughts on South Africa*, although a number of other writings, produced as direct interventions into South African political life, are of equal significance: the 1896 political essay *The Political Situation*, the 1897 allegorical novella *Trooper Peter Halket of Mashonaland*; the anti-war pamphlet *An English South African's View of the Situation* published immediately before the South African War; and in 1908, in the wake of the 1907 strike on the Rand and the run-up to the post-war settlement, the pro-federalist and anti-unionist pamphlet *Closer Union*.[111] Across these writings, Schreiner insisted that non-white South Africans should be admitted to the suffrage on absolutely the same conditions as whites. Even if many non-white people were less 'civilised' and more child-like than whites – something it must be emphasised Schreiner thought about its Boer population as well – she argued this was the result of cultural factors and certainly not biological ones and would change over time.

Some Schreiner scholarship has insisted on Schreiner's 'social Darwinist' and so racist views. However, throughout her life she promoted universal suffrage and full citizenship rights for everyone, insistently rejected any notion of biological determinism, and her views about 'race' changed and she left behind many of the earlier assumptions that she, like other liberals, had used to think about the different populations of people in South Africa. What changed her thinking was greater knowledge – "Later on, my feeling for the Boer changed, as did, yet later, my feeling towards the native races; but this was not the result of any training, but simply of an increased knowledge".[112] The sources of her increased knowledge about the Boers are well known;[113] those changing her ideas about black people remain considerably under-investigated, although there are some small clues.

Firstly, Schreiner's analysis, from her 1890s essays on, focused on the role of capital in southern Africa in creating and maintaining a submerged class of labour defined around 'race' criteria, over and against which all whites formed an opposing class group, so that the labour question in its 'race' form permanently shaped South African society. Along with this, she became increasingly aware that the problem wasn't only a matter of labour and capital, but involved deep-seated prejudices that whites, including her, held about the supposed inferiority of black people. The catalyst here seems to have been her realisation that this paralleled the prejudices men had about women, borne on her when a group of African political leaders wanted all women banned from a political meeting and she in turn had reacted by not wanting to work with them again.

Secondly, Schreiner actively supported and was influenced by the Indian passive resistance movement in South Africa; and her respect for the ethical principles underpinning it went hand in hand with her admiration for Gandhi and its other leaders. She also became increasingly aware of the growing militancy of South Africa's other non-white populations about 'race' issues, and also the ways in which education, political analysis and organisation could transform people into agents of their own destiny, with the turmoils in Matabeleland and Mashonaland (later annexed as the two Rhodesias, then becoming Zimbabwe and Zambia) in her *Trooper Peter*.

Thirdly, from around the mid-1890s Schreiner came to know black people in a very different way, as political agents rather than victimised peoples, including as writers and journalists using the power of ideas and the written word in a socially and politically transformative project as she had herself (for instance, the Schreiners gave financial help to the writer Sol Platje in his journalistic activities, and he named one of his daughters after her).[114] Schreiner also increasingly perceived links between 'the problem of men' and that of 'race'. In late 1911 the fourth General Missionary Conference of South Africa established a Commission of Inquiry into 'the so-called Black Peril', which Schreiner distributed questionnaires for.[115] The Commission investigated whether white women were at risk of rape and other sexual violence from black men, and concluded that it was black women who were most at risk and mainly from white men. Schreiner's stance is indicated in her letter of 26 December 1911 to the secretary of 'Commission VI', Mr J. Henderson, that "My feeling of course is that peril which has long overshadowed this country, is one which exists for all dark skinned women at the hands of white men".[116]

From her admiration for Toussaint L'Overture as a man of genius in the 1890s on,[117] Schreiner read the biographical, political and analytical writings of black radicals, especially from the USA, and she had a particularly high regard for the analytical ideas of W.E.B. Du Bois.[118] By the time she left South Africa in late 1913, she had publicly rejected the Women's Enfranchisement League for its segregationist franchise policy, criticised the government's handling of strikes on the Rand, objected to the increasing segregationism of South African trades unions, and opposed the Natives Land Act.

War, Pacifism and Social Change

Olive Schreiner arrived in England at the end of 1913, after a short stay went to Italy for medical treatment for her heart condition, then travelled to south Germany to visit her father's birth-place. She returned on one of the last ships leaving Holland for England through the help of a friend, the Dutch feminist, pacifist and birth control campaigner Aletta Jacobs, with whom she had been travelling. She remained in England for the duration of the 1914–1918 War, indeed until mid-1920. For many people, their overwhelming impression of Schreiner during this period was of a woman in ill-health and also very bitter about the war, although Alice Corthorn (who at this time didn't accept the reality of Schreiner's heart problems – it took the post-mortem report to convince her) thought it was the rift with Cronwright that had most changed her.[119] The ill-health is witnessed in a passport photograph taken in England in August 1920 a few days before she returned to South Africa, which shows an Olive Schreiner who could have been eighty-five rather than her actual sixty-five.[120] The two wars and the political events in South Africa were contributory factors perhaps, together with the estrangement from Cronwright, but the persistent ill-health of a woman with chronic disabling asthma and congenital heart problems must be seen as the dominant factor.

Schreiner was involved in the peace movement and had written anti-war allegories during the South African War, as well as writing analytically about war in *Woman and Labour*. Feminism, pacifism and the possibility of revolutionary change in the face of autocracy were among her preoccupations during her sojourn in England from 1914 to 1920. During the 1914–1918 War, she experienced frequent hostility from landladies and from strangers, because of her German name linked to her sometimes vocal pacifism, and she was summarily made to leave a number of lodgings and social gatherings by people's xenophobic reactions.[121] She remained in close contact with Betty Molteno and Alice Greene, Alice Corthorn, Adela Villiers Smith, Constance Lytton, Havelock Ellis and Edward Carpenter, and she made some new but less close friendships. However, she was increasingly alienated from people who supported the war in any way (like Emily Hobhouse, for instance), and the friends closest to her were Betty Molteno and Alice Greene (who had left South Africa permanently in 1912 and were living in England), both Quakers who shared her total pacifism.

In spite of her severe health problems, by 1917 Schreiner had produced "The Dawn of Civilisation", a lengthy but unfinished piece of writing concerned with war but more particularly the genesis of aggression in men and in women. Her expressed concern was that it should be published, writing to her brother Will in 1917 that "I am seldom well enough to do anything. If I should not finish it I wish the part that is written to be published".[122] She also said this to Cronwright-Schreiner when she left England for South Africa in 1920, because she was sure she would not live much longer. Over the course of the war, she attended many of the military tribunals that conscientious objectors appeared before, and wrote some anti-war allegories and public letters on conscientious objection.

Schreiner and Cronwright did not meet from October 1913 to July 1920. When he finally arrived in England, having retired and started out on a 'round the world' trip, he commented in family letters sent to his brother Alfred in South Africa about how changed and aged by illness she was. The extent of their estrangement can be gauged by the fact that, despite Schreiner's manifest incapacity and continued physical decline, Cronwright stuck to his plan of holidaying in England to be followed by Europe and the USA, and not for one moment did she think he might change his schedule. Six weeks after Cronwright's arrival in London, in mid-August 1920 Olive Schreiner returned to South Africa by ship with her nephew Oliver and his wife and baby, too ill to be able to pack for herself or to travel on her own.

Schreiner was shaken by the many retrograde changes that had occurred in South Africa and predicted a long bitter struggle around 'race' issues that would eventually end with all power and influence being wrested from white hands. She stayed initially with members of her family, particularly her sister-in-law Fan, widowed by Will's death in June 1919; and then moved to a boarding house at Oak Hill in Wynberg, a suburb of Cape Town. Industrialisation and urbanisation as a consequence of the war, as well as political changes, had markedly changed South Africa. In her last letter to Cronwright, Olive Schreiner wrote that, if she had realised about these changes she would not have returned, because "It doesn't seem to me that this is Africa".[123] At some point during the night of 10–11 December 1920 she died, sitting in bed with her glasses on and still holding the book she had been reading. Her siblings Katie, Alice, Fred, Ettie, Will and Theo, as well as her father, all died from the same heart complaint, in her case fully confirmed by the post-mortem she had arranged to be carried out after her death.[124] It is clear that what Cronwright depicted in *The Life* as a 'fictitious' heart problem and for years had ridiculed behind her back was the cause of Schreiner's many years of painful suffering and then her death. She was temporarily buried in the family plot in Cape Town. Cronwright read the news of her death in a London newspaper before the telegram sent to his bank was re-routed to his lodgings. He immediately telegraphed his brother Alfred to take possession of Olive Schreiner's belongings, particularly her manuscripts. He returned to South Africa over two months later, having gathered a lot of material for the biography he intended to publish.

On 13 August 1921 – the anniversary of the date the previous year she had sailed for South Africa – the lead-coffined bodies of Olive Schreiner, her baby daughter and her dog Neta were sealed in a stone sarcophagus on the very top of Buffels Kop, outside Cradock, at the foot of which she had first lived after her marriage. The coffins were carried by African workmen to the top of Buffels Kop, accompanied by some of her friends but no members of the Schreiner family. Before they started, Cronwright read from one of Olive Schreiner's favourite poems, Robert Browning's "The Grammarian's Funeral": 'Let us begin and carry up this corpse, Singing together'. At the top, before the coffins were placed in the sarcophagus, he read part of Tennyson's "In Memoriam".

During 1921, Havelock Ellis and Cronwright-Schreiner corresponded about the planned biography of Olive Schreiner, what to do with her many surviving letters, and concerning a number of unpublished Schreiner manuscripts, some of which Ellis had in his keeping and others of which Cronwright had found in her papers. Their activity was seminal (I use the word advisedly) in shaping for a considerable time how Olive Schreiner and her writings were seen. In 1923 Cronwright-Schreiner published Olive Schreiner's collected South African essays in *Thoughts on South Africa* and also her *Stories, Dreams and Allegories*. He then returned to England to collect material for *The Life* and *The Letters*, both published in 1924. Also a shortened and edited version of "The Dawn of Civilisation" (which appeared first as a short two-part essay in the *Nation and Atheneum* in 1921) was added to the 1924 second edition of *Stories, Dreams and Allegories*. In 1926 Cronwright-Schreiner published the novel *From Man to Man*. Then, in 1929, he published the cast-off *Undine*, which Schreiner had assumed destroyed by Ellis at her request, insisting it was never to be published.

In 1923, Cronwright-Schreiner legally reverted to his original name, removing the Schreiner from it. In London, he married Lyn Gunn, nèe Bush, in June 1924. Their daughter Cronlyn was born in July 1925. He died in 1936, following a stroke some months earlier.

Concluding a biographical account with its subject's decline and death is of course traditional. But it is worth pointing out that, in spite of Olive Schreiner's worsening health and her knowledge by the end of 1919 that she was dying, the period from the end of the 1914–1918 War until her death also contained hopes and joys for her. The war itself had ended, and with this came new political beginnings, as people who had lived under harsh autocratic rule (that of Britain as well as Russia, Germany and the Austro-Hungarian Empire) began to pressure for political, civil and economic rights. Schreiner hoped that the dreams and plans that had fuelled the activities of her and her comrades in the 1880s and 1890s were stoking the fires of radical change anew, changes she passionately wanted to change South Africa too.

The 1880s and 1890s had been experienced by Schreiner and her friends and comrades as a time of enormous optimism during which all things seemed possible: everything could change, immediately and for the better. In the very first letter she wrote to Ellis, she had asked, "Does it ever strike you, it often does me, how within the sixteen miles that make London, lie all the materials for heaven on earth, if only something could come suddenly & touch our hearts one night... I haven't faith in anything that promises to raise us by purely material means".[125] Socialism and feminism were seen as not far-off aspirations but rather as practical means of bridging the 'purely material' and the things that 'touch the heart'. 'The future' that Schreiner invoked in various of her allegories and also in the dedication of *Dreams* – 'To a small girl-child who may grasp somewhat of that which for us is yet sight, not touch' – was felt to be almost within reach, perhaps to be realised in her lifetime, and certainly by the children already growing up. As Schreiner commented much later, this overwhelming sense of hopefulness had lent fervour and passion as well as an innocence to the politics of the time:

> no one who did not live through it can ever know the joy, and hope, and passion of enthusiasm with which we worked in those years in the eighties. I was talking of it with Keir Hardie and tears came into both our eyes when we spoke of it. But it was not for nothing. The solid, stolid (call it sordid if you will), but real advance in the condition of the working classes in England is the result of that movement, begun and carried on almost entirely by a small handful of men and women mostly of the 'upper' classes and all of ability. It was the brilliant sunrise, without which there could not have been any day...[126]

I am reminded here of how the biographer Richard Holmes came to rethink the 1780s from the viewpoint of a 'child of 1968'. Writing about hearing the news of the radical uprising in Paris 1968 on the radio, he comments in terms one can imagine Olive Schreiner would have identified with, that:

> suddenly the idea of 'the Revolution' came into my head... the sense of something utterly new coming into being, some fresh, immense possibility of social life, a new community of hope, and above all the strangely inspired note – like a language – that sounded in the voices of those who were witnessing it. It was a glimpse of 'the dream come true', the golden age, the promised land.[127]

Schreiner's remark about the 'brilliant sunrise' suggests that the memory of the 1880s not only remained with her but also provided a platform from which she contemplated many later political events. It explains the renewed sense of hopefulness with which she viewed the activities of the militant suffragette movement, a hopefulness crushed by the 1914–1918 War as it had been crushed earlier by the South African War. However, her hopes revived around the Bolshevik revolution in Russia, increasingly militant political activity in Ireland and India, and the break-up of the Austro-Hungarian Empire. Schreiner's letters to her younger friend Ruth Alexander during 1917, for instance, are filled with joy at the demise of autocracies in Europe and disgust at British and French intervention in Russia, and Nevinson described her at a meeting of the 1919 Club toasting the Russian revolutionaries.[128] In Cape Town she talked about herself as a Bolshevik and Sinn Feiner to acquaintances, strongly expressed her support for Indian home rule, and eagerly anticipated revolutionary change in Russia and the demise of British imperialism.[129]

In these last few years, there were also more discouraging political developments, including the strong anti-feminist mood in post-war Britain in spite of some women gaining the vote, but more particularly the extension of segregationist and punitive measures against black people in South Africa.

However, in the last weeks of her life Schreiner collected money for the large number of African women in prison in Bloemfontein in the Free State of South Africa for opposing the introduction of 'passes', and sent a contribution to the embryonic ANC. She retained until the very end her strong conviction that organic but organised social movements such as these would eventually win the day.

Notes

1   Rive 1987.

2   Schoeman 1989, 1992.

3   Chapter 4 discusses the major interpretations, also short annotations are provided of a range of secondary sources, so I do not 'name names' in this chapter.

4   This idea of 'Schreiner biocriticism' comes from Gray 1975.

5   OS to Havelock Ellis, 25 January 1888, HRC Schreiner, Draznin 1992 p. 441. Due to the greater accuracy of Draznin's transcriptions, this collection is referenced wherever possible.

6   OS to Mary Brown, early 1889, SAL Schreiner, Rive 1987 p.148.

7   See Keegan 1996 for an overview of the historical background.

8   Emily, as the baptismal register shows, and not 'Emilie' as erroneously repeated in many sources.

9   This had also happened in 1842, when he was dismissed by the London Missionary Society. The trading prohibition was to protect black people from exploitation, although Gottlob Schreiner's infringements probably were intended to be helpful rather than profiteering. But he also had extensive family obligations and his ministry was conducted in what seems an all-round incompetent way. See Schoeman 1989 pp.118–20.

10 This was the extent of the formal schooling Schreiner received, unlike her brothers, who attended 'good schools' and then either college or University, and it rankled with her. She commented to Ellis (OS to Havelock Ellis, 21 July 1884, HRC Schreiner, Draznin 1992 pp.106–108) "I have never been to school you know or had one sixpence expended on my education. When I think of all the advantages that other people have I sometimes feel bitter... It isn't that one can't teach oneself everything, one can, but it's such a fearful cost of strength".

11 OS to Havelock Ellis, 28 March 1884, HRC Schreiner, Draznin 1992 pp. 38–40.

12 OS to Betty Molteno, 22 May 1896, UCT Schreiner, Rive 1987 p. 277.

13 The Schreiner siblings shared this medical 'dream'. For Will Schreiner, it formed a kind of 'ideal life' against which, when depressed, he contrasted his over-worked reality; see Walker 1937.

14 Renier 1984.

15 Mary Brown received the manuscript of An African Farm in England in 1880, then consulted a publisher in Edinburgh who proposed revisions which Schreiner largely completed before leaving Africa in February 1881. From the second edition on, An African Farm is dedicated to Brown, although she had reservations.about this public association with freethinking radicalism (Mary Brown to Alice Hemming, 15 October 1884/1885, UCT Schreiner).

16   For some clues as to the earliest period of Schreiner's time in England, see Brown 1937, Liddington 1984 pp. 56–8. Schreiner and Eleanor Marx could have met as early as June 1881 in Eastbourne, and my own view is that Marx was the source of her contacts with British socialism. See Wheen 1999 on Karl Marx and family.

17   Cronwright-Schreiner 1924a pp.136–7.

18   Cronwright-Schreiner 1924a p. 370.

19   OS to Edward Carpenter, nd March 1908, NELM Schreiner SMD 30.32.d.

20   Carpenter 1916 p. 229.

21   As Schoeman (1991) points out, it was not so intellectually isolated as Europeans supposed, key books reached the Colony within a short time of publication, and their ideas had wide circulation through the lending libraries that even small towns possessed.

22   Cronwright-Schreiner 1924a p. 67.

23   *An African Farm* p. 83; the epigraph appears at the start of Part 2.

24   Such a view of asthma has been medically discredited for some considerable time now, although Berkman's (1989) study was the first Schreiner scholarship to recognise this.

25   It was probably the oldest sister Katie who suffered the most, as letters from her brothers Fred and Theo after her marriage suggest; see Wits Findlay Papers A1199, also Findlay 1954 pp. 163–5.

26   OS to Rebecca Schreiner, February/March 1896, Rive 1987 pp. 266–70. Whenever I reference the Rive collection without noting an archive source, this is because Rive has quoted a letter from Cronwright-Schreiner's *The Letters* which no longer exists. As the Rive collection is generally easier to obtain, I reference it rather than *The Letters* where appropriate.

27   There were also large areas of agreement between the siblings, in particular regarding 'the Native question'. In fact, because of Will's earlier much more illiberal views on 'race' matters, for a long period Olive Schreiner was closer to Ettie than to him (Theo's religious fundamentalism prevented closeness in spite of his radicalism on 'native' issues).

28   This included in relation to her doubts about marrying Cronwright, as a letter to Edward Carpenter makes clear; see here OS to Edward Carpenter, 18 July 1893, 1 August 1893, Sheffield Carpenter.

29   Story-telling was widely recognised as a special gift she had, which held successive generations of children (and adults) enthralled.

30   OS to Havelock Ellis, 2 May 1884, HRC Schreiner, Draznin 1992 pp. 46–8.

31   In part presumably because, as the head of a fee-paying school, he was concerned about parental attitudes and the effects on recruitment to the school.

32   "Dream life and real life" in November 1881 (later published in Schreiner (1909) *Dream Life*), "The Adventures of Master Towser" in March 1882 (later published in Schreiner (1923) *Stories*), and "The Lost Joy" in 1883 (later published in Schreiner (1891) *Dreams*); a fourth, "My first adventures at the Cape", appeared pseudonymously as the work of 'Paulinsky Smith' in 1884 (later published as Schreiner 1992).

33   OS to Havelock Ellis 5 April 1889, Rive 1987 p.154.

34   See Wheen 1999 for Marx and her father in Eastbourne and Ventnor in 1881–82.

35   This happened following her discovery that the then-recently widowed Aveling was secretly planning to marry another woman, although other factors were involved as well. See Kapp 1976, Part V.

36 Olive Schreiner destroyed many letters before leaving South Africa in 1913, so that she retained these is testimony to the importance they had for her – others that she kept were from her Mother, Will and Cronwright-Schreiner himself. For Cronwright-Schreiner's letter-burnings, see his journal, 3 June 1921, 5 September 1922, 22 Nov 1924 (NELM Schreiner SMD 30.1.a, b, and d).

37 This demonstration and Stead's 'The Maiden Tribute' articles in the *Pall Mall Gazette* were influential in radicalising many people's views about prostitution; the government's introduction of a Bill to increase the age of female sexual consent was linked. See Bland 1995.

38 Olive Renier (1984 p. viii) comments that during various crises in her life Alice Corthorn destroyed all letters and her diaries, bar one volume.

39 In a letter to Mary Sauer (nd March 1891, SAL Schreiner, Rive 1987 p. 188–9), Schreiner refers to Corthorn as "the woman I love almost best in the world".

40 Renier 1984.

41 HE to OS, 20 February 1884, HRC Ellis, Draznin 1992 p. 334.

42 Two high altitude semi-arid bush-covered areas in South Africa of stupendous grandeur and beauty.

43 James Hinton was seen as a radical because of his views about women's spiritual equality with men. It became known in the circles Ellis and Schreiner moved in, which included the widow and other women associates of Hinton, that Hinton had had 'polygamous' sexual relationships with a number of them. Objecting to Hinton and 'Hintonism', Olive Schreiner also saw these relationships as an exploitative abuse of power on Hinton's part. However, she refused to condemn the women involved, including Maud Weldon, the 'bigamous wife' of Hinton's son Howard; when he was prosecuted for bigamy, she went everyday to the court to support Mrs Weldon.

44 Ellis was a polymath who also edited plays, a new edition of Shakespeare introduced by well-known figures, a 'popular' science series, translated work by the Italian criminologist Cesare Lombroso, and was a prolific writer on literary matters. By the 1920s he had become a 'pundit', writing popular pieces containing what had by then become received wisdom on sexual matters. See Grosskurth 1980.

45 The British Progressive Association was "a small group of freethinkers, cooperative pioneers and ethical socialists who came together for lectures and discussion. Through the Association Ellis, who acted as secretary, made contact with Thomas Davidson, the founder of an equally small Fellowship of the New Life... which envisaged a new social community.... A succession from the Fellowship in January 1884 led to the founding of the Fabian Society" (Rive 1987 p. 41). There were overlaps in membership and attendance at meetings of the Association and the Fellowship.

46 Edith Lees, who later married Ellis, was responsible for the running of the Fellowship cooperative household; thus when in her novel *Attainment* she wrote that 'fellowship is hell', she knew what she was writing about.

47 OS to Will Schreiner, 12 May 1912, UCT Schreiner.

48 OS to Havelock Ellis, nd. February 1884, HRC Schreiner, Draznin 1992 pp. 34–5.

49 An attached note says it was to appear in his (1932) *Views and Reviews*, although in the event it did not; see HRC TIF Armstrong MSC.

50 "The world is crashing about you... Your dearest friends are being dragged to prison; & theory that you have been interested in are being practically tested; cruel & wicked wrong is being done to innocent little children – & yet you look with astonishment and disapproval on another... not untouched by it!... & give you £200 a year you would curl yourself up in abstract study & thought for the rest of your life." OS to Havelock Ellis, 25 January 1888, HRC Schreiner, Draznin 1992 pp. 441–2.

51 OS to Havelock Ellis, 29 July 1884, HRC Schreiner, Draznin 1992, p. 114.

52 For instance, Ellis emotionally completely withdrew from his wife Edith Lees in 1919, around her linked physical and mental decline and then death from diabetes. Schreiner's view was that if Edith's behaviour was the result of "the diabetes affecting the brain" (OS to HE, 29 March 1916, HRC Schreiner OS.5b-x) then she should not be in an asylum, as Ellis was proposing; this was Edith's great fear and the cause of the final rift between them. See also Grosskurth 1980.

53 See Sheila Rowbotham 1977 for still the best succinct account of Carpenter and his place in radical circles.

54 A proposed chapter on "The intermediate sex", which was his response to the Oscar Wilde trial, was withdrawn from his 1896 published *Love's Coming of Age* because of Allen and Unwin's nervousness about possible prosecution. It appeared in the 1906 second edition and then, with related essays, it was published in *The Intermediate Sex* in 1908, again by Allen and Unwin.

55 His relationship with Kate Salt was less happy than this, which suggests that Schreiner provided much of the running in working out a modus vivendi between them; see here Stanley 1992b.

56 See for instance OS to Edward Carpenter 13 October 1914, NELM Schreiner SMD 30.32.q.

57 Symons 1899.

58 Cronwright-Schreiner 1924a p.187.

59 In 1897, Symons visited Schreiner and Cronwright when they were in Italy following the publication in London of her *Trooper Peter Halket of Mashonaland*. It is difficult not to wonder what Symons the aesthete made of the hyper-manly Cronwright.

60 For example, OS to Karl Pearson, 20 June 1886, London Pearson, Rive 1987 pp. 84–5; also see extracts from letters to her probably from Pearson in Cronwright-Schreiner 1924a pp. 355–6.

61 See Bland 1990 and 1995 and Walkowitz 1986 for interesting but rather different accounts.

62 Before Schreiner had returned to South Africa he had become a close friend, though she disagreed with his evangelism and uncritical support for Rhodes.

63 To Pearson, Schreiner commented "it left out one whole field; to me, personally the most important one" (OS to Karl Pearson, 12 July 1885, London Pearson, Rive 1987 p. 65); his paper was published in Pearson 1887.

64 One was Caroline Haddon, James Hinton's sister-in-law, who Hinton also had a sexual relationship with. There were also anonymous letters saying the same thing, which Schreiner suspected were written by Cobb.

65 Given the usual emphasis on the relationship between Pearson and Schreiner, it is instructive to note that twenty years later what remained in Schreiner's memory was the betrayal by a woman (that is, Elisabeth Cobb); see here her letter to Adela Villiers Smith, 12 December 1910, *The Letters* p. 297). Regarding the gossip, see Schreiner's comment to Carpenter that "You must always stick up for Ellis if you ever hear anyone talk against him; he's one of the quite purest, noblest souls, and people don't understand him" (OS to Edward Carpenter, 5 February 1889, Sheffield Carpenter, Rive 1987, p. 151), while see OS to Havelock Ellis (10 December 1886, HRC Schreiner, Draznin 1992 p. 424) regarding the anonymous letters.

66   Thus, in a purple aside, Nadine Gordimer (1983 p. 96) comments "About sex, she lied to herself continuously – protesting to her men friends that she wanted 'love and friendship without any sex element' in letters whose very syntax paces out yearning sexual desire". If so, I have yet to read them.

67   See here Burdett 2001 for a very interesting discussion of this, although I cannot agree with the overall 'message' of her argument across Chapter 2 of her book, that Schreiner's response to Pearson's ideas in effect determined hers, that her two 'Woman' articles and *Woman and Labour* were written "to fit her argument as closely as possible to the kinds of demands Pearson might make, but yet to turn it to different conclusions" (p. 49). Thus, for instance, I find little sign of Pearson having an influence on the detailed analysis in Schreiner's 'sex book', although its title, *Woman and Labour*, certainly has a dig at his work and she clearly disliked his – and many other people's – ideas about 'women's place' and her argument rebuts contemporary views about this. Their 1880s exchanges on the topic (for instance, OS to Karl Pearson, 10 September 1886, London Pearson; Rive 1987 pp.103–105) also suggest that when she was more influenced by him she envisaged the form her analysis would take very differently from what eventuated.

68   See here OS to Edward Carpenter, 21 January 1889, Sheffield Carpenter.

69   OS to Karl Pearson, 6 June 1890 and 11 November 1890, London Pearson, Rive 1987 pp.173–4, 177–8. OS to Havelock Ellis, 12 June 1890, Rive 1987 pp.174–5.

70   A fictionalised reworking of this appears in *FMTM*, when Drummond explains to Rebekah the circumstances in which he writes.

71   Gregg 1955 p. 39.

72   OS to Karl Pearson, 11 November 1890, London Pearson, Rive 1987 pp.177–80.

73   OS to Havelock Ellis, 25 April 1890, Rive 1987 p.170; and OS to Karl Pearson, 6 June 1890, London Pearson, Rive 1987 pp.173–4.

74   Expressed particularly in letters when she first returned, including in OS to Havelock Ellis, 5 April 1890, 20 April 1890, Rive 1987 pp.167–8, 169–70; and OS to Edward Carpenter, 19 April 1890, Sheffield Carpenter, Rive 1987 p.169.

75   See Monsman 1991 on Schreiner and landscape.

76   With this being a key feature of Afrikaner mythology; see Cauthen 1997.

77   Regarding the Philistinism of whites, see OS to Havelock Ellis, 27 November 1889 and especially OS to HE 15 April 1890, Rive 1987 pp.162–3, 168–9; also OS to Edward Carpenter, 31 January 1890, Sheffield Carpenter, Rive 1987 p.164.

78   Rebecca Schreiner had converted to Catholicism soon after Gottlob's death, and lived for many years (until she 'de-converted') as a paying guest attached to a convent in Grahamstown.

79   See OS to Havelock Ellis, 25 April 1890, Rive 1987 p. 170.

80   Molteno was headmistress of a well-known girls' school in Port Elizabeth. Greene also taught in the school. They were inseparable, and Schreiner saw their relationship as one of the perfect loves she had known.

81   Schreiner had intended to publish it in 1896, then in 1901. After the war, the fundamental unity of whites around racist policies had become clear, and she realised publication was no longer viable.

82   Schreiner's admiration always contained a 'but', for even in mid-1890 she thought Rhodes ought not to accept the Prime Ministership of the Cape, given his control of the British South Africa Company chartered by Britain to operate in Matabeleland and Mashonaland meant a conflict of interest; see OS to W.T. Stead, 12 July 1890, Rive 1987 p. 175.

83 Strictly-speaking, 'the Boers' were the trekkboer pastoralist farmers, whereas increasingly over this period other Boer people were becoming the rapidly urbanised, educated, professional Afrikaner middle and upper class. As Tamarkin (1996) interestingly explores, until the South African War and after, there was no great separation of interests between Boer and English in the Cape.

84 'Explaining' the Jameson Raid and events in Matabeleland and Mashonaland would require explaining the changing course of the politics and economics of Africa in the context of European imperialism – and all in a footnote! These were bound up with Cecil Rhodes' territorial ambitions, on his own behalf but also of British imperial expansion in Africa. The complicity of Rhodes (and Chamberlain) in the Raid became clear in two official inquiries, in the Cape and then in London, in spite of attempts by the British government to cover this up.

85 Originally having pan-Afrikaner aspirations, under the leadership of Jan Hofmeyer the Bond developed as a sub-party in Cape politics, adopting a 'line' distinctive from that of the Afrikaner Transvaal and Free State and usually supportive of British imperial policies. In providing the key support for the second Rhodes government, it became the most powerful grouping in Cape political life. See Tamarkin 1996.

86 Rhodes' sexuality is still usually written of as an absence, a failure to act out what might have been his feelings about men. That he might have been sexually involved with many of his 'band of brothers', including Jameson, or have made use of 'sexual services' from men, including black men, is apparently still unthinkable. See for instance Rotburg's (1988) otherwise excellent account.

87 Gregg 1955 pp. 27–8.

88 He legally changed his name to Cronwright-Schreiner, while she was usually known as Mrs Schreiner. Generally I refer to him as Cronwright unless the discussion includes publications that appeared under his married name. His father was a successful shopkeeper, and, while his brothers entered professional occupations, his own work when Olive Schreiner met him was as a farm manager; he later became a land agent and auctioneer. From archive papers at NELM, he clearly had early literary ambitions and after Schreiner's death wrote a number of unpublished stories as well as keeping a diary and a journal. Given his productivity in terms of quantity of writing, it must have been galling to have witnessed his wife's continuing fame in the face of – in his terms – very little activity.

89 He had already corresponded with her about An African Farm in 1890, but this was the first time they met.

90 See here OS to Edward Carpenter, 18 July 1893, 1 August 1893, Sheffield Carpenter.

91 OS to Will Schreiner, 20 February 1894, UCT Schreiner, Rive 1987 pp. 232–3, her emphasis.

92 OS to Cronwright-Schreiner, nd. January 1893, Rive 1987 p. 218. The 'note' is a promissory one.

93 In fact she had pointed out the great likelihood of this happening before their marriage and had consequently planned on them living apart; it was through his insistence that she came to live at Krantz Plaats; see OS to Will Schreiner, 27 October 1893, UCT Schreiner.

94 See OS to Betty Molteno 1 November 1897 and 16 December 1897, OS to Will Schreiner 17 November 1897; OS to Fan Schreiner 15 December 1897; all UCT Schreiner.

95 OS to Edward Carpenter, Christmas Day 1892, Sheffield Carpenter, Rive 1987 pp. 216–7.

96 Her letters to Will Schreiner, read against hindsight knowledge of Cape and wider South African events of the time, testify to this. See here the UCT Schreiner collection.

97 Her very last letter to Cronwright-Schreiner, for instance, commented on the rise of the National Party in South Africa, the fact that the mining capitalists were backing Jan Smuts, and promised him more news about these things. See here OS to Cronwright-Schreiner, 9 December 1920, NELM Schreiner SMD 30.33.k.

98 As Jan Hofmeyer played within the Afrikaner Bond. Rose Innes had championed the growth of a number of Progressive Associations in the Cape; Schreiner wanted them in every town and village and across all four settler states; for the political work of the Transvaal Associations, see Wits Historical Papers A603 Transvaal Progressive Association 1905–7.

99 The South Africa Conciliation Committee was attached to the pro-Boer wing of the Liberal Party. Schreiner's friend, the Labour leader Keir Hardie, accompanied Cronwright to many of the meetings.

100 OS to Isie Smuts 24 May 1906, copy in SAL Schreiner 2.12.45.

101 Schreiner and Cronwright climbed Buffels Kop together not long after their marriage. The land was purchased at that time as their burial-place; the re-interment in a sarcophagous of Schreiner with her daughter and her dog was long planned.

102 While not likely in realist terms, it is clearly not present in the text as a realist description but rather as a symbolic device.

103 She described it, using the title of James Thompson's poem, as 'The City of Dreadful Night', a place of human corruption because founded for and devoted to the sole purpose of making money.

104 What this was remains unknown, but may be connected with bitter comments made in Cronwright's journals after her death about 'harrowing & angering' letters from her over this period and his unhappiness about her 'madness' and 'suspicions'; see his journal, 5 Sept 1922, 15 Dec 1921 – 30 Sept 1923, NELM Schreiner SMD 30.1.b, c, d. My conjecture, no more, is that Schreiner might have discovered him having adulterous relationships and reacted in ways that paralleled Rebekah's to Frank's adulteries in *FMTM*.

105 When martial law was declared, they were away from their Johannesburg home, staying on a farm near Hanover because of her asthma but expecting to return before war was declared. In spite of Cronwright's later protestations that nothing so precious as a manuscript on the 'woman question' could have been left behind, their baby's clothes, a lock of her hair and photograph were left and destroyed with other possessions by looters and shows they were completely caught on the hop. It is so unlikely as to be effectively impossible that they would willingly have left these in Johannesburg, so other important things would not have been either.

106 Married to the West End physician and would-be litterateur Dr J.H. Philpot, she had been a close friend of Elisabeth Cobb's in the 1880s; Schreiner's 'friendship by extension' ended when the relationship with Cobb did; Schreiner also thought Philpot was implicated in the gossip about Ellis. Philpot had South African family connections.

107 OS to Cronwright-Schreiner 27 March 1913, SAL Schreiner MSC 26, 2.16.139a.

108 As First and Scott (1980 pp.315–20) comment, in spite of suppressing any mention of differences in *The Life*, Cronwright none the less kept Schreiner's letters about this. He also kept falsified copies of his own letters and her replies, which he carbon-copied and sent to his brother Alfred. See NELM Schreiner SMD 30.34.a, b, c, d, e, and f.

109 Cronwright-Schreiner 1924a pp. 361–2.

110 SAL Schreiner MSC 2.1.29. Schreiner also wrote to her friend Mimmie Murray, from a farm in Porlock near Graaff-Reinet and president and founder of her local WEL branch, about these developments over a lengthy period of time; see here OS to Mimmie Murray, NELM 2001.24, Mrs Murray Letters.

111 This was published in book form in Britain in 1909 through the good offices of Constance Lytton, a close friend of Schreiner's; see here OS to Edward Carpenter, 19 February 1909, Sheffield Carpenter.

112 Schreiner *Thoughts*, p. 17.

113 Interestingly traced in Schoeman 1991 and particularly Schoeman 1992.

114 See Willan 1984.

115 General Missionary Commission on the so-called black peril, 1912/1913, Cory MS 14.847.

116 OS to J. Henderson, 26 December 1911, Cory MS 14.847.

117 See here OS to G.W. Cross 21 April 1898, Cory MS14.462.

118 See Zamir 1995 on Du Bois's ideas, and Du Bois 1903 for a book that Schreiner particularly admired because it was 'written from the inside' of black experience; see also OS to Edward Carpenter, 3 March 1906, NELM Schreiner SMD 30.32.f.

119 Renier 1984 p.11.

120 Stanley 2001a.

121 See OS to Havelock Ellis, 16 October 1914, *The Letters* p. 340.

122 OS to Will Schreiner, ?1917, UCT Schreiner.

123 OS to Cronwright-Schreiner 9 December 1920, NELM Schreiner SMD 30.33.k.

124 See the 'Report on post-mortem', Appendix C, Cronwright-Schreiner 1924a p. 390. Two letters in the NELM Schreiner collection are also pertinent. In the first, in 1898, John Brown sent to Cronwright-Schreiner a confidential letter from a consultant Olive Schreiner had seen, who Brown had contacted without her knowledge and who replied to him that "...her trouble is chiefly the loud complaint of an over taxed nervous system. There is, in the first place, no organic mischief about the heart, although her emotions are directed to that organ..." (Dr Rogers to Dr John Brown and sent by him to Cronwright-Schreiner, 12 Oct 1898, NELM Schreiner SMD 30.35.a). They secretly agreed a response based on the fictitious nature of her illness which also included Alice Corthorn. The second letter from John Brown concerns the autopsy report which proved the factual nature of her supposedly fictitious heart complaint: "... The 'coronary arteries' which were found so much 'occluded' are the only arteries which supply the substance of the heart with blood. Being for many years in the state they were found in, the heart has for all that time been staved of the blood necessary to enable its filters to [be] nourished, so that they could contract, and so drive the blood through the body. This is the cause for all her life long sufferings – & eventually her death. How does our poor knowledge give us any means of curing this state of matters, or of alleviating the suffering the poor patient has to endure." (John Brown to Cronwright-Schreiner, 16 Dec 1920, NELM Schreiner SMD 30.35.h).

125 OS to Havelock Ellis, 2 May 1884, HRC Schreiner, Draznin 1992 pp. 46–7.

126 OS to Cronwright, 8 May 1908, *The Letters* pp. 278–9. The quotation continues "Of course, Ed. Carpenter's book touches us in a way it can't others, just because it brings us back to that time..."; the letter-extract provided by Cronwright-Schreiner (the original was destroyed) does not say which of Carpenter's books this is. It is likely to have been either the 1906 *Love's Coming-of-Age* or the 1908 *The Intermediate Sex*.

127 Holmes 1985, pp. 74–5. Sheila Rowbotham (2000) makes a similar point and in ways more directly speaking to my own experience. Perhaps each generation has its own 'brilliant sunrise' (although mine, occurring in the 1970s and connected with the rise of the gay movement and the eruption of feminism within it, is not entirely coterminous with Rowbotham's), but I think perhaps only where the promise and the possibility of radical change is part of the zeitgeist.

128 She commented in August 1917 that "I fear England & France will come to the autocracy's help again as they did after the Japanese war & crush down the movement for freedom" (OS to Ruth Alexander, 22 August 1917, SAL Schreiner MSC 26, 2.1. 8) and later that "...it's not the fighting, it's the lying & the injustice that is the worst of all...Oh the wickedness of this league of curs with Russia" (OS to Ruth Alexander, nd 1917, SAL Schreiner MSC 26, 2.1.10).

129 Louis Herrman to Zelda Friedlander, 20 March 1957, SAL Schreiner MSC 26, 6.1.3.

Chapter 3
Olive Schreiner's Writings

Introduction

This chapter introduces the wide range of concerns that Olive Schreiner brought under the sign of what is now called 'feminist theory' and the different genres of writing she used in doing so. I discuss these discursively, looking at ideas and their development rather than details of 'plot and character', beginning with some comments on the place of writing in Schreiner's life, then the main themes and analytical ideas developed across Schreiner's writings. In doing so, I comment briefly on relevant aspects of the context her work was written in which have not been covered in previous chapters.

Schreiner's writings are discussed here in the approximate chronological order they were written in – 'approximate' because neither her letters nor her novel *From Man to Man* can be neatly confined to one period of time. Her letters were written across most of her life – the earliest archived was written in 1871, and the last on the day she died. Probably about half of the letters extant at her death were destroyed by Cronwright-Schreiner, but there are still around 5,000 in archive sources and most have never appeared in print; they are thus an important and still considerably under-utilised 'work' in their own right. The unfinished *FMTM* was edited and revised a number of times and is almost as difficult to 'place' chronologically as the letters. Substantial but incomplete, it haunts some commentators even more than Schreiner herself; it is also in my view a greatly under-estimated novel, one that has risen in my estimation each time I have re-read it. Consequently my account of Schreiner's writings starts with her letters, because of their central importance for understanding her ideas, relationships and the shifts and changes of her life; and it concludes with *FMTM*, because of the way it has been used as a metaphor for characterising her life.

I discuss Schreiner's writings in a broadly chronological way rather than thematically for a number of reasons. Firstly, 'writing, as such' was the core of Schreiner's life, the centre of her activities and her thoughts – even the otherwise grudging Cronwright recognised its defining importance for her. Looking at her writings chronologically throws light on how she responded to external events during her writing lifetime, and it also enables these to be related to 'what she did with them'. Secondly, Schreiner's ideas are sometimes treated as always 'already there', with little distinction made between her thinking in her late teens and twenties, and in her fifties and sixties. In fact her ideas developed and her analyses changed, in some respects markedly so, and a chronological approach enables these changes more readily to be discerned. Thirdly, Schreiner perceived a distinct change in her emphases and ways of working which she characterised as a move from 'interiority' to 'exteriority'; and a chronological approach enables an assessment of this. And fourthly, Schreiner has often been presented as a failed writer, perhaps because of taking her own comments about what she failed to write at face value. Looking chronologically at her work puts the emphasis firmly on what she did write and did complete, and thus better enables its assessment as a body of work, as an oeuvre.

The overview of Schreiner's writings given here is inevitably shaped by my particular interests and viewpoints, although I have attempted to sketch out Schreiner's ideas in as even-handed a way as possible. But of course, I want to emphasise, readers should read Schreiner's published writings themselves, rather than relying on 'interpretations', mine or any other.[1]

Writing, As Such

Writing was an important matter for a woman who wrote at least three and perhaps four novels, hundreds of individual allegories, a set of essays on South Africa, an allegorical novella, three important political pamphlets, a book of feminist theory and related articles preceding it, an unfinished analysis of war and aggression, numerous public letters on political topics, and something like 10–12,000 private letters, not to mention journals and diaries. Therefore an indication of Schreiner's ideas about the 'place' of writing, both in her life and as a social function, is in order.

Writing, Schreiner commented to her friend Betty Molteno in terms many other writers have echoed, and having a baby are comparable kinds of activity – "it may be a great labour & half kill you, but if you don't feel it's a great joy & bliss to suffer the agony of writing it, & a reward in itself, you're not fit to write it!!"[2] She also saw writing as an important factor in achieving social change because ideas 'travel':

> *That complex of knowledge and thought ... which for the want of a better term we are accustomed to call 'the spirit of the age' ... is created by the action of speech and mainly of opinion ossified and rendered permanent, portable, in the shape of literature ... Probably to no man is the part played by literature in creating this unity so clear as to the writer himself ... The thoughts which have visited him in his solitary night will have brought him into communion, closer than any physical contact, with men and women in every corner of the globe ... His kindred are not only those dwelling in the same house with him, but that band of men and women all the world over of whatever race or colour in whom his thought is germinating; for him almost alone at the present day is the circle of nationality ... obliterated by a still wider, which knows no distinction of speech, race, or colour – his readers are his people, and all literary peoples his fellow-countrymen.[3]*

Schreiner used the term 'writing' to include a number of activities, from the sudden germination of a thought or idea, thinking it through, repeatedly telling it aloud to refine it, then writing it down, subsequently reworking it, through to final revisions and publication. Her commitment was to 'writing, as such', to telling 'externally' and on paper the stories or ideas she told herself 'internally', and not to any specific form or genre of writing. She articulated this in terms of the social impact that writing could have, harnessing it to her feminist, socialist and humanitarian principles and commitment to social change. Her basic desire was to make 'real' the 'ideal' that had been glimpsed in her mind,[4] and this remained fundamental to how she understood her writing and perceived its successes and failures. Schreiner's writing is consequently best understood as a means, not an end: a means of her grasping a thought only barely glimpsed, which could then be made actual by thinking it into life, through giving it representational shape in first spoken and then written language.

Schreiner used a range of experimental literary devices, including deploying mixed genres, interrupting narrative, disrupting temporal sequencing, subtly ironicising the heroic, and using symbolism to undercut a surface impression with another more meaningful one. She had ethical and political purposes in writing the way she did, embedded in her rejection of 'the stage method' and employment of 'the method of life' in her polemical and analytical as much as her creative writings. Her authorial use of what she described as 'ribbed' and 'plain' styles of writing, as well as the more structural devices just listed, was also part of her departure from realist conventions that presumed writing as a referential and representational medium.[5]

Writing, then, was not a commentary on an ethical and political domain of activity; for Schreiner, 'writing, as such' was already fully part of this. In addition, the 'consumption' of writing by readers was something she saw having ethical and political consequence, because of the power of ideas to travel frontiers and create communities of like minds in ways that, as the quotation above puts it, 'know no distinction of speech, race, or colour'. This was not a conclusion Schreiner advanced glibly, but had arrived at from feeling pulled between the immediate and often heart-rending claims of needy people wanting sympathy and material help, and the more abstract claims of writing, engrossing in its own right, but potentially able to change the social and economic circumstances which occasioned people's demands on her. At the point she finally resolved this tension, in the later 1890s, her worsening asthma and heart problems had made inroads on her physical energy and affected her intellectual energy and ability to concentrate, something of enormous sadness and regret to her.[6]

For Schreiner, writing was work and so to be thought of like other kinds of productive and social labour. Consequently unnecessary intrusions into her time and energies (the threat of Cronwright's mother and sisters living with them in Johannesburg in the 1890s, for instance) rendered her fiercely resistant. And when things necessarily prevented or impeded her writing (her pregnancies and miscarriages and most particularly her asthma and worsening heart condition), she experienced self-punishing thoughts about 'what might have been'. Even Cronwright-Schreiner, usually so quick to disavow her productivity, commented in *The Life* on the necessity of work in this sense for her and the toll that not being able to do it took.

Schreiner frequently emphasised the incomplete nature of her writing project compared with what she had conceived in her mind, and in her later letters she lamented her failures and what she might have done had her asthma and heart condition permitted. The temptation is to take these comments (as Cronwright did) entirely at face value. While Schreiner's own disappointment is entirely understandable, it seems to me that constructing a balanced assessment now, more than eighty years on from her death, requires looking beyond this, relating her self-criticisms to what she actually produced, examining what her work overall 'adds up to' and evaluating this in its own terms, not just against the greater 'might have been'. Doing this is the purpose of this chapter.

The Works

Her letters

Olive Schreiner's archived letters are the single most important source regarding her writing, political views and involvements, and also her life, family, friendships and marriage. Her letters show the extent of her political interests, her keen involvement in family life and depth of feeling for people, and the seriousness of her commitment to the public concerns and analytical ideas she promoted. They also point up how responsive she was to her correspondents, rather than being 'egotistical' as a letter-writer.[7] There is a very different 'feel', for instance, to Schreiner's letters to her friends Havelock Ellis, Edward Carpenter and Karl Pearson; or to her brother Will and sister-in-law Fan; or to the politicians James Rose Innes and John X. Merriman; or to Rose Innes and his wife Jessie. Also the kinds of letters Schreiner wrote to the same correspondent – her sister Ettie, for instance – when she was a young woman are very different from those she wrote in later life.

Schreiner felt strongly that letters were entirely private communications and should never be made public. Therefore when she left South Africa for England in 1913 (and expecting to die there), with sadness but feeling its necessity, she destroyed large numbers of letters she had received and requested her correspondents to destroy hers or else to return them so that she could do so. Then, in completing *The Life* and *The Letters*, Cronwright-Schreiner systematically destroyed all the other letters he was able to.[8] But even so, a large number have survived in archive collections, covering her adult life from late adolescence on.

There are three published collections: *The Letters of Olive Schreiner*, edited by Cronwright-Schreiner; *Olive Schreiner Letters Volume 1 1871–1899*, edited by Richard Rive; and *My Other Self: The Letters of Olive Schreiner and Havelock Ellis, 1884–1920*, edited by Yaffa Claire Draznin.[9] While inevitably providing a less comprehensive picture than the archive collections, they are of course considerably more accessible and together give a flavour of 'what she was like' by conveying something of how she expressed herself. There are some 'cautions to readers' as well as indications of the particular strengths and weaknesses of these collections that can be indicated.

The first collection of Schreiner letters, *The Letters of Olive Schreiner*, was published by Cronwright-Schreiner in 1924. This is now widely recognised as heavily bowdlerised as well as being highly partial in the selections of both letters and correspondents included. *The Letters* contains extracts from around 900 letters in total, but with no more than a single sentence taken from some, while others are actually cannibalised parts of different letters grafted together. And many of Schreiner's relatives and friends refused to send him letters, feeling that Olive Schreiner would have been horrified at his project of 'biographising' her, while others greatly distrusted his intentions.[10]

This collection gives a skewed impression of Olive Schreiner as a letter-writer and also about who her key correspondents were. Cronwright-Schreiner's selections are also often oddities that point up her troubles with landladies and illnesses and remove not only her kindness and humour but, more importantly, her political ideas and involvements. They over-represent Havelock Ellis, certainly an important correspondent earlier in her adult life, but with equally significant ones overall including Schreiner's mother, her brother Will, Eleanor Marx, Betty Molteno and Alice Greene, Constance Lytton, Adela Smith, Edward Carpenter and Cronwright-Schreiner himself. In addition, some thirty inconsequential letters to Isaline Philpot are included, presumably to obviate any gossip that her relationship with Cronwright-Schreiner might be suspect.

The result removes all the major correspondences of Schreiner's young adulthood bar Ellis, and all the major correspondences of her maturity as well. *The Letters of Olive Schreiner* none the less remains an important as well as curiously interesting source, for it contains many extracts from letters now destroyed. However, the issues of selection, censorship and bowdlerisation sketched out here need to be kept in mind and readers be aware of the problems in drawing any conclusions from the material it includes.

Richard Rive's *Olive Schreiner Letters Volume 1 1871–1899* was published in 1987 and is probably the single most important contribution to Schreiner scholarship; indeed, Rive's emphasis in articles and other publications on the importance of the archive letters began to be influential even before its publication. His intention was to repair the problems of Cronwright-Schreiner's version and to give a rounded overview of Schreiner's interests and correspondences from 1871 to 1920, and some 550 letters are included in what was intended to be the first of two volumes.[11]

Many of the letters in Rive's collection have been edited, some of them substantially so; and others are unaccountably reprinted from Cronwright-Schreiner's collection even though the originals exist in archive sources and are different from Cronwright-Schreiner's version. Rive's editing work is not always made transparent to the reader, while sometimes the material he excised as holding "little real interest for readers today"[12] actually contains important evidence of Schreiner's political interests and concerns. Also readers are given a skewed impression of the importance of some correspondents in Schreiner's life: too many letters proportional to the total archived from some people are included, and too few from others. In addition, the editorial notes often omit or seem unaware of the feminist or socialist affiliations of various of Schreiner's correspondents,[13] with the result that her political contacts and involvements are less fully visible than they should be.

Still, these are problems about work that is at basis excellent and which certainly provided major new information and insights that underpinned much Schreiner scholarship subsequently, and so should be kept in proportion. Overall, Rive's collection has made an extremely important contribution to Schreiner scholarship and has been crucial for changing interpretations and understandings of her work.

The 'tone' of Schreiner's style of letter-writing has sometimes been assumed from her early letters to Havelock Ellis, which dominated Cronwright-Schreiner's collection. The third collection of Schreiner letters, *My Other Self: The Letters of Olive Schreiner and Havelock Ellis, 1884–1920*, was published in 1992, edited by Yaffa Claire Draznin. This collection focuses on both sides of the exchange of letters between Schreiner and Ellis,[14] and Draznin's bibliographic and editorial work is fully transparent, meticulous and quite exemplary. The result throws an extremely interesting and perhaps unexpected light on one of Schreiner's important friendships.

As Draznin's useful "Introduction" notes, the importance of this correspondence lies, not in individual letters from either Schreiner or Ellis, but rather because of the way this set of letters illuminates their relationship overall. This is not to say that there are not interesting individual letters here, and more accurately transcribed than in Rive's collection or other published sources,[15] but rather that Draznin's work, in bringing together both 'sides' in the chronological order these letters were written in,[16] reveals a more important dimension. This concerns its internal dynamics, with Ellis constraining a particular kind of response from Schreiner. This not only involved Ellis' need for emotional support of a kind and degree she found increasingly unacceptable and avoided or 'managed' in her letters, but also Schreiner's self-censoring of the assured and confident tone that marks her other letters of this time, and her omission of anything about people and activities Ellis disapproved of.

The result of Draznin's editorial work substantially changes understanding of the relationship between Havelock Ellis and Olive Schreiner. What was earlier taken to indicate Schreiner's emotional dependency now appears substantially the effect of Ellis' emotional demands; and what was earlier seen as an egalitarian relationship between a 'New Woman' and Ellis as a 'new man' now shows just how much of the 'old Adam' he retained. It thereby throws a side-light on those of Schreiner's early allegorical writings, in particular "Three dreams in a desert", which propose that women's freedom entails stopping 'carrying' men emotionally. And certainly Draznin's collections sets standards for transcription and editing that are exemplary.

Each of these three edited collections of Schreiner letters is partial in coverage, albeit in different ways and for very different reasons: Cronwright-Schreiner's because it bowdlerised and cannibalised and deliberately misrepresented; Rive's because only one part of the planned two volumes appeared and because editing removed, or failed to provide, some important material; and Draznin's because it is explicitly concerned with one particular exchange of letters. Consequently it is important to provide some brief information about the archived letter collections (and see also the Appendix).

The archive collections of Schreiner's letters give a rather different view of the woman than any so far published account. They show Schreiner's responsiveness as a letter-writer, the care she took in maintaining friendships and family relationships, her kindness and humour, her interest and proficiency in the details of domesticity, as well as in the debates and controversies of public political life, and her keen attention to political and economic developments inter/nationally. Some of the important concerns characterising the archived letters include Schreiner's involvements with feminism and socialism; her analyses of imperialism, capitalism and international finance; her theorisation of labour and 'race'; political life in South Africa before, during and after the War of 1899–1902; federalism versus union; the nature of nation-states; the emergence of state racism, her analysis of militarism and war; and her thoughts on changes in Europe and Africa following the 1914–1918 War. Many of these things either do not appear in the edited collections, or else appear as less important than they actually were for Schreiner. These concerns are not insignificant ones, and they are important to understanding the kind of woman, and the kind of social and political analyst, she was. The material in Schreiner's letters on them also throws light on her published work, and writings intended for publication but never completed. The archive letters, then, are of incomparable importance.[17]

The novels, finished and unfinished

It is surprisingly difficult to answer what appears to be an apparently straightforward question: how many novels did Olive Schreiner write? The simple answer is three, *The Story of An African Farm*, published in 1883, and two others published posthumously, *From Man to Man* in 1924, and *Undine* in 1929. Immediately, however, other questions have to be asked. Precisely what is meant by 'a novel' and should Schreiner's *Trooper Peter Halket of Mashonaland*, published in 1897 and now usually referred to as an 'allegorical novella', be counted or not? What is the status of *Undine*, which Schreiner had completed but abandoned as 'never to be published'? And how should "New Rush" be seen, for although a full manuscript of this title no longer exists, the archival evidence suggests that this novel was completed by Schreiner and read in draft by Philip Kent and Havelock Ellis in mid-1884.[18]

These questions bring to light some interesting things about how Schreiner wrote. All three of the now extant novels, and probably also "New Rush" (which may or may not be coterminous with a partly, or even wholly, completed story called "Diamond Fields"), seem to have had a common point of origin. This was in the early 1870s when Schreiner lived in the diamond mining camp at Kimberley with her brothers Theo and Will and her sister Ettie and started writing in a serious way; then over time strands within this work separated out from the common source and took on increasingly distinct forms of their own. Thus *Undine* and *An African Farm*, for instance, share an opening episode concerned with the change of the physical landscape from day to night, and an accompanying change in the emotional and ethical landscape in the mind of a wakeful child listening to a clock ticking away seconds and also human lives.[19] These two novels and also *From Man to Man* feature a karoo farm, and parents who are either dead or otherwise distant and removed from the life of its child denizens; and all three are concerned with the wavering line between 'dream life' and 'real life'. In addition, in Schreiner's few extant journals[20] and her letters, many more titles of pieces of writing are mentioned alongside or in succession to those of the three published novels. Consequently the question arises as to whether these indicate the existence of yet more novels that Schreiner was writing and which were perhaps abandoned or lost.

After following these mentions through her unpublished as well as published letters, the view I've come to is that Schreiner's fictional writing had its origin in allegorical 'scenes' or 'episodes', to which the many mentions of titles in her journals and letters refer, and that her novels developed by a number of these scenes or episodes being expanded and fitted together around an emergent narrative line and the development of characterisation. The plethora of such titles that exist in Schreiner's archive papers, her frequent remarks about 'writing allegories all the time' and that her other kinds of writing 'threw themselves' into allegorical form, and her comment to Arthur Symons that allegories were "the very essence of art" and of her writing,[21] all support this.

Schreiner's first-completed novel is *Undine*, the manuscript having as its sub-title 'A Queer Little Child', which is also the title of the first chapter of the published version.[22] The manuscript copy is beautifully copied out and fully complete and Schreiner gave it to Havelock Ellis in autumn 1884; she later wrote to him that it was never to be published. On one level *Undine* is pure juvenilia, tyro work, a novel with a 'real time' narrative based around an extremely unrealistic plot.[23] But on another level, *Undine* is a complex and ambitious, if not successfully realised, project. This novel is constructed around the allegorical frame of the Greek myth of the water-nymph *Undine*, who died because the human man she left her natural habitat for did not love her in return. It contains a number of echoes of Goethe, one of Schreiner's favourite authors, who wrote about the same theme in the story of Mignon, the 'queer little child' who also died for want of love, in *Wilhelm Meister*.[24] In Schreiner's novel, Undine is indeed a queer little child, one who grows up to be an unworldly young woman. As in the Greek myth, Schreiner's Undine crosses water, both literally from Africa to England, and symbolically when she comes to love a man, Albert Blair, she knows to be cold and cruel. She then later re-crosses water literally, returning to her true home of Africa and goes to the mining camp in Kimberley. However, symbolically Undine is unable to return to ordinary life and the arrival in Kimberley of the dying Albert Blair heralds her own death from fever.

Undine exemplifies an idea, and its plot and much of its characterisation has allegorical significance and weight, rather than being 'realistically' conceived or drawn. It is not surprising that Schreiner failed to bring off this book as a fully realised project, not least because she was such a young and inexperienced writer. But it is surprising that as a novice she should have conceived and completed such a 'structural' piece of writing, and also that she did so at a time when novel-writing in general, let alone novels written by uneducated young women living on colonial frontiers, was rarely conceived in structural terms and as a whole in this way.

Undine is certainly juvenilia, however. Albert Blair is too icily a 'piece of perfection' to be believable, the stories within stories in the book are too separate from the main plot, the plot is arranged around events which are too epiphanously dramatic. But once prised loose from the conventions of the realist Victorian novel and being seen as a failed example of this, and re-read as something different in kind, an experimental and non-realist novel conceived on structural lines, then *Undine* looks far more interesting and its status consequently needs rethinking with this in mind.

The Story of An African Farm was published in two volumes by Chapman and Hall in 1883, became an instant bestseller, and its sales and translations world-wide continued to provide not only Schreiner with a regular income from royalties for the rest of her life, but also Cronwright-Schreiner after her death.[25] *An African Farm* still continues to sell in a variety of 'popular' editions. It has received a number of very different present-day interpretations, re-readings which in interesting ways parallel those of Schreiner's contemporaries, being seen as juvenilia, as a failed romance in which the heroine unaccountably dies, as badly plotted with wooden characters, as almost pure autobiography, as oddly missing the thrills and spills and kills of Africa, as an over-moral Christian tale, and so on.[26]

An African Farm was published under the pseudonym of Ralph Iron.[27] It has three central characters, tied emotionally and by circumstance and events through living together on a karoo farm: Lyndall, a forthright, independent-minded and orphaned English child; her homely placid cousin Em, daughter of 'mixed' Boer and English parentage, who will inherit the farm when she is adult; and Waldo, the dreamy artistic son of the farm's German overseer, old Otto. Tant' Sannie, second wife and widow of Em's father, presides over the farm and holds authority in the eyes of white and black alike. The farm is by itself out on the karoo, under the merciless sun by day and transformed by the moon at night. The farm's African workers come and go, giving only the barest outward show of subservience and openly contemptuous of Otto's naiveties; its African and Indian house-servants give allegiance only to Sannie, the source of power although not of justice. A feckless itinerant Irish adventurer, Bonaparte Blenkins, arrives; Sannie and Otto in their naivety, but not the children, believe his boastful taradiddles; he courts Sannie, usurps Otto (who dies of a heart attack when sacked from his job), and terrorises the children, culminating in the savage beating and near death of Waldo. His evil reign is ended, not by a just adult power or by Christian mercy, but instead by chance through a comic mishap involving Sannie and her very fat and very rich niece Trana.

The adult Waldo, Lyndall and Em are in their different ways each permanently marked by their childhood: an epigraph from Alexis de Tocqueville precedes the first volume of the novel, indicating that the key to the development of moral character lies in responses to childhood experiences rather than 'inner' qualities. Waldo is deeply damaged and scarred by Blenkins' reign of terror; his inner will has been broken and something essential has gone from him.[28] Lyndall has the independence and quality of will that Waldo lacks; but she is a woman and her ability to act, and thus to become, is severely constrained by the limits imposed on women regardless of their qualities or gifts. Em on the surface appears to be unscathed; none the less her simple desires are thwarted by circumstance: Gregory Rose, the callow young man who reciprocates her love, comes to passionately care for Lyndall after she returns from boarding school; and although eventually he and Em marry and have children, Em knows there is a greater love that will never be hers.

The epigraph to the second part of An African Farm – 'a striving, and a striving, and an ending in nothing' – is taken from earlier in the novel, when Waldo's dog Doss plays with and then casually kills a dung-beetle which had spent hours collecting and rolling up debris, as it turned out pointlessly. Waldo goes from the farm out into the world, but has little definition of character or will to enable him to make this a constructive experience; Lyndall returns to the farm and then leaves again, driven by her need to do and to be, but utterly limited in the choices she can make and sexually involved with an Englishman she morally despises; and Em stays at home, but is defeated none the less.

The structure of An African Farm is 'odd'. Its organisation of narrative, plot and characterisation is multiply cross-cut by silences, elisions and intrusions that are 'out of time and place', as well as by a number of 'stories within stories'. Some crucial elements of plot remain absent from the narrative (for instance, what happened while Lyndall was at school, and how she became involved with the Englishman). People come and go, even though the conventional requirements of plot are that they should not. Thus Lyndall leaves the novel half-way through and re-appears only through a story told by the minor character of Gregory Rose; the Englishman appears for one brief evening only; Waldo dies of a heart attack like his father when he ought to live in contentment on the farm. In the end only the villain, Bonaparte Blenkins, prospers. He gets exactly what he desires, for he marries Sannie's rich niece Trana, who quickly dies and leaves him her fortune. There are 'comic' intrusions into 'tragic' events, featuring Sannie, Trana and Blenkins. There are two lengthy allegorical intrusions: the first is the "Times and Seasons" sequence, concerned with the development of morality and ethics; and the second is "The Hunter's Tale", an allegory told by a passing traveller Waldo meets on the outskirts of the farm. There are two particularly important stories told within stories: Gregory Rose's story of looking for, finding and then nursing Lyndall, who dies from a fever after she gives birth to a child who dies; and Waldo's story of his adventures in the world and his subsequent return to the farm. And as well as these 'set piece' allegories, there are also a number of shorter allegorical moments tucked away in the details of the plot, of which the dog Doss casually snapping off the legs of the beetle, and the deaths of animals cruelly killed – Waldo's elderly horse ridden to its death by an acquaintance, and an ox beaten to death by its owner, Waldo's employer – are the most notable.

In addition, Schreiner's portrayal of African and Indian characters in *An African Farm* emphasises both their lack of independent agency within the domestic setting, and also their suppressed anger, sullenness and resentment which spills out onto those even less consequential in the scheme of things than they. Her landscapes sketch in the shadowy formations of Africans who come and go without gratitude or tie of affection at the borders of the domestic and the untamed, and are contemptuous or sullenly angry at the naiveties and exploitativeness of whites. In doing so she represents with considerable accuracy the inward-looking insularity of colonial life on the frontier, its apparent imperviousness to the African world it was actually a part of, the immensely corrupting and damaging consequences of their way of life for the white colonists themselves, and the barely suppressed bitter resentment and anger of the Africans they lived among but not with. It remains a riveting read.

Both *An African Farm* and *Undine* were completed and the former had already been published by the time Olive Schreiner met Havelock Ellis in London in 1884. Schreiner's letters to Ellis, and reports on manuscripts read for Chapman and Hall,[29] show that another Schreiner novel had been completed and submitted to this publisher. Between 1884 and 1886 it was substantially, and in Schreiner's view deleteriously, changed around comments and suggestions made to her. This was *From Man to Man*, which subsequently went through three further periods of revision and also a transfer into typescript. Originating in Schreiner's great burst of creative energy in her young womanhood, *FMTM* is also marked by ideas and experiences later in her life and accompanying shifts in the book's 'message' and structure. In addition, after Schreiner's death it was also edited and perhaps modified in now unknowable ways by Cronwright-Schreiner. A temporally 'out of place' and extremely readable piece of work, I discuss it at the end of the chapter.

Stories, dreams and allegories

The three books containing selections of Schreiner's allegories and allegorical short stories are *Dreams*, published in 1890; *Dream Life and Real Life*, published in 1893; and *Stories, Dreams and Allegories*, published posthumously in 1923. All three make use of the idea of 'dreams', that half-sleeping and half-waking state in which people's imaginations and fantasies are often extremely active. Dreaming is a liminal state of mind that provides a route-stop between everyday realities and a world of allegorical landscapes and significances. Some of Schreiner's allegories are organised around a dreamer dreaming; in others, the reader is immediately plunged into an allegorical landscape, or else in an apparently realistic one that later assumes allegorical significance.

The stories in these collections have allegorical structure as well as content. Events take place in symbolic landscapes: stark and cratered mountains, tempestuously rushing water, over-hung forests thick with trees, a desert under a burning sun, a ruined chapel at the end of a promontory, a woman's study which a male visitor briefly enters and then leaves. They also feature characters that are formalised to one degree or another. The most formalised personify symbolic or ethical meanings, such as 'God', 'Goodness' or 'a Hunter', for instance, while others, such as 'Woman' or 'Man', are employed as empty categories around which an ethical point can be made. Some writings in these collections are 'more story' and 'less allegory', and involve a greater degree of plot and narrative structure and also more rounded characters who develop over the course of the plot. Others contain little of these usual accountrements of story-telling and are 'all allegory', consisting of one or more tableau-like episodes in which there is little character or plot but instead an event propels a sometimes brief ethical inquiry and rapid conclusion.

'Stories, dreams and allegories', the title given by Cronwright-Schreiner to the variable quality of work published in the posthumous collection of 1923, is an appropriate description of the three related genres of writing that Schreiner intertwined. In addition, 'dream life and real life', the title of an earlier collection of allegories and also the longest story in this, also indicates the shift of consciousness Schreiner was concerned with exploring and the ambiguities involved in distinguishing what is 'real' and what is 'dream'.

Schreiner wrote or talked to friends about the genesis of a number of her best-known allegories. Regarding "I thought I stood", written in 1887, Mary Brown described arriving at Schreiner's lodgings to find she had been up most of the night writing, having the evening before been to a feminist meeting during which sanctimonious comments about sexually 'good' and 'bad' women had outraged her; the idea for the allegory then flashed into her mind.[30] In a letter to Adela Villiers Smith, Schreiner described the genesis of the "Prelude", "The Child's Day", now published as the start of *From Man to Man*. She was sitting at her desk "when suddenly, in an instant, the whole of this little Prelude flashed on me. You know those folded up views of places one buys; you take hold of one end and all the pictures unfold one after the other as quick as light. That was how it flashed on me. I started up and paced about the room. I felt absolutely astonished ...".[31] The origin of the allegorical novella *Trooper Peter Halket of Mashonaland* in 1896 was very similar: she wrote to her friend Betty Molteno that the idea of the story came complete into her half-sleeping and half-waking mind one morning as she woke, at a time when she felt horrified about the genocide happening in Matabeleland and Mashonaland.[32] Even though in conception it arrived complete, there were some months of re/writing before its form on paper came near her original idea, as her letters testify.

The purpose of Schreiner's allegorical writing was not to 'tell a story', but rather to convey an ethical message in an elaborated metaphor. Its ethical basis was sometimes socialist or feminist or anti-war; sometimes it concerned the literal and symbolic ties of sisterhood, the vulnerabilities of children or the abuse of animals; and it sometimes dealt with fundamental themes, such as how people respond to the passing of time, failure to achieve their goals, or behave in the face of wrong-doing. Although the figure of 'God' appears fairly often in Schreiner's allegorical writing, she used the term in a kind of 'post-Christian' way. A freethinker, she had originally completely eschewed using the term 'God', thinking this would only confuse readers by implying a Christian meaning to the word.[33] Later she resumed using it because of the positive ethical connotations it had for many people, but always with a sharp sting in the tail/ tale to ironicise Christian pretensions and hypocricies. But her doing this has resulted in precisely the confusions she had earlier worried about, leading not just many contemporaries, but a good few present-day readers as well, to ignore the sting and assume her message was indeed Christian. Schreiner was rueful or dismayed about such readings, but could never quite accept these came directly from the terms she used. An illustration here concerns "In a Ruined Chapel", published in *Dreams*, an allegory in which the teller of the tale sleeps within a ruined chapel, beneath its walls painted with frescoes of Christ and the Madonna, and dreams of a man speaking with God and an angel. She thought interpreting this allegory in Christian terms was an almost wilful misreading, for she saw it as concerned with the virtue of forgiveness in human relationships and she intended its particular setting and the figures of God and the angel to be seen as heavily ironic, given the actual paucity of forgiveness in Christianity.

As I suggested earlier, allegory was the basis of the way that Schreiner wrote. She re-worked her allegories so as to strip from them any detail that had accrued in the writing process. An example here concerns "Workers", a short allegory written in 1887 and published in *Stories, Dreams and Allegories*, where the manuscript (one of the few to escape destruction by Cronwright-Schreiner) shows Schreiner striking out detail from its sentences.[34] And when the allegorical genesis developed instead as a short story, she successively added detail during the writing process, with her novels being structured around allegorical episodes or tableaux joined narratively together with considerably more development of character and plot. *From Man to Man* is a good example of this, for in journals and letters Schreiner comments about having written 'stories' with titles that correspond to some chapter headings in this novel, and also that she has joined together some of these.[35]

A watershed: the Wollstonecraft fragment

Crowding social engagements, her problematic feelings about Pearson, the resentful importuning of Bryan Donkin when she refused to marry him, and seemingly endless demands on her from women wanting her support or help, led Schreiner to move from lodgings into a convent in Kilburn and then another in Harrow,[36] places where single women could board and visitors could not enter. Schreiner thereby regained a good deal of solitude and the consequent opening of her mind necessary for her to write. During this time, and especially the period following when she travelled through France, Switzerland and Italy, she wrote most of the allegories which appeared in *Dreams* and in *Dream Life and Real Life*, and many others as well. Schreiner saw her 1889 return to South Africa as a shift in her intellectual concerns from interiority to exteriority; however, her 'allegorical turn' of the later 1880s occurred in a period apparently marked by the concerns of exteriority and what she described as 'scientific work'.

During much of her time in England, Schreiner was concerned with the 'sex book' her letters to Karl Pearson refer to and which is also described in some detail in the introduction to *Woman and Labour*. She was relatedly immersed in reading and thinking about prostitution, both its effects on women and her rejection of it being seen as 'the problem of women' (rather than that of men). Alongside this, before she left England for Europe Schreiner had agreed to write an introduction to a centenary edition of Mary Wollstonecraft's *A Vindication of the Rights of Woman*.[37] Schreiner's proposed "Wollstonecraft Introduction" was never completed, and what exists now is only a short fragment of a draft in a typescript of doubtful status: the typescript was edited and prepared by Cronwright-Schreiner from a manuscript sent to him by Havelock Ellis in November 1924, with the manuscript then being destroyed. The typescript has subsequently been published by Carolyn Burdett with an introduction by her.[38]

Cronwright-Schreiner suggests the draft fragment was 'dashed off' in 1886 when Schreiner was in Italy and she did no more work on it but sent it to Ellis, who kept it until he sent it to Cronwright-Schreiner. Schreiner's contemporary letters suggest this is actually likely to be an early draft which had been superseded by a longer version or versions which were written but later lost or destroyed.[39] Certainly Olive Schreiner described its contents in a letter to Havelock Ellis in November 1888 in terms very different from the surviving fragment – "My Mary Wollstonecraft is going on. It is all poetry from the first to the last. There are six or seven allegories in it; I've tried to keep them out and I can't …".[40] And while the short opening sentences of the typescript might, but only by considerably straining the point, be seen as a kind of blank verse, there are certainly not six or seven, nor even two or three, allegories within it. Indeed, only if a conversation with a black woman Schreiner says occurred when she was a child, contained in a long footnote, is seen in these terms could it be said to include even one.[41] The precise status of the Wollstonecraft fragment with regard to Schreiner's developing ideas, then, is 'not known'; however, there is good reason for supposing Cronwright-Schreiner's typescript is indeed an early draft superseded by later ones.

The typescript begins by criticising Wollstonecraft's work – it lacks genius because Wollstonecraft doesn't argue but asserts; and Schreiner's positive comments about Wollstonecraft as a woman contrast with her criticisms about the argumentative style of Wollstonecraft's book. Schreiner's own concern is with pinpointing the "two *principles* acting on each other ... which we call male and female"[42] and tracing how these affect different life forms from lichen to birds to apes to humans and also among humans from one age to another. Schreiner's discussion rejects a developmental social Darwinist model, seeing other species and earlier stages of human history as more egalitarian, and also arguing that in societies where "muscular power is largely superseded by other forms of force in material production ... the process of [sexual] differentiation is not continuing, and ... in such society there is a tendency in the male and female forms to become increasingly similar".[43]

Schreiner intended to treat Wollstonecraft 'as a woman' and use this as a vehicle for a theoretical exegesis which would "hold the substance of all my thoughts on the man and woman question".[44] However, the more Schreiner pursued this, the more problems became apparent, and she expressed her difficulty in finding a form to hold 'all of her thoughts' to Pearson. Letters during 1888[45] show something of this: her arguments and explanations continually 'threw' themselves into allegorical form; and by the time she wrote to Ellis in November 1888 the draft was 'all poetry', a rather vague statement; more specifically, she wrote that it was composed by six or seven allegories, commenting that she loathed the 'long legal arguments' she could more easily produce. There are no clues about 'what happened next', just a letter to Ellis of February 1889 which reports that she is completing "The Prelude" to *From Man to Man*, and that "Mary W & every thing else can go to the D-. Tell Rhys so!".[46]

My conclusion, *contra* Cronwright-Schreiner, then, is that there was a lengthier piece of writing about Wollstonecraft's *Vindication* in a more advanced form than the surviving typescript, but this was abandoned unfinished because of a failure in form, rather than content. Schreiner commented that in its 'reduced' form, her Wollstonecraft "Introduction" consisted of a number of allegories. I think it likely these took on independent life and are either to be found in the three published collections and/or were perhaps, with the draft "Introduction" itself, in a trunk of her things which was lost en route to visit her mother in late 1889.

Writing to Ellis about her return to South Africa, Schreiner commented that "I look and look at ... material things ...I suppose it is after these long, long years buried in abstract thought ... that I turn with such a keen kind of relish to the external world".[47] Her attempt to write the Wollstonecraft "Introduction", by 'throwing itself' into allegorical forms about abstract matters, seems to me to represent a watershed in Schreiner's writing because it re/turned her to interiority, while out of it came her decision to return to Africa, something which represented her positive choice of the external world and an 'objective life' and all that this entailed.

South African writings: of politics, citizens and states

Between her return to South Africa at the end of 1889, and leaving again in 1913, Olive Schreiner published a number of political essays and pamphlets, the allegorical novella *Trooper Peter Halket of Mashonaland*, and *Woman and Labour*. While these have different origins and analytical concerns, their histories are closely intertwined; each is concerned in some way with labour; each examines the issues cohering around the value accorded to the different classes of people who perform it. They witness Schreiner as a 'returned South African', occupying a liminal social position having been overseas for a decade, writing as a relative outsider on the 'distinctive problem' faced by the country; and then becoming an insider again, making a number of interventions in South African political life, but drawing on her international reputation and contacts and a feminist analysis in doing so.

The essays Schreiner wrote about South Africa's peoples and problems after her return were published in British and American journals. She intended to draw them together with some additional chapters as a book, *Thoughts on South Africa*. This was halted initially by Schreiner's realisation that the second Rhodes ministry of 1893 was fundamentally reshaping Cape political life, and she produced an outspoken analysis of these changes read at a public meeting in 1895 and published in 1896 as *The Political Situation*. She then returned to her South African essays, and a "Prefatory Note" to the intended collection written in February 1896 explained that, because of the Jameson Raid, "the Boer has been struck a sore blow by the hand that stroked him" [i.e. Rhodes] and it was now "necessary that he, with his antique faults and his heroic virtues, should be shown to the world as he is".[48] But then in June 1896, Schreiner's attention turned to the events surrounding the uprisings in 'Rhodesia' by the Ndebele and the Shona and what she saw as genocide by the paid mercenaries working for Rhodes' Chartered Company, and she became immersed in writing *Trooper Peter*, published in December 1896.

Publication of Schreiner's South African essays was then halted again through another series of political and personal events. There was the birth and death of her daughter, a number of serious miscarriages and various moves across the country, while around 1897–99 some unknown but momentous change occurred in her marriage, with her energies consumed by things she could neither talk nor write about. She also thought that the economic interests analysed in *The Political Situation* were behind the increasingly confrontational attitude of the British imperial government towards the Boer Republics of the Transvaal and the Orange Free State. A polemic, *An English South African's View of the Situation*, published in a range of outlets in late 1898 and early 1899, warned of 'the Monopolists' and their domination of political events from behind the scenes and argued passionately against the by then certain war. The English version (it was rapidly also published in Dutch) was being reprinted when war between Britain and the Boer Republics began and Schreiner withdrew it from publication so as not to profit from this.

During the period of the South African War, publication of any new work was not possible for Schreiner because she lived for most of it under martial law in Hanover, with its provisions with regard to censorship particularly stringently applied to her. She had written a number of short anti-war statements for the volkscongresses and peace meetings held across South Africa during 1900, while her enforced seclusion and regimented confinement for the last two years of the war provided the conditions for a new burst of creativity, out of which came *Woman and Labour* as well some concentrated work on *From Man to Man*.

As the war started, Schreiner published two linked essays on "The Woman Question" in the USA. These extended her analysis of 'sex parasitism' in "The Boer Woman and the Modern Woman's Question", and of 'race parasitism' in "The Psychology of the Boer", both originally published in the early 1890s and conceived as components of *Thoughts on South Africa*. As the War ended, Schreiner returned to *Thoughts* and wrote some additional footnotes and a new "Introduction". But it rapidly became clear to her that the post-war rapprochement between Britain and the Boers was removing civil and political rights from black South Africans, and this decisively brought publication plans to an end, for some of its basic premises had been overtaken by events.

While *Thoughts* had missed its political moment, a casualty of the events leading to war and then the changes occurring in its wake, Schreiner's analysis of where these events would take South Africa in the future continued, in her letters, and also in an essay published in 1908 in South Africa and 1909 in Britain. This was *Closer Union*, concerned with the form that a closer constitutional relationship between the four settler states might take. It was produced as part of Schreiner's 'behind the scenes' activities in opposing union and supporting federalism, a position she held from the early 1890s, and it centrally raised questions about the relationship between 'race', labour and citizenship.

Schreiner's South African writings are fascinating on a number of levels. Firstly, they were written as direct political interventions in a society that excluded women from its political life. By their very existence, they were a public affront to the masculinist preserve of South African, and not just Cape, politics of the time. Secondly, they combine a sharp analytic edge with a sometimes highly polemical argument. Schreiner was a very unwilling public speaker, but comments about the few occasions she did so suggest she was both powerful and persuasive, with similar qualities characterising her polemical writing, which I think best thought of as 'writing aloud'.[49] Thirdly, as well as analysis, they are also concerned with prediction, with looking forward to where current events might lead. As well as this being unusual for a social analyst, it is also striking how accurate Schreiner's predictions for the future of South Africa in economic, 'race' and social terms were. And fourthly, the scope of her analysis covered questions of labour and 'race', the role of monopoly capital, imperialism and its interconnections with capitalism, liberal and radical organisation, different kinds of states and the rights of citizens within them. Schreiner didn't 'know her place' analytically any more than socially, for she refused to be confined to 'women's issues' conceived narrowly. I now look in more detail at these writings, focusing on themes concerned with 'politics, citizens and states', particularly regarding labour and 'race' within this.

Thoughts on South Africa

Thoughts on South Africa is an interesting and still contentious book.[50] It provides considerable evidence of Schreiner's political prescience, but looked at with hindsight it also reveals where the fault-line in her analytic thinking about the connections between capitalism and 'race' lay in the early and middle 1890s: in eliding the specifically colonial presence of whites in the four settler states, and positioning black Africans in a child/parent relationship with them. Its opening essay starts with a kind of travelogue, a journey through a landscape. The 'figures' in this landscape are central in later essays, but are heralded here by Schreiner's outline of "the core of the social and political problem" of South Africa – that it contains "the most marvellous diversity of races" but "no possible line which can be drawn across it will separate the colours one from another, or even combine their darker shades".[51] Consequently its political boundaries (those of the settler states) "have no relation to the racial divisions of the people beneath them and therefore have in them, at the core, nothing of the true nature of national divisions".[52] Moreover, Schreiner sees the remaining independent 'native' states also being drawn into this configuration, prey to commercial interests and so intruded upon by guns, railways and other accoutrements of 'civilisation', and eventually to be annexed or subjected to Chartered Company control.[53]

In her exposition of 'the problem', Schreiner takes the white presence as a given, the result of emigration into empty lands, and sees the early Boer trekker-farmers and English settlers in equal competition with groups of black people also on the move, migrating from elsewhere into the apparently empty plains.[54] She emphasises the resulting complex heterogeneity of the racial mixtures of peoples 'on the ground' but structured around a hierarchy of colour, of settler over 'native'. Colour here is not seen as coterminous with 'race' – "Our race question is *complicated* by a question of colour", as Schreiner puts it;[55] and at the time of writing her main concern was with that other 'racial' confrontation, with defending the Boer pastoralists in the face of monopolist encroachments and British imperial intransigence.

Schreiner was fully aware of the anomalousness of the Boer farmers. She notes their lack of rootedness in metropolitan culture, their earlier slave ownership and consequently troubled relationship with the British imperial presence, leading to them trekking to new frontier areas. She discusses the Boers' way of life, its simplicity, poverty; its homogeneity in atomised familial groups on isolated farming homesteads; its subsistence-basis and predictable annual rhythms; and its resultant distinctive social patterns, including an inward-looking anti-intellectualism, early marriage, and an equally valued but highly gendered division of labour. She particularly comments on the language the Boers spoke, an archaic and truncated form of Dutch she thought unable to express subtleties, cutting off its speakers from intellectual developments in the rest of world. Schreiner was also aware that the characteristics she associated with the Boers in fact made them anomalous within the Afrikaner population as a whole (which was increasingly urban and educated), but she argued that it was stereotypes about the 'primitive' Boers that fuelled British imperial disregard for the Republics of the Transvaal and the Free State and so she wanted to accord value to their positive characteristics. And however 'outdated', she saw their way of life as anti-capitalist and also having unusually egalitarian relations between men and women, both attributes she highly valued.

In *Thoughts*, Schreiner discusses divisions of labour between Boer women and men and the consequences of the equal worth of 'domestic' and 'non-domestic' labour, in a situation where marriage was not based on romantic ideals but practical considerations, with both parties having similar expectations, similar levels of education and interest, and also comparable duties, obligations and pleasures. Boer women were almost alone among people of European origin in having no part in contemporary woman's movements, in Schreiner's view because this "in its ultimate essence is '*The Movement of a Vast Unemployed*'" and Boer women were certainly not that.[56] She also notes the decrease in European societies of women's traditional labour, and points out that 'sex parasitism', the dependence of one gendered class of person upon the labour of another, had become a possibility.

Boer women already had equal labour equally valued, and Schreiner suggested this was the product of the pre-industrial and 'primitive' life of the Boers, mid-way between the pastoral native Africans and 'civilisation'. Such comments, and her remarks about Afrikaans, explain the largely negative response of Boer and Afrikaner people to publication of those of Schreiner's essays that appeared contemporaneously. Nevertheless her account was intended as complimentary, located as it was in her anti-Darwinist analysis that 'civilisation' and industrialisation actually constituted a moral and ethical, and also a social, step *backwards* and not forwards for humanity. For Schreiner, 'civilisation' was quintessentially problematic, because she saw 'progress' as always a matter of equality and justice, rather than technological development.

Thoughts deals with the issues surrounding 'race' and racism mainly in connection with 'the problem of slavery' and its result in mixed race people – companion essays on South Africa's other black populations were planned but not written. Outlining three 'branches' of African peoples, Schreiner's focus is the supposedly 'anti-social' characteristics of 'half-castes', people of mixed race, asking "whether this anti-sociality is inherent ... or is accidental, dependent on external and changeable conditions",[57] and suggesting the latter. Schreiner saw the mixed race population as the product of largely forced sexual relations between the most vulnerable of enslaved women and the most despotic of Boer slave-owners. The children who resulted had 'no place', certainly not among whites, nor within black communities either. The popular view, notes Schreiner, is that mixed race people are born 'anti-social', resulting in criminality in men and prostitution in women. Against this, she insists on 'lack of social place', for while the social position of mixed race peoples had improved, there was still not the "solid social matrix about him, which inevitably results in social training ... nothing is left but an awfully isolated 'I'". Her conclusion is that "Had he been begotten by Cherubim upon Seraphim and born before the throne of God, and then transported to a slave compound, to grow up raceless, traditionless, and believing himself contraband, we should in all probability have had a being with the same anti-social characteristics we often have today".[58] In spite of this, because of the social consequences and possible unknown 'laws of inheritance', Schreiner argues that "in a country situated such as South Africa is to-day, for cowardice and recklessness perhaps none equals the action of the man who ... originates such a cross of races ... because the pain and evil resulting ... must be borne by others ... because the results of his action must go on for generations ...".[59] She was considerably surprised at the hurt and anger her comments produced in non-white readers; consequently, in a note on "The Value of Human Varieties" added in 1901, she emphasised her 'profound sympathy' for mixed race people, but in patronising terms that reiterated the very problem these readers had perceived.[60]

Schreiner argues that no groups of whites were by definition more, or less, racist, with it being different material circumstances which produced the different responses of whites. Her focus is instead on how the 'race' problem in South Africa is refracted by capital and monopoly, particularly the activities of financial syndicates monopolistically controlled by 'interests' that were largely non-resident. These were the 'great labour employers' in the diamond and gold mines of South Africa, and they treated their black labour force, not as people, but as a commercial asset, a machine, as mere labour force or power. Thus Schreiner at this point in time formulates 'the native problem' of South Africa as entirely a labour question, as the labour question of Europe and America complicated by two factors, those of monopolism and race – "the native is not a person hated or beloved, but a commercial asset ... For them [the monopolists] the native problem is a nutshell: 'In how far, and by what means, can the rate of native wages be diminished, so raising profits?' ...".[61]

For Schreiner, this relationship of capital to labour was compounded because almost the entire body of the labouring or proletarian class was black: whites of whatever class or occupation by origin quickly became overseers, managers, or occupied other positions of authority in relation to black labour. Attempts by the labouring class to better their conditions were met by an overt hostility which was apparently class-based, but actually founded on racial prejudice, and employer syndicates used the spectre of black labour as a demonised threat against their white overseers and managers. Against this, Schreiner argues the only way to contain the power of the monopolistic control of diamonds and gold would be for black and white employees to combine.[62] But she was aware the labour movement was deeply flawed, its radicalism marred by two 'symptoms', "that the man who is trying to free himself from the tyranny of class still does ... maintain that of sex ... [and] strives jealously to exclude men who are not of his blood".[63]

Schreiner asserts the 'moral imperative' she sees characterising the liberal response to 'race': for the liberal, "if the native be his equal in mental power and moral vigour, his place is beside him; but, if the African native be not his equal ... then there rests upon him the mighty obligation of all strength towards weakness, of all wisdom towards ignorance, of the God towards the man: 'Rank confers obligation'".[64] Variants of this argument, depicting black people as 'little brothers' or as children hand in hand with whites, are used in various of her writing at this time and show her unable at this point to conceive of black people as fully equal:

> It would be a lie to say that we love the black man, if by that is meant we love him as we love the white. But we are resolved to deal with justice and mercy towards him. We will treat him as if we loved him: and in time the love may come ... When we have dealt with the dark man for years with justice and mercy and taught him all we know, we shall perhaps be able to look deep into each other's eyes and smile: as parent and child.[65]

The prose here, as in much of Schreiner's writing, is performative, an injunction or an encouragement to her, by implication white, readers, and so discerning whether these were 'really' her own views is simply not possible. In addition, it should be noted that the views about 'race' expressed in *Thoughts* were considered subversively progressive when Schreiner originally published them in article form, and any sensible re-reading needs to recognise this. Regarding 'race' matters, it also should be noted that a significant shift in the way she thought about these occurred subsequently, encouraged by changing and more retrogressive political circumstances, and an increase in her personal knowledge of black people. Two pieces of her work are particularly relevant to this, *The Political Situation* and *Trooper Peter Halket of Mashonaland*.

The political situation

Schreiner wrote *The Political Situation* as an explicit political intervention. It was read by Cronwright-Schreiner on a highly public occasion in Kimberley Town Hall in August 1895 under the noses of Rhodes and the 'Monopolists' it lambasts; and it was published under their joint names in early 1896.[66] Initially it was popularly supposed Cronwright-Schreiner was its author, but, while he gained substantial initial credit for it from the black community in the Cape, being invited to stand as the 'native candidate' for Queen's Town in the following election, it soon leaked out who the actual author was.

In May 1893 Rhodes had resigned and jettisoned the three liberals (Sauer, Merriman and Innes) in his cabinet, and with support from the Afrikaner Bond was invited by the Governor to form another ministry, composed by Bondsmen, the former Prime Minister Gordon Sprigge and other conservatives. A number of pieces of retrogressive legislation were then introduced; in particular, the 1894 Glen Grey Act 'settled' land rights on black Africans in Glen Grey, but in very small land-holdings and with the requirement that these could be inherited only through primogeniture, with the effect of creating strong 'push factors' driving black men in increasing numbers onto the labour-market. Alongside this, the Cape franchise was successfully limited through a redistribution measure; while unsuccessful attempts were made to introduce a 'strop' bill, a 9 p.m. curfew for black people, and a 'pass' system. Together these measures constituted an early, albeit in part unsuccessful, attempt to establish what was known later as 'apartheid'. With them, Schreiner's essay also listed the alienation of public land, the monopolistic control of mineral rights, Chartered Company control of adjacent territories, and taxation of necessities but not of diamonds or alcohol, as components of the 'persistent tendency' for retrogressive legislation in the Cape.[67]

It had by this time become clear to at least some observers of Cape politics, including Olive Schreiner, that its old political life, with its high degree of individualism and low degree of organisation, had become anachronistic. The Bond was successful largely because it operated more like a 'party' in the modern sense; and Rhodes could operate effectively unopposed because the opposition was both fractured and also open to being 'squared', as he would have phrased it.[68] The emphasis on the individual, not principles and policies, predisposed even liberal politicians to cooption in return for their own individual political advancement – "coquetting with any and every party which appears likely to aid them to office and power", as Schreiner put it.[69] James Rose Innes responded by encouraging Progressive Associations in Cape Town and Port Elizabeth, but for Schreiner this was too contained, arguing in *The Political Situation* that a liberal political grouping should institute branches in every town and village and act in an organised and concerted way around an agreed set of principles.[70]

'Liberal' is used in *The Political Situation* in its late nineteenth century meaning and is more akin to what would now be called a social democratic position. For Schreiner, the founding principles of liberalism took a particular 'turn' in the South African context, in relation to labour, taxation and the franchise, with people's response to the first being the key to their position regarding the others. This was because for her the labour question "assumes gigantic importance, including as it does almost the whole of what is popularly termed the Native Question; that question being indeed only the Labour Question of Europe complicated by a difference of race and colour between the employing and propertied and the employed and poorer classes".[71] Because of the importance of 'race' matters, South African liberalism would take a distinctive and, she hoped, more radical turn. And while Schreiner proposed that Rose Innes should be invited to lead the Progressives, she emphasised that the "most vital and world-wide movements ... such as those of labour and women, have not been organised or led by one commanding intellect"; it was instead their grassroots base which gave them life and force.[72]

Schreiner's comments about 'monopolists' and 'capitalists' in *The Political Situation* were certainly not mealy-mouthed about Rhodes, the Chartered Company, or the deleterious effect of the formation of the cartels, syndicates and monopolies it was promoting. The lure of its mineral wealth meant that it was not just diamonds and gold, but South Africa itself, that was regarded as a mere 'field' for extracting wealth from;[73] and economic power bought political power and control in the Cape legislature. Schreiner's concern here was with minerals and profit, but, because of events elsewhere in southern Africa, her analysis then shifted dramatically towards the role of military force in expansionist activities.

Trooper Peter

Trooper Peter Halket of Mashonaland was written about the uprisings against the frontier regime of Chartered Company rule by the Ndebele and their fiefs the Shona in June and July 1896 in the areas now Zambia and Zimbabwe.[74] Chartered Company rule involved corporal punishment, the expropriation of land, and the forced labour of men. The uprisings involved brutal killings of whites, followed by extraordinarily punitive reprisals including mass killings and rapes and the burning of kraals and fields by combined Chartered Company mercenaries and British imperial troops. In Matabeleland, peace was negotiated by Rhodes with some personal bravery involved and agreement to ameliorate the repressive white regime, although the structure of Company rule in fact remained the same. Mass starvation followed, exponentially increasing the necessity for Ndebele men to sell their labour to the settler population. Similar events took place in Mashonaland, again involving the systematic burning of kraals and fields, the equally systematic rape of women and murder of children and the elderly, and the summary execution of men under more than usually brutal conditions.

Schreiner was on holiday on the Kowie River, Port Alfred, in July and August 1896 in the wake of a serious miscarriage, and "as I opened my eyes there was an allegory fully fledged in my mind! A sort of allegory story about Matabeleland. So I'm here writing hard ever since", although she had earlier commented she felt stunned by the events in Matabeleland to the extent that "I seem to have no feeling left".[75] *Trooper Peter* was completed in November 1896 and in December she travelled to England with the manuscript. Schreiner was accused of exaggerating in *Trooper Peter*, and people were particularly shocked by her inclusion of a photograph of white men watching black men being hanged from a tree, their feet nearly touching the ground but not quite.[76] Schreiner, though, was sure of her ground and emphasised that her contacts had provided her with reliable detailed information. These contacts included acquaintances of Cronwright-Schreiner's from Johannesburg, appalled but publicly quiescent 'Company men', young troopers in shock, and a trail of black Africans who found their way to her home. Subsequently a journalist, Frank Sykes, who accompanied one of the British military columns, provided the same description of summary hangings outside Bulawayo that Schreiner had referred to.[78]

In *Trooper Peter*, Schreiner indicted Rhodes by name as not only morally but also directly personally culpable. This was scandalous enough; however, the literary means Schreiner employed in the book made it blasphemous for many readers. It was published in early 1897 while the Committee of Inquiry on the Jameson Raid was hearing Rhodes' evidence, and also having its remit circumscribed by Chamberlain so that the matters the book deals with were ruled out of its jurisdiction. The anonymous readers' reports on *Trooper Peter* commissioned by its publisher veered between dismissing it as slight but verbose, and condemning it because "one is sorry to see so many inflated nothings put in the mouth of his [that is, Peter's] Saviour".[79] Reviewers frequently responded to it as an evangelical Christian tract and thus as either laudable or blasphemous (a review in *Blackwood's Magazine*, for instance, insisted on the presumptious folly of using 'Our Lord' as an 'extraordinary Interlocutor', and also saw this as an ineffective way of making a political point which the reviewer sympathised with).[80] *Trooper Peter* none the less had a enormous popular impact, its first (and large) printing sold out rapidly, and it was almost immediately translated and published in a large number of languages.

Trooper Peter now tends to be seen as an artistic failure because of its textual interruptions by propagandist and verbose speeches and its seemingly Christian message,[81] an approach which sees Schreiner wanting to write a conventional Christian moral story but failing. However, the book's temporal interruptions and disjunctures purposefully 'do things' to what kind of moral message it inscribes, and in fact it savagely attacks Christian hypocrisy.[82]

Part I is a 'dream' narrative. The Chartered Company trooper, Peter Simon Halket, is lost and spends the night on a koppie, staring into a fire and drinking cheap brandy. He thinks of his washer-woman mother, the little cap she had knitted for him, and the way she had taught him to pray and to be 'good'. He hears footsteps, prepares to shoot what he thinks will be a Shona rebel but finds is a white man, a Jew. Peter tells the man a 'story within the story' about his sexual exploitation of black women, joining the troop, turning Maxim guns on kraals, murdering women and children, shooting black men, sometimes blowing their skulls off, blowing up caves where fleeing elderly people and pregnant women hide, but not being able to stomach watching men be hanged.

The reader becomes aware, although Peter does not, that the man in the frock with wavy hair and bare feet is Jesus Christ.[83] The man becomes a questioner or interlocutor, leading Peter to think about how his story relates to his – and British – professed beliefs. The man then tells a second 'story within the story', relating a large chunk of a Cape Town preacher's tedious sermon. After three disavowals, Peter falteringly realises who the man is and his own moral duty; but the man vanishes.

Part II is a 'realist' narrative. Peter, found by his troop, is guarding a bound man; the reader is aware he is the husband of a woman Peter had bought for sexual purposes, but who stole his ammunition and ran away. A third 'interruption' occurs, in which 'a Colonial' travelling with the troop tells 'an Englishman' the story of Halket attempting to persuade the troop Captain not to execute the man by saying he was not a spy but defending his country; Halket's punishment is that he is made to guard the man and has been told he must shoot him the next morning. Peter frees the man, who silently escapes; Peter is shot by the Captain and then immediately buried.

Peter's death, apart from the escape of the Shona man, is utterly futile. It is also deliberately written as a tear-jerker of bathic dimensions, with Peter buried under a little stunted tree with his empty brandy flask and the cap his mother had knitted. Schreiner employs ironies lavishly mixed with overblown sentimentalities to attend her savage condemnation of the 'morality' that underpins Peter's act of Christian duty followed by martrydom: his brandy flask as a grave-marker, his little knitted cap, his murder by his own troop commander, the indistinguishable mound that is his grave. *Trooper Peter* invokes a fairy story of a washer-woman in her cottage with roses on the walls and it contains a picture-book version of Christianity that emphasises its hypocrisy – that people profess it but they don't live it, and that 'Christian redemption' excuses evil by suggesting that a last minute 'I'm sorry' buys moral indemnity. From the beginning, the reader is made to be a 'knowing reader', because of the textual assumption that Peter's tale of abuse, rape and murder will distance the reader from this thoroughly obnoxious little man. This distance between the protagonist and the reader is then compounded because the reader, but not Peter, rapidly becomes aware that 'the man' who appears during Peter's night on the koppie is in fact Jesus Christ. And Schreiner tellingly uses Christianity's moral teachings against it: its Jesus Christ is an implausible European man in a frock from a child's picture-book, conjured up by Peter's subterranean sense of guilt mixed with the fumes of Cape brandy; and its moral teaching iniquitously proposes that a life of lies, theft, rape and murder can be 'paid for' by a single death-bed act of redemptive sacrifice.

'On behalf of' Schreiner, and also, presumptively, the knowing reader, the Englishman travelling with the troop emphasises the 'real' moral point of the book, one that is more fundamental than just pointing out religious hypocrisy. While he had not believed in a literal 'God', none the less he comments he had believed "in something greater than I could understand, which moved in this earth, as your soul moves in its body ... [but] I do not believe it anymore. There is no God in Mashonaland". However, this too is treated as merely another unaccountable madness: "'Oh, don't say that!' cried the Colonial, much distressed. 'Are you going off your head, like poor Halket?'".[84] *Trooper Peter*, then, seduces Christian readers into the realisation that they aren't true Christians, emphasises the fundamental evilness of even the 'true' kind, and seditiously dismisses the idea there is any *a priori* underlying ethical purpose to anything.

Schreiner also had specifically feminist concerns in *Trooper Peter*, a book about imperialism and genocide. British imperial expansionism in southern Africa was occurring through the Chartered Company on the cheap, on the quiet; and its project was directed towards the possession and control of land on the one hand, but on the other the production of a proletarian labour force expropriated from land and dependent on wage-labour. But it was not just the labour of proletarianised men that Schreiner was concerned with, but also that of women on small land-holdings and as domestic servants and sex workers in the homes and cities of white South Africans. The one was as necessary, but no more, than the other. There were severely gendered outcomes to the expansionist project, then. There is a strong 'figure/ground' effect in *Trooper Peter* that concerns the highly gendered *modus vivendi* of imperial expansionism. There is a male fore-ground to the book: Peter with his brandy on the koppie, Jesus sat round Peter's fire, the troop Captain and the troopers, the Shona man bound and tied, a Colonial man and an Englishman sharing a tent and talking. But the book's African women are none the less *figuratively* central to its *ethically* central 'story within a story'. Thus the narrative that Peter Halket relates to Jesus contains multiple instances of sexual expropriation and sexual terrorism which had occurred 'off scene', including sexual assault, rape, the Maxim-gunning of women and children in Shona kraals, blowing up elderly women hiding in caves, thereby exposing the fundamentally gendered nature of the expansionist project.

The role of the Chartered Company in Mashonaland is pinpointed and Rhodes' complicity is named. Peter fully supports Rhodes' policy of expropriating land, parcelling it out to white settlers, and introducing forced labour – "We don't come out here to work; it's all very well in England; but we've come here to make money, and how are we to make it, unless you get niggers to work for you or start a syndicate? ...'". He compares this with the British, who would "let them have the vote, and get civilised and educated, and all that sort of thing";[85] the irony being, of course, that Peter is a murderer and rapist and vastly more uncivilised. The events surrounding the writing and publication of *Trooper Peter*, not susprisingly, contributed to major changes in Schreiner's analysis of 'race' and capital, aspects of which can be seen in the next essay she published.

An English South African's view of the situation

Peter Halket's 'we don't come out here to work' statement derives from Schreiner's earlier identification of economic 'parasitism' as central not only to gender and class but also 'race' relations. Her analysis of the role of monopoly and finance capital in relation to parasitism continued in *An English South African's View of the Situation*. An anti-war polemic, within it she comments on the role of diamond and gold monopolies as well as the expansionism of the Chartered Company. Schreiner saw Rhodes as central, not as an individual 'personality', but because he symbolised the underlying system that produced him, writing to Merriman:

> *We fight Rhodes because he means so much of oppression, injustice and moral degradation in South Africa; – but if he passed away tomorrow there still remains the terrible fact that something in our society has formed the matrix which has fed, nourished, and built up such a man! It is the far future of Africa during the next twenty-five or fifty years which depresses me. I believe we are standing on the top of a long downward slope. We shall reach the bottom at last, probably amid the [upheaval] of a war with our native races (then not the poor, savage but generous races whom we might have bound to ourselves by a little generosity and sympathy, but a fierce and half-educated, much brutalized race, who will have [come into their own].) I always see that day fifty or sixty years hence, and it is with reference to it that I judge of many things in the present.*[86]

An English South African's View was Schreiner's response to political circumstances in 1898 and 1899, involving not only the Chartered Company and Rhodes' involvement in De Beers and the Rand gold fields, but also the British and German imperial presences, and the political machinations of the Transvaal government under Paul Kruger as well. Her 'voice' within it is deliberately polemical and highly emotive – she was attempting to stir her readers into active opposition to the coming war between Britain and the Boer Republics.[87] The role of Milner as Governor of the Cape and the conduit of mis/information back to the imperial government was crucial when the clash of interests between British imperialism and the Transvaal came to a head, ostensibly over the franchise in the Transvaal, which excluded the large number of 'uitlanders' or foreigners from voting. Kruger's eventual offer to base the franchise on five years residency, an earlier demand of Milner's, was rejected; British troops were moved from India to South Africa; and the Transvaal presented an ultimatum about this to Britain.[88] Schreiner's polemic argued that those who were 'betwixt and between' British and Boer had a particular viewpoint which should be heeded: "Our position is unique, and it would seem that we are marked out ... for an especial function".[89]

In an open letter to the London *Sun*, a contemporary pro-Liberal newspaper, Schreiner pinpointed the origins of the war in "an endeavour on the part of a small but exceedingly wealthy and powerful section of persons to gain possession of the Transvaal gold fields".[90] Earlier, in the first essay in *Thoughts*, she had also predicted that in any war there were features of Boer life that would prevent an easy or quick victory by British troops. *An English South African's View* also emphasises the minority position of English-speaking South Africans, their lack of grievance against the Boer States and split loyalties, the uncertain success of British intervention, and that regardless of the military outcome a war would sever the last ties with Britain as a 'mother country'.

An English South African's View starts dispassionately, outlining events up to the point that war became likely; then it becomes a rising crescendo of polemic appealing passionately to British readers from the particular situation of an 'English South African'. Indeed, Schreiner argues, all white South Africans were increasingly 'in the middle' because of the growing prevalence of British-based education and English/Afrikaner inter-marriage. She also emphasises that the growing unity of whites had occurred in part through the worsening situation of black Africans: the harvest of the previous five years (that is, since the Glen Grey Act and the events in Matabeleland and Mashonaland), she insists, will be reaped by both English and Boer.[91]

Schreiner notes only in passing in this essay that the white populations of South Africa were settler societies, and her attention is very much on the new economic developments following the discovery of diamonds in the Kimberley area and then gold on the Rand in the Transvaal.[92] This had led to a very large number (around 80,000) of predominantly male uitlanders from all over the world pouring into the Transvaal during a very short period of time, with the accompanying 'invention' of Johannesburg as a consequence, quickly followed by the concentration of land-holdings and the creation of syndicates to create monopolistic control and maximise profit.[93] Although 'capitalism' and 'monopoly' were world-wide phenomena, for Schreiner in South Africa they were taking a very distinctive 'shape'.[94] For the speculators, financiers and syndicates, South Africa was merely a "hunting ground, a field for extracting wealth"[95] which was channelled to Europe. They also used their wealth and power to influence – Schreiner's term is corrupt – South African public life by fixing parliamentary elections, ministerial appointments and political deals to further their business interests. While Schreiner is clear much of this was lawful, she notes it could happen only because these developments had happened so quickly that adequate measures had not been introduced to ensure that the governments concerned could regulate these industries. By contrast, in Chartered Company land, she observed wryly, 50% of all profits from gold and diamonds went to the government (i.e. the Company controlled by Rhodes, the financier Alfred Beit and their associates).

Schreiner's answer to the question of 'who gains' from the coming war is unequivocal – "In the background we catch sight of misty figures; we know the old tread; we hear the rustle of paper passing from hand to hand, and we know the fall of gold; it is an old familiar sound in Africa; we know it now! We know it now! There are some who think they will gain!".[96] In this war, South Africa might finally be 'pacified', but this would take enormous resources and the imported British soldiers "with each step … are breaking the fibres, invisible as air but strong as steel, which bind the hearts of South Africans to England. Once they are broken they can never be made whole again …".[97] Later events of course proved Schreiner's analysis of the deliberately provocative stance of the British Government and the effects of the war to be correct.

Schreiner's thinking about monopolistic capitalism was connected with her ideas about balances of power and how to preserve differences within political states, in this essay concerning the more liberal political and legal rights in the Cape, while also ensuring unity in, for example, matters of defence. She wrote to her brother Will in September 1899 that:

Ultimately, I fear, (I say I fear because I believe that small states tell for more in favour of the freedom and good government of mankind than large) all South Africa will be more or less united in one sort of united States; but one of the first principles of statesmanship in South Africa from my point of view is to keep all our states as small and separate as possible .... No doubt you have gone over the whole ground quite as carefully as I have myself. I would like to know on what a thoughtful mind like yours bases its desire for Union.[98]

Will Schreiner later became a vocal proponent of federalism, indeed the leading parliamentary voice opposing the proposed constitutional changes that led to the Act of Union in 1910. His reasons closely followed those of his sister, regarding balances of power and influence and what both had come to think was the crucial need to defend the civil, legal and political rights of black South Africans.

Closer union

Schreiner rehearsed many of her ideas about federalism in the too-ing and fro-ing of letters to Will, her sister Ettie, Betty Molteno and Alice Greene and other friends who shared her increasingly militant stand. Her earlier view that 'the native question' was subsumed within the question of labour changed, as did her wider analysis of the relationship of labour to the state. From well before the South African War ended, she was concerned that the white 'races' of South Africa would recognise the fundamental unity of their interests, as the old pastoral life gave way to one dominated by capitalism and urbanisation, and so combine in common purpose. Schreiner's view of the post-war constitutional Convention planning the new form that the state, as well as government, of the four colonial powers would take was unequivocal: "All those men on the Convention know that the real force hurrying them on is crush the native – cheap labour – new mines – the native territories".[99] But there was more involved here too.

For Schreiner, the key problem was "How, from our political states and our discordant races, can a great, healthy, united, organized nation be formed?"[100] She favoured a central government concerned with defence and 'vital problems', while leaving the individual states otherwise self-governing. Union in South Africa, she had commented in *Thoughts*, was the "speculator's dream of breaking down all interstatal lines which have stood out as so many small ramparts behind which freedom could hide".[101] That is, the state in a union could act in an authoritarian way to the benefit of capital, overriding differences and dissent; while federation allowed for internal differences and ensures that pockets of relative liberalism on 'race' matters could survive as beacons for future changes.[102]

Within this framework, Schreiner's critique of imperialism takes on an additional dimension. Imperialism is rule through an external and imposed force, but, even if it were not dependent on external force, for her it would still be an unmitigated evil because "Imperialism spells the death of all healthful readjustments and developments ... Imperialism is the euphonious title of a deadly disease ... It increases in virulency in proportion as it is extended over more distant spaces and more diverse multitudes, till it becomes at last the death shroud of the nations".[103] British and other imperialist ambitions embody autocracy and are "a nightmare, perhaps only seriously conceived of as a possible reality in the mind of the ignorant man in the street of all nations, eaten up, as such minds are, by a stupendous national egotism".[104] This is of course another performative statement, for she was well aware that this 'stupendous national egotism' not only possessed 'the man in the street', but politicians and governments too.

Closer Union resulted from a set of questions about the future structure and government of South Africa posed to Schreiner and other prominent people. Her replies were published in the *Transvaal Leader* in late December 1908, then in London in 1909 as a short book, and they also reflect her longer-term concerns with imperialism, autocracy and state formations. In particular, *Closer Union* emphasises Schreiner's general commitment to federalism, not just in the South African context – "I believe a body of small highly organised social units self-governing, but uniting together for the furtherance of certain common aims, to be the highest form of social organisation yet evolved for humanity, and that which, probably, will ultimately prevail throughout the world, at least for a time".[105]

Closer Union is also concerned with the franchise, and, although a 'franchise fanatic', as she described herself in *An English South African's View*, Schreiner proposes an education qualification within full adult suffrage. When the second Rhodes ministry had attempted to limit the franchise by including an educational as well as a property qualification, liberals had criticised the 'race' implications as unacceptable. Schreiner's argument in *Closer Union* reverses this, proposing that their great desire for political rights would encourage black people to gain basic educational skills where they might not have done so otherwise.[106] Recognising that the qualification would "tell heavily against the natives", Schreiner suggests that those living under 'tribal tenure' should elect a number of representatives to the Federal Parliament, while other adults should come under the ordinary franchise arrangements.[107] However, she is insistent that all residents should have the franchise on the same conditions and without distinction of race, colour or gender, emphasising that the idea that anyone born in South Africa should "be refused any form of civic or political right ... is one which must be abhorrent to every liberalised mind. I believe that an attempt to base our national life on distinctions of race and colour, as such, will, after the lapse of many years, prove fatal to us".[108]

Schreiner's comments about 'the native question' are developed at length in *Closer Union*, because for her this is "the root question in South Africa; and as it is our wisdom in dealing with it, so will be our future", in this 'our' referring partly to the future position of whites, partly to society as a whole.[109] Although divided at the time she was writing, Schreiner perceived the basic unity of interests between whites eventually leading to 'inextricable blending' through inter-marriage,[110] and it was the economic importance to whites of its heterogeneous 'Bantu' majority that Schreiner saw as the basis of this 'root question'. The black population refused to die out, grasped whatever opportunities there were, and could be neither exterminated nor transported by whites "because we want him! We want more and always more of him – to labour ... and to buy our goods"; and her argument here is situated firmly within her view of labour as the source of value – "They are the makers of our wealth, the great basic rock on which our State is founded – our vast labouring class".[111]

Schreiner also comments on 'race' as the defining problem of the twentieth century. The walls between continents are breaking down and formerly distinct peoples are becoming closely inter-related and "The world on which the twenty-first century will open its eyes will be one widely different from that which the twentieth century sees at its awakening. And the problem which this century will have to solve is the accomplishment of this interaction of distinct human varieties on the largest and most beneficent lines, making for the development of humanity as a whole ...".[112] South Africa could play an important part in this, she argues, because it is one of the first countries to be brought face to face with this necessity; it also has the advantage that its black population, unlike that of America, had never experienced "the dissolving and desocialising ordeal of slavery", but instead has an instinct for freedom and is very socially minded.[113] But because they are the source of the problem, and because of their position of dominance, she sees white South Africans as bearing the responsibility for the social reconstruction required. For Schreiner, this will be a long and difficult task requiring humanity and justice, but is also absolutely necessary.

"But if we fail in this? ... then I would rather draw a veil over the future of this land".[114] In fact Schreiner doesn't draw a veil at all, but points out precisely what the effects will be. Whites might gain economically in the short term, but in the longer-term not only would black South Africans be reduced to being treated as "a mere engine of labour", but they would also be demoralised and deskilled at the very time when the world's other labouring classes were gaining skills.[115] And beyond this, "a far more subtle and inevitable form of evil must ultimately overtake us", a nemesis lying in the fact that "If we raise the black man we shall rise with him; if we kick him under our feet, he will hold us fast by them".[116] Brutalising and degrading other people produces these very qualities in those who do it, and so for Schreiner all the populations of South Africa would rise or sink together; she perceived the country standing "at the parting of the ways; and there is no [white] man or woman ...[who] can absolve themselves" from moral responsibility for what would then happen.[117]

Schreiner's comments about the nemesis beyond the veil are prefaced by "I would not willingly appeal to the lowest motives of self-interest".[118] Clearly, however, the entirety of *Closer Union* was conceived with the purpose of appealing precisely to the self-interests of whites. It is in their best interests, her argument runs, that the civil and political rights prevailing in the Cape but not the other settler states should be preserved in a federal system; it is in their best interests that, longer-term, black South Africans should become fully equal; it is in their best interests that, even as 'a machine of labour', black people should be treated with dignity, humanity and justice; and it is in their best interests not to be morally damaged by treating other people heinously. Indeed, these things are also necessary, she proposes, because they are inevitable in South Africa as they are elsewhere in the world. It seems to me that it is in this context that her comment that "The dark man is the child the gods have given us in South Africa for our curse or our blessing; we shall rise with him, and we shall also sink with him" should be located.[119] Whether Schreiner was also appealing here to self-interest in using the 'whites/adults and blacks/children' metaphor she had used in earlier writing, but now with a more radical underpinning hidden from her readers, or whether she 'really' held this view, cannot now be discerned. But what *is* clear is that her overall analysis has changed significantly, with regard to questions of 'race' in South Africa, and also with regard to her ideas about the relationship of labour to different forms of state.

By the time *Closer Union* was published, Schreiner's two-part essay on "The Woman Question" had appeared in American journals some years before; she had revised *From Man to Man* and its analysis of 'race' and sexual exploitation immediately before the publication of *Closer Union*; and also around 1909, she had begun work on the text of what became *Woman and Labour*. Thus between 1908 and 1910, she was working on 'the woman question' while also rethinking 'the native question' in relation to labour, states and notions of citizenship, and she expounded her ideas about these matters in some of her letters from this time as well. Schreiner had become incensed by trades unions operating increasingly segregationist politics (*Closer Union* comments on this, as do some of her published letters); and she had cast a sharp eye on the increased state regulation of the movement, marriage and child-rearing of black people. She had also taken increasing cognisance of the highly gendered effects of the expropriation of land, in the commandeering of black men as 'engines of labour' and black women as domestic and sex workers.

Thus, for instance, *From Man to Man*, probably last reworked around 1907, presents a very clear indictment of white men's extraction of sexual services from black women in its portrayal of the philandering Frank and his 'I'm the centre of the universe' gratification of his sexual and other pleasures and his total lack of concern for the effects on other people. In Chapter 2, I noted Schreiner's part in the 1911 investigation of 'the so-called Black Peril' and her conviction that "that peril which has long overshadowed this country, is one which exists for all dark skinned women *at the hands of white men*".[120] Chapter 2 also refers to her opposition to the introduction of the Natives Land Act and her fierce rebuttal of segregationism in the women's suffrage societies. As a consequence of this latter, she was excluded from the unveiling of the Women's Monument in Bloemfontein in 1913 which commemorated the women and children who died during the War;[121] and this must have confirmed to her the determined Afrikaner nationalism and racism increasingly dominating political life in the new Union. When Schreiner returned to South Africa in 1920, the creation of a narrowly instrumental and sectional, and also segregationist, white state that *Closer Union* had warned against had become a reality.[122]

Women and labour: value, care and civilising men

> It is because so wide and gracious to us are the possibilities of the future; so impossible is a return to the past, so deadly is a passive acquiescence in the present, that to-day we are found everywhere raising our strange new cry – 'Labour and the training that fits us for labour!'.[123]

Woman and Labour is the most important analytic work to emerge from feminism over the period of Schreiner's life, and indeed for a good while after her death. It has been unjustly criticised in re-readings which have presented it as promoting Darwinist, maternalist and essentialist ideas, for these are misreadings of its clearly stated anti-Darwinist and anti-biologist arguments. Its analysis is a far-reaching one, considerably more so than Charlotte Perkins Gilman's *Women and Economics, A Study of the Economic Relation Between Women and Men as a Factor in Social Evolution*, published in 1899, with which it is frequently compared.[124] As its sub-title suggests, Gilman's book offers an account of the 'economic relation' between men and women and her analysis is quite specifically concerned with what would now be termed gender issues, while Schreiner's deals with fundamental aspects of society, production and labour in general and women's part within this. There are other important differences I want to sketch out.

Firstly, while Gilman is not uncritical of Darwinian ideas about evolution and its impact on social life, her position can best be characterised as a 'reform Darwinist' one which, in spite of the radicalism of some of her proposals, in fact assumes the conjugal relationship between women and men will be untouched because grounded in 'facts' of biology. This is very different from Schreiner's view that, for social change to occur and a just society to exist, men have to change in fundamental ways, to become 'civilised' by their relationship to child-care and other forms of social care and therefore changed in a root and branch way. Secondly, for Gilman mechanisation is seen in positive and progressive terms, enabling new forms of social organisation through radically changed divisions of labour in society. But for Schreiner, mechanisation was part and parcel of a much more fundamental set of economic shifts which were radically re-inscribing notions of social value, and which had highly negative implications for women. And thirdly, for Gilman socialised domestic labour is perceived as the solution to the problem of women and work, whereas, for Schreiner, relying on a lower-valued group of people for domestic labour is an expression of the problem.

Woman and Labour interestingly mixes theory, polemic and irony, and its 'strange new cry' acted as a singularly powerful call to women and to pro-feminist men when first published. It advances a social labour theory of value within a framework concerned with wide-ranging sources of economic and social change; it pinpoints 'the problem of men' within this; and it anticipates and rebuts objections to its analysis and conclusions. Its broad argument is developed around the key term of 'parasitism', used to characterise the situation in which one whole group or class of people are enabled by technological or other economic developments to live off and be dependent upon the labour of another group or class. Parasitism is analysed in *W&L* around the particular socio-economic circumstances which make it possible for women to be in a parasitic relationship to men, although, as I noted earlier, Schreiner had also used the term more briefly elsewhere to characterise the relationship between whites and the emergent black proletarianised labour force in South Africa.[125]

Parasitism, previously a possibility only for individuals or sub-sets of superordinate groups, Schreiner sees in *W&L* as having taken on a very different meaning contemporaneously. The root change occurring was that 'mechanical force' was fundamentally transforming the nature of labour power, mechanising and making redundant those forms which utilised only sheer physical labour, significantly increasing the demand for skilled and technical and scientific forms of labour, and displacing and changing who did what throughout capitalist economies as a consequence.[126] With attendant changes, Schreiner argues that the result was that traditional female labour (in food harvesting and preparation, making material for clothes, and so forth) was being replaced by mechanical means, by socialised forms of labour (in the form of, for example, factories making clothes, and schools educating children), and also by the marked decline in the need for and the value attached to child-bearing itself. These changes, she emphasises, were also affecting women because the 'dislocations' that accompanied them decreased their chances of (hetero)sexual partnerships; and it also increased prostitution because women's unemployment was increasing as a consequence.

Schreiner is very concerned that her analysis overall should not be misrepresented because of the particular focus on sex parasitism in *W&L*, important though this is. She insists that neither the extent of the paid and domestic labour that women carry out, nor its economic as well as social importance, is sufficiently recognised; and she emphasises that it would be quite wrong if her analysis of parasitism should "lead to the impression that women's domestic labour at the present day ... should not be ... most highly recognised and recompensed".[127] She also insists that the need to eradicate sex parasitism does not mean women should take over the share of domestic labour and child-care that men ought to have, not least because of "how essential to the humanising and civilising of man, and therefore of the whole race, was an increased sense of sexual and paternal responsibility, and an increased justice towards woman as a domestic labourer".[128] And although similar kinds of work could be performed just as well by both men and women, convention decreed that women "on the ground of her sex alone shall receive a less recompense", and for Schreiner this was the cause of profound indignation and a great wrong to be righted.[129]

The origins of *W&L* lay in the "Woman" book Schreiner had worked on in the 1880s. As she outlines in the "Introduction" to *W&L*, this had contained three initial chapters on 'the sex function' and its bearing on 'the modern sex problem', to which she had later added another on women's situation in "the most primitive, the savage and the semi-savage states"; and these were completed by the end of the 1880s.[130] Then just before the South African War, she had written another chapter, on "the causes which in modern European societies are leading women to attempt readjustment in their relationship to their social organism".[131] Traces of this appear in Schreiner's letters of this period, particularly to Betty Molteno and Alice Greene, and it is related (to put it no stronger) to the two-part essay on "The Woman Question" published in mid 1899.[132] The manuscript was left in Johannesburg with other personal possessions when the declaration of war prevented the Schreiners from returning; and, as noted in Chapter 2, her papers were largely destroyed by looting British soldiers. Probably in late 1910 and early 1911, she re-wrote the part of it concerned with woman's labour and parasitism, using "The Woman Question" as the base; the result was *W&L*.[133]

W&L looks at the origins and current forms of sex parasitism and also the kind of future society that could result from it. In doing so, it differentiates between the men's and the women's labour problems, discusses the relationship of parasitism to prostitution and to war, and provides a strongly non-essentialist view of sex differences. Its conclusions anticipate arguments against women seeking new forms of labour, rebutting these by looking at the Woman's Movement and the relationship between the 'New Women' and the 'New Men'. Schreiner's main objections to parasitism are connected with her views about 'evolution' (a term she doesn't use in a Darwinian sense, but instead to indicate any period of rapid and extensive change) and also to her social labour theory of value.

Schreiner's analytical attention is drawn to the notion of parasitism for a specific reason, connected to the scale, not just the pace, of economic change, for "Something that is entirely new has entered the field of human labour, and left nothing as it was". This is that "crude muscular force ... sinks continually in its value in the world of human toil; while intellectual power, virility and activity, and that culture which leads to the mastery of the inanimate forces of nature, to the invention of machinery, and to that delicate manipulative skill often required in guiding it, becomes ever of greater and greater importance to the race".[134] While the 'modern world' has no need for much of what was formerly essential male labour, these same changes have opened up many new forms of labour for men, so that, overall, "Never before ... has the man's field of remunerative toil been so wide, so interesting, so complex, and in its results so all-important to society ...".[135] The same changes had very different effects for women, Schreiner points out, for these not only massively reduced the need for women's traditional forms of labour, but also "where there has not been a determined and conscious resistance on her part, have nowhere spontaneously tended to open out to her new and compensatory fields ...".[136] Indeed, as Schreiner notes, the new forms of labour available to men not only mechanise these but also gender-invert who carries them out.

For Schreiner, the 'Women's Labour Problem' is "the propelling force behind that vast and restless 'Woman's Movement' which marks our day. It is this fact ... which awakes in ... European women their ... cry for new forms of labour and new fields for the exercise of their powers".[137] She is careful to specify *European* women here, for these changes were first experienced in the industrial and capitalist regions of the world, because of the way capitalism and its "increasingly perfected labour-saving machinery" impacted on the lives of "the large mass of women in civilised societies who form the intermediate class between rich and poor".[138] She thought in the following fifty years these changes would be experienced by all women and men in European capitalist countries, and then other societies, in what was becoming a world economic system. Schreiner's eye is on the likely effects, that:

> it will be quite possible for the male half of all civilised races (and therefore ultimately of all) to absorb the entire fields of intellectual and highly trained manual labour; and it would be possible for the female half of the race, whether as prostitutes, as kept mistresses, or as kept wives, to cease from all forms of active toil, and ... sink into a condition of complete and helpless sex-parasitism.[139]

Schreiner objected both to the phenomenon of sex parasitism and also to its possible implications. She thought that social and economic change was occurring because of continuing human adaptation to new circumstances and conditions; however, a parasitic group or class stultifies, it stops developing and then limits the adaptive potential of other groups or classes it is symbiotically connected to. Ultimately, she suggested by using historical analogies, this could lead to the collapse, not merely of the power of dominant groups in a society, but also a whole society. It should be noted, though, that Schreiner was not making a causal argument about parasitism and is careful always to write in terms of 'possible' and 'quite possible', and she sees parasitism as linked to wider economic and social factors, with it being these which promote both the parasitism and the social decay.[140]

It is important to note two things here. One is that her discussion of sex parasitism in particular is written in a highly polemical rhetorical style; she is making an argument and making it at full volume, as it were. The other is that her argument about sex parasitism is not – and nor was it meant to be – a literal description of 'how (married) women are', as some particularly flat-footed present-day commentators have suggested. It rather points to social systemic tendencies, to underlying structural possibilities, to the ways that fundamental social and economic changes then underway might come to impact on *all* women's lives – not just those who were married – because of how men might use these. Schreiner's argument about sex parasitism is frequently taken out of context and misrepresented, so it is worth reiterating that she is not saying that sex parasitism is a literal description, and nor is she saying that its occurrence is determined by the changes underway. She had emphasised at the start of the book, in what are in effect instructions to her readers about how to understand the place of sex parasitism within it, that women's social, domestic and paid forms of labour were extensive, under-recognised and under-valued. Her point is that the existence of sex parasitism at a systemic level had become possible, and she thought that the possible consequences of this for women needed guarding and organising against.

Schreiner saw prostitution as fundamentally related to, indeed as a quintessentially defining form of, sex parasitism, and she argued that unless this was recognised it could not be adequately responded to, morally or politically. For her, the existence of prostitution affected the way that all men thought about all women, and women's freedom was ultimately conditional on ending prostitution: "Always in our dreams we hear the turn of the key that shall close the door of the last brothel; the clink of the last coin that pays for the body and soul of a woman; the falling of the last wall that encloses artificially the activity of woman and divides her from man ...".[141] Her analysis of prostitution, however, rejects the idea that there are 'good' and 'bad' women in sexual terms, insisting there is no sharp dividing line between the 'sex functions' women performed in prostitution and in marriage where there was any degree of economic dependence on men. As a consequence, Schreiner proposes, 'civilised' women could more easily cross this line than the supposedly 'primitive', whose productive labour was absolutely necessary for their societies.[142]

W&L sees the Women's Movement of its day as "an impressive, irresistible and quintessentially modern force for change.[143] Its arguments, policies and ways of working might sometimes be muddled or expressed in unacceptable ways, but Schreiner insists that great social movements don't succeed through "chopped logic" but because they are underpinned and propelled by structural and material factors "which, pressing upon the isolated individuals, awakens at last a continuous, if often vague and uncertain, social movement in a given direction. Mere intellectual comprehension may guide, retard, or accelerate the great human movements; it has never created them ..."; she also emphasises that the leaders of these "have been ... themselves permeated by the great common need ... they have not themselves created the wave which bears themselves, and humanity, onwards".[144]

W&L strongly rejects biological or evolutionary determinism, dismissing the idea there are fixed 'natural' gendered characteristics that suited men and women for different kinds of labour and so different occupations. Schreiner insists there is no evidence of any correlation between brain function and reproductive function. And, even if broad general gender-based patterns still existed in a future completely equal society, she argues it would still be wrong to prevent any individual from undertaking the kind of labour they were most suited to, even if their particular aptitudes departed markedly from the general pattern.[145]

The idea of 'labour' that *W&L* develops includes social and domestic as well as paid forms of labour. It also analyses war as a form of labour cutting across divisions between the social and the economic, for women have not only "always borne part of the weight of war, and the major part", as labourers and producers, as nurses, as sufferers from its effects, but also through a relationship which is "far more intimate, personal, and indissoluble than this. Men have made boomerangs, bows, swords, or guns with which to destroy each other; we have made the men who destroyed and were destroyed! ... No woman who is a woman says of a human body, 'it is nothing!'".[146] And while Schreiner argues that women differ from men in their relation to and feelings about war, she rejects seeing this in terms of biological or reproductive difference: support for or opposition to war "is in no sense related to any particular form of sex function",[147] but comes about because women know experientially 'what the cost is', in a way that men do not. This is because of their day-to-day caring responsibilities, which puts them "at a slightly different angle" to war and to some other aspects of human life than men.[148] Her emphasis on men taking equal responsibility for caring work is both a matter of social justice, then, and something she sees as helping civilise and humanise men, making them more truly human. Also, because Schreiner's non-essentialist view is that women are less war-like because of their experiences of social mothering (she later changed her mind about this during the 1914–1918 War), so she proposes that men's equal involvement in social mothering would have a similar consequence for them too.

This is what would now be termed a 'social constructionist' approach to mothering, and it is developed around Schreiner's twin insistence that there are no sex differences at the point human life begins, and that even after puberty most aspects of the body and its functions are not affected by 'sex modification'. Sex differences increase 'as the body approaches reproduction' and decrease away from it; Schreiner points out that the eye is one of the most complex organs but is entirely sexually undifferentiated, and she perceives the same lack of difference regarding intelligence, the emotions and desires. In fact, Schreiner's analysis eschews essentialism even regarding reproductive differences themselves, emphasising as it does that, when different life forms are compared, then "all forms of psychic variations are found allying themselves now with the male sex form, and then with the female": although such differences may exist systematically between males and females within one species, they do not between species.[149]

W&L concludes by anticipating and rebutting objections to its arguments. It is difficult to take seriously, Schreiner comments, any criticism which suggests that women's labour should be confined to 'sex functions' only. Considerably more than half the world's labour has always been performed by women, and anyway this argument is actually directed at the woman professional, not the servant or factory worker or mother, to whose strenuous labours men have no objections at all. She also points out that the objection that women's labour would be somehow 'less productive' than men's is not proven, and it might actually be more productive because women's lesser musculature and greater mental agility might better fit the 'labour of the future'. Her point, however, is not whether one sex 'excels' over the other, but that people find the labour which best suits their abilities.

Schreiner's response to the view that 'future labour' might be beyond women because of inherent mental incapacity is four-fold. Many of women's present occupations require much mental ability, and she briskly insists that the housewife with many tasks exerts more mental capacity than the accountant carrying out only one; where women have been free to express their abilities they have been very able; women in universities and professions have performed at least as well as men; and many people know at least one woman who is a "chained eaglet", and "it is upon our knowledge of that woman that we base our certitude".[150] And rebutting the criticism that, even if her arguments are correct, the equality she wants would result in a diminution of sexual attraction and affection between women and men, Schreiner argues the reverse is actually true, that the Woman's Movement was significantly contributing to better relations between women and men. She comments on this through an evocative image:

> sexual love – that tired angel who through the ages has presided over the march of humanity, with distraught eyes, and feather-shafts broken, and wings drabbled in the mires of lust and greed, and golden locks caked over with the dust of injustice and oppression ... – shall yet, at last, bathed from the mire and dust of ages in the streams of friendship and freedom, leap upwards, with white wings spread, resplendent in the sunshine of a distant future.[151]

Schreiner emphasises that the Woman's Movement is part of a much wider set of social changes already happening 'on the ground', and although the 'New Woman' was much remarked upon, she points out that the linked existence of the 'New Man' was conveniently ignored.[152] She saw both as products of the general changes she had analysed, changes which were part of social 'evolution', not in the Darwinian sense, but rather a time of far-reaching change – "It cannot be too often repeated ... that our societies are societies in a state of rapid evolution and change. The continually changing material conditions of life, with their reaction on the intellectual, emotional, and moral aspects of human affairs, render our societies the most complex and probably the most mobile and unsettled which the world has ever seen".[153] Schreiner saw sex parasitism, the Woman's Movement and its demand for labour, and the emergence of the New Women and the New Men, as all components within this; and for her neither 'evolution' nor 'change' necessary entailed progress, but could also occasion detrimental and retrogressive changes as compared with earlier periods of human history, with the new possibility of sex parasitism being a case in point.

Schreiner's argument enshrines heterosexuality, albeit of a new and improved variety; and this is another elision in her formal thinking. Given the omnipresence, then and now, of institutional heterosexuality and Schreiner's pinpointing of the need for radical change in men to achieve social justice, this emphasis is consonant with her political and also her analytical purposes; however, some brief comments in letters particularly to Molteno and Greene hint that some more radical rethinking might perhaps have been occurring 'behind the scenes'. Thus while Schreiner's discussion focuses on sex love, her argument also touches on wider social relations, including those of friendship and comradeship, between women and men; and an exchange of letters with Betty Molteno shows she certainly did not intend these ideas to apply only insofar as women were involved in sexual or other relationships with men.[154]

'Labour' in W&L is conceptualised in a way that goes far beyond any narrow economism and includes not only 'productive' but also all the 'social' forms of labour. Indeed, for Schreiner *all* labour was 'social labour', in the same way that Marx had analysed labour power: a person's labour bestows value on a commodity or a service beyond the thing itself. Her analysis of social labour encompasses domestic labour, child-bearing and child-care, and also any kind of 'sex function' which involves remuneration, as within prostitution, or the trading of sex for economic gain or support of any kind, as within marriage. This results in a highly inclusive interpretation of labour, encompassing social, sexual and domestic forms of work as well as paid employment. It conceives of 'the labour market' in broad terms around social as well as economic production and reproduction, positions marriage and domestic relations within this, and emphasises the importance of an egalitarian involvement in caring work and other forms of social mothering of both women and men as a matter of social justice. It is only relatively recently that feminist thinking has caught up with Schreiner's analysis of value accruing to social forms of labour including 'caring' activities, and with her conceptualisation of prostitution in terms of 'sex work'; and by and large it still has not done so regarding her theorisation of war as part and parcel of 'productive labour' for those directly employed in or economically supported by it outside of periods of actual warfare.[155]

Many of the ideas discussed in W&L appear, in outline at least, in Schreiner's earlier work, but within this book Schreiner has a more effective analytic armoury at her disposal. Its analysis constructs a well-articulated argument about the origins and processes of social change as well as social stasis; this encompasses relationships, emotions and also material life; it is as concerned with 'social labour' as with paid 'productive' labour; it deals both with individual conduct and with social systems over time; and it holds Schreiner's feminist, socialist and humanitarian concerns firmly in concert. *Woman and Labour* also successfully refuses the disjuncture between materialism and idealism that Schreiner had earlier raised with Ellis and with Pearson in the 1880s, because its theory takes the form of a materialism fully infused with idealism, or rather of an idealism which is entirely materialistic in its foundation. In doing so, it escapes the theoretical impasse which bedevilled much feminist analysis after it was written, because until recently immersed in a mind-frame which treated materialism and idealism as binaries.

As I noted earlier, in spite of – or perhaps because of – the complexities of its analyses and the radicalism of its ideas, *W&L's* arguments about sex parasitism and social mothering have been subject to serious misreadings. It is time, it seems to me, for a renewed detailed reconsideration of this book, regarding not only its ideas and arguments but also its place in Schreiner's thinking and in the development of feminist ideas at the time of its publication.

Peace and war: from social mothering to the genesis of human aggression

> [this] *problem ... is probably the most complex and the most important which has ever faced the human intellect ... It stretches across the globe; its roots go down into the deepest fibres of human nature ... we must deeply consider those elements in human nature and in national relationship which make universally for peace or war, for co-operation or antagonisms, between individuals or nations ... On all sides we must creep out of our wretched little trenches of national hatred and antagonism, dug for us by ignorance and the desire for vulgar domination and empire, which has ensnared us all; and we must meet on the ground of our common humanity.*[156]

Olive Schreiner's analysis of war in *Woman and Labour* is an optimistic one. That is, it assumes social mothering, social labour, does indeed lead to greater value being given to human life, and that men's equal participation in it will therefore lead to a less war-ridden world. *W&L* was written in the long shadow of the South African War, but this was accompanied by the rejection by many people in Britain as well as South Africa of the war-mongering and jingoism that accompanied it, and also the existence of many peace meetings and congresses held across South Africa. Schreiner's very different experiences of the 1914–1918 War, in particular that very few people shared her total anti-war views, led her to think again about aggression, to analyse it at an inter-personal and not only an inter-statal level. As the 1914–1918 War progressed, Schreiner's developing ideas about the genesis of aggression and its links to militarism resulted in some significant changes in her thinking, as shown in the much more pessimistic analysis of "The Dawn of Civilisation". However, I begin my discussion of Schreiner's analysis of 'peace and war' with the allegorical stories she wrote during the South African and the 1914–1918 Wars, and then look at the published letters she wrote about conscientious objection and pacifism, for these provide an interesting coda to her thinking about war in *Woman and Labour* and "The Dawn of Civilisation".

In Schreiner's 'war allegories' she comments on the meaning of war, its effects on society, and also social relations after hostilities end.[157] Her thoughts are focused as much on the consequences of war as its conduct or origins, emphasising how past events underpin current resentments and so future conflicts. Thus the powerfully written "Eighteen-Ninety-Nine" accounts for the historical origins of the South African War in the early period of colonisation and warfare between Boer and African peoples, which produced a lineage of attachment to the land through ties of history and 'blood' in a way that the Boers saw as conferring rights of unending possession. Even though Boer ownership in the sense of control might be forcibly ended by a war with Britain, possession in this more fundamental sense of 'Ons Land' cannot be. Boer men constitute this lineage through their readiness across the generations from boys to old men to forcibly defend it, while Boer women do so by ensuring continuing life and succession regardless of the difficulties and by insisting that men 'do their duty'. Thus with the last of their men-folk killed in fighting and much of their farm destroyed, the mother and daughter-in-law in "Eighteen-Ninety-Nine" still plough the land, sow seeds, ensure a harvest for those who will survive even though they know they personally will starve before then. Schreiner uses the idea of a future 'harvest' metaphorically, to invoke a legacy of bitterness, the seeds of revenge, and the harvest of independence – "they passed slowly on pressing in the seeds ... that were to lie ... and rot there, seemingly, to die ... and then, when the rains had fallen, and the sun had shone, to come above the earth again ... for the next season's harvest!".[158]

Control is not possession, then, proclaims "Eighteen-Ninety-Nine". Indeed, control achieved through acts of forceful acquisition is ultimately meaningless: a musket and footstool looted by British soldiers from the farm in "Eighteen-Ninety-Nine" are merely curiosities when divorced from the context that gave them value. Also the violence of war has a curious illogicality to it that mirrors the illogicality of dreams themselves. In the undated allegory "The Great Heart of England", for instance, it is "for the wearing of the Green" that brings the bayonets and bullets. The dreamer-dancer has nothing else to wear than this green garment, and "when I have got it on I go down the street, dancing, dancing, dancing ... And then there is a sudden stop, there is a gleam of bayonets, and a sound of guns firing; and then all is silence".[159] This dream sequence, with its odd imagery and plays on words and peculiar dream logic, is very powerful, not least because for the waking dreamer the nightmare actually starts when the sudden silence propels them awake.[160]

There is a similarly odd, but also seemingly inevitable, logic to the dream sequence in "Who Knocks At the Door", written in 1917. This starts with a dreamer falling asleep thinking of the death and destruction reported in a newspaper they had been reading. And then "I found myself in a great forest. On every side the stems of trees tower up above me like the aisles of some vast cathedral, and high above my head the wind struck their mighty branches together. It seemed to be one of those primeval forests ... [and] I wandered in that impenetrable darkness".[161] The dreamer eventually arrives at a great building looming out of the darkness and echoing with the sound of music. The dreamer peers through a window, sees a scene illuminated by thousands of glittering lights with gorgeously dressed beautiful people; but there is a strange undercurrent which erupts into a scene of terrible carnage, men stabbing and killing each other and women shouting them on, a butchery by people in a blood-red frenzy. The dreamer stumbles away and finally awakes.

The grief and horror that the watcher feels in "Who Knocks At the Door" is the entire substance of "The Cry of South Africa" (which is literally a cry, 'give us our dead'), a much slighter piece of blank verse written by Schreiner on the occasion of the military execution of three men in Hanover, the village she lived in during the South African War.[162] Grief is also the denouement and the meaning of the title of "The Great Heart of England", where the dreamer awakes in a cold sweat remembering carnage, but also listening for the heartbeat of compassion for suffering that Schreiner polemically invokes in her title.

These allegories gain substantially from being grounded in detailed landscapes. For instance, the dreamer falls asleep on a koppie in "Seeds A-Growing", with the hill and the sunshine and the plants described; and these provide the setting, literally the grounding, that the dreamer falls asleep on and wakes up to. It starts with the dreamer on the koppie, "at my feet were the purple fig-blossoms, and the yellow dandelion flowers were closing for the night",[163] and it concludes with the sun sinking and the dreamer passing the barbed wire gate into the village under martial law with its jeering guards. The seeds here are those that will flower in resistance, then freedom. Schreiner's other war allegories also use landscape in a similar way – for instance, the primeval forest and towering hall in "Who Knocks at the Door" are described in detail within its symbolic landscape, which constitutes a 'moral geography' that the dreamer inhabits and which marks life and death in fundamental ways.

These allegories provide a powerful indication of Schreiner's feelings about war. Corrupt and evil in itself, worked into the fundaments of society, war also produces a sense of injustice among those defeated and so gives rise to future conflicts and future wars. The defeated merely wait for revenge or restitution; people are killed for their beliefs and for defending their own land; and the nightmare of war does not end when open conflict ends, for the pre-conditions of the next conflict are embedded in the settlement of the old. And, while this cycle of vengeance and retribution is repeated, there can never be a just society.

Woman and Labour, however, proposes that there is a way of bringing the cycle of war, injustice and revenge to an end: men must become fully civilised and fully humanised; as and when men fully share in caring and other social labour, they will feel about human life as women do. But as I noted earlier, Schreiner's ideas about war underwent major change during the 1914–1918 War. Important differences opened up between Schreiner and many friends, including Ellis, Carpenter, Gandhi, Hobhouse and Will Schreiner, and she was unable to accept that their albeit provisional support for Britain could coexist with pacifism or indeed an ethical response of any kind.[164] As well as these private events in Schreiner's own life, she was very aware of radical changes to public moral life. She personally experienced xenophobic reactions from many people because of her 'German' name; she was disturbed by the almost total support for the war; she commented to Ellis how combative and aggressive people were at even peace meetings; she was astounded that many feminists supported British militarism, although recognising some rejected this;[165] and she was truly appalled by the vociferous pressure that many blood-thirsty women put on men to join the fighting.

Schreiner felt strongly that people should have the right to object to militarism by refusing to participate in fighting. She found the immense social and personal pressures to enlist that men were subject to both horrible and distasteful; she also saw the introduction of conscription, a compulsory system of 'call up' into military service, as ethically and politically unacceptable. In spite of her health problems, she was actively involved in campaigning against conscription, including supporting individual men, attending tribunals hearing cases of conscientious objection, writing open letters for publication, and attending a number of meetings with government ministers to put the case for conscientious objection to be treated as a legitimate reason for non-combatism.

During 1915 and 1916, Schreiner published probably around half a dozen open public letters about conscientious objection and pacifism, mainly, as she wryly commented to Carpenter, in the very papers and magazines where they would do least good because their readers were already sympathetic.[166] In these, Schreiner emphasised these men should not feel abandoned or alone in their views and recognise the 'higher service' they were undertaking by living out their ethical principles. Even if only one person publicly objects to something which is wrong, indefensible, she argues, this act will be remembered in the future while the evil that occasioned it will be forgotten; and so they should heed the inner voice of ethical principle. There are many other people who share their convictions and beliefs, she points out, but because of their age or sex they are not "called upon to stand beside you", particularly people who "from early childhood, owing to ... some feeling with regard to the ultimate ends of human life ... have never felt ourselves justified in taking or assisting in taking the lives of our fellow-men".[167]

Schreiner's attention is on the future and how the cycle of repetition can be broken. Firstly, there should be no bitterness expressed towards those who do fight, nor any antagonism towards those on the opposing side. Secondly, she suggests society should be more concerned with the "religion of the future";[168] that is, not religion, but the future itself, a better future which should be actively worked towards. Schreiner conjectures about the nature of the peace that will come, commenting in 1916 that "Those of us who have lived through a long and desolating war know that it may end in a so-called 'peace,' more destructive than the war itself, which may continue to be the ground of war and of human antagonisms and conflicts, long after the men who have framed it have passed away".[169] A peace which is merely a cessation of hostilities is no real peace at all, for this must be based on the principles of justice. Schreiner's fundamental concern is with the causes and prevention of war in general, and consequently her analytic focus is directed, not to the causes of particular wars, but rather to "those elements in human nature and in national relationship which make universally for peace or war, for co-operation or antagonisms, between individuals or nations".[170]

There are clear links between Schreiner's comments in these public letters, and the concerns expressed in her extended discussion of aggression and war begun, but not completed, in "The Dawn of Civilisation". These involve her ideas about the underlying 'causes' of war in the desire for domination which 'ensnares us all'; and the need for individual commitment to live out a principled stand against all aggression, as well as war and militarism. "The Dawn of Civilisation" exists in three related but not coterminous versions: a short two-section article which Cronwright-Schreiner published after Schreiner's death, and two rather different archive manuscripts, one in South Africa and the other in the USA. Bracketing matters of provenance, I draw on all three in providing an overview of Schreiner's ideas about the causes and consequences of war and its underpinnings, in social institutions but also regarding 'personal' or psychological characteristics,[171] in this very last piece of work in her writing life.

In the published shortened version of "The Dawn of Civilisation" (referred to here as "The Dawn" to differentiate it from the manuscript versions), Schreiner comments that, atypically, she has allowed 'a personal element' to enter her discussion, because "only by a very simple statement ... it might perhaps be possible for me to make clear to some of my fellows that such a being as the universal conscientious objector to war does exist. We are a reality! ... you have to count us in!".[172] Generally, the more personal an issue was, the wiser she thought it was to deal with it impersonally, for otherwise particular feelings of anger and hurt would intrude into what should be a dispassionate process of thought and analysis. War and peace have this 'personal' quality for Schreiner because they 'stand for' things which she considers 'organic' or fundamental. Most people experience a 'psychic compulsion' with regard to war, she argues, an inner and almost unconscious compulsion to behave and respond in particular ways, which is the source of their aggressive reactions to people who do not share their views. But she rejects seeing this as universal, just as in earlier work she had rejected the existence of other supposedly 'innate' behaviours or characteristics, because, while most people's response may be aggressive, that of people like her was an equally compelled objection to war and its underlying causes, and indeed to aggression itself.

Schreiner's point here is that, while some people object to war because of religious or other beliefs, and others to a specific war, people like her experience a more fundamental objection to *all* war, even while recognising there are important differences between wars fought, for example, for dominance, trade expansion, glory, the maintenance of Empire, against an aggressor, or to oppose invasion. And these people, she emphasises, not only object to war itself, but also "if possible more strongly to those ideals and aims and to those institutions and methods of action which make the existence of war possible and inevitable among men".[173]

Although it is not possible for any individual to stop a war, in "The Dawn" Schreiner proposes there is a domain of action in which people can help make a better world. Thinking about this as a child, and feeling intensely unhappy about her inability to change the pain and suffering in the world, she had slowly become aware that "this one thing only can you do – in that one, small, minute, almost infinitesimal spot in the Universe, where your will rules, there, where alone you are as God, strive to make that you hunger for real! ... This is all you can do; but do it; it is not nothing!".[174] At its conclusion, "The Dawn" calls on people who do not approve of war to become 'conscientious objectors' to the institutions and methods which make war possible, not only to armed hostilities. In the longer term, Schreiner proposes, the awareness she had gained as a child had "in the course of a long life's experience, become a hope, which I think the cool reason can find grounds to justify".[175]

Schreiner's grounds for this hope are discussed in some detail in the two manuscript versions of "The Dawn of Civilisation" and are concerned with the individual, gendered and social characteristics and traits which give rise to the 'compulsion' to aggression. In discussing 'the causes of war', Schreiner comments that warfare between nations is rather like fruit on a tree: the harder it is cut, the more it will grow back. Attempts to 'prune', to cut away, particular wars are merely palliative because they treat war as somehow abnormal, whereas she sees it as the product of "causes [which] lie deeply intertwined in the most primitive and deeply-seated instincts of human and animal nature"; she insists that war coexists with all forms of societal organisation and is never caused by individuals, no matter how powerful they may be.[176]

In analysing the genesis of aggression in these overlapping manuscripts, Schreiner argues that there are "primitive instincts and passions and the habits formed unconsciously by early training and from imitation" which give rise to a liking for conquest over others. She refers to the human liking for force and conquest as an 'animal delight' covered by only a thin social veneer; and she wonders whether children's pleasure in playing at 'killings and maiming' is inborn or the result of learning. Whichever, as with 'sex differences' in *Woman and Labour*, Schreiner is adamant that: "This instinct exists equally in the male and the female, though in the female in an inverted and more complex form".[177] Consequently she insists it is only partially true that women are less touched by aggression than men. On the one hand, women seem less predisposed to open physical aggression and so this may "form one of the few characteristics which really does mark off the sexes"; but on the other, this still exists in women albeit "somewhat disguised in complimentary forms", including women's vicarious support for and enjoyment of men's aggressive behaviours, and Schreiner suggests there is a 'distinctly sexual' element in this.[178]

While arguing that the vicarious thrill of violence is experienced by many women, Schreiner recognises that others find this abhorrent, and also that such feelings may seem unreal or incomprehensible to men as well as women who are 'cool and far-seeing', or who have been neither directly nor indirectly involved in warfare. But Schreiner is very clear that these people too could experience a 'frenzy of hatred' under different circumstances, for this is something she sees as the product of external circumstances, and especially collectivities of people being swept along the same mass emotional trajectory.

There are some strong continuities as well as differences between Schreiner's analysis in *Woman and Labour* and in "The Dawn of Civilisation". In both pieces of work, she specifically rejects linking militarism and warfare to men only, and pacifism and a greater valuing of human life to women only. In both of them, she sees 'sex differences' in any innate sense as barely existing in either men or women; where they do, she sees them as 'plastic' and shaped almost entirely by social factors. And in both of them, insofar as mothering means that women value life more highly, then she argues that men can and must share this through social labour; and, insofar as men are more warlike, women share this trait vicariously. What has changed between *Woman and Labour* and "The Dawn of Civilisation" is that her earlier analysis focuses on the factors encouraging greater social labour, 'mothering' as a shared form of social labour, and an increased valuing of human life; while in her later analysis she has become concerned with the ways that women and men share in social aggression, with this underpinning her understanding of the genesis of warfare and the social institutions linked to it. Earlier I described Schreiner's analysis of warfare in *Woman and Labour* as an optimistic one. By the time she wrote "The Dawn of Civilisation", her analysis had become considerably more pessimistic, in part because rooted in her later conviction that, although governments start and institutions underpin wars, it is people who consent to them because of deep-seated feelings about aggression and conquest, and in part because she was convinced that this 'compulsion' had been only barely constrained, let alone modified, since 'the dawn of civilisation'.

Perhaps Only ...

From Man to Man seems to me one of the great feminist novels of the last century, although most present-day assessments, including from feminist critics, see it as narratively problematic, too polemical or otherwise flawed. Schreiner started writing *From Man to Man* probably in the early 1870s, at the same time as *Undine* and *An African Farm*. Rejected for publication by Chapman and Hall, during 1884 and 1885 she substantially revised the manuscript in ways she found increasingly unsatisfactory.[179] It was put 'on ice' while Schreiner worked on other pieces of writing; then during three subsequent periods of time it underwent further major revision and/or extension. After her death, Cronwright-Schreiner edited the typescript and some remaining manuscript to the form in which the novel was published by him in 1924. Because he destroyed Schreiner's typescript as well as her manuscript, it is now impossible to be certain what impact he had on the novel as Schreiner left it.[180] His "Introduction" to *From Man to Man* apparently provides a good deal of information about this, suggesting that he had had to make major changes to produce a publishable book.[181] However, what he wrote about *Undine* and Schreiner's terrible handwriting, erroneous punctuation and spelling, compared with the actually pristine manuscript, suggests he is likely to be exaggerating the confusions and problems of this manuscript and so his own work in 'correcting' it.[182]

    From Man to Man assumes mythical status for some commentators, as a work Schreiner was supposedly constantly revising and was purportedly still working on when she died (indeed, in one highly romanticised variant, she is erroneously portrayed as working on it with a pen in her hand when she died). *FMTM* has been viewed as a kind of symbolic representation of Schreiner's life, a metaphor for what is sometimes depicted as an unsatisfactorily unfinished and incomplete person, as well as novel. But this is mythology and not actuality: prosaically, the manuscript was revised during four documented periods of time (between 1884 and 1886, between mid 1888 and spring 1889, during 1901 and 1902, and in 1906 and 1907; and was re-typed in 1911),[183] Schreiner always read with a pen and (tsch, tsch) wrote in the books she read, and the book she was reading when she died was the memoirs of Ismail Kemel Bey. The myth of the constant revision of *FMTM* in fact began with Cronwright-Schreiner's "A Note on the Genesis of the Book" in its first edition,[184] which provides what is presented as a list of mentions of it in Schreiner's journals and letters. However, a close look at the actual documents shows that many do not in fact comment about work on the manuscript, but simply record topics, like marriage and prostitution, dealt with in it; in fact only a minority are concerned with Schreiner actually writing or revising the manuscript itself.

From Man to Man shares a number of structuring features with Schreiner's earlier concerns in Undine and An African Farm. At the emotional centre is the karoo farm, both of the sisters Rebekah and Bertie in different ways flee from the farm, while Rebekah as an adult returns to another farm and finds solace there. The novel starts, both literally and symbolically, with children and the moral and other puzzles that confront them, together with the unpredictable almost random nature of adult authority and its frequent ill-will. There are emotionally absent parents, and authority is displaced, residing initially with 'old Ayah' on the farm and then later with Rebekah's sexually errant and morally betraying husband Frank. And only slowly does Rebekah, not so much rebel, as eventually find some kind of moral authority within herself as a 'figure in a landscape', the landscape of the farm.

From Man to Man also bears distinctive hallmarks of Schreiner's adulthood and maturity. It is centrally concerned with the nature of sisterhood and its bonds and responsibilities. In doing so, it provides a powerful critique of marriage and moral (rather than specifically sexual) corruption, showing the complex ways in which sex parasitism characterises both sisters' lives. Pivotal to this is the knowledge the reader accrues about Rebekah's self-indulgent husband Frank, a man unable to tell the difference between his own pleasures and what is honest or right. An ethical parallel is provided through the character of Mrs Drummond, an adulteress (including with Frank) who is relentlessly vain and petty-minded, and who uses gossip to hound Rebekah's younger sister Bertie, who is actually far less 'sinning', sexually and also morally, than she. Bertie had been seduced by her tutor when very young; she 'confesses' this to her suitor, Frank's brother, the starchy and conventionally 'moral' John Ferdinand. He rejects her and then later betrays her confidence by telling Veronica, the woman he has married, about it – and she in turn tells Mrs Drummond. Mrs Drummond's 'sin' is not her sexual looseness but rather her complete lack of probity in relationships and the consequent tissue of lies her marriage is wrapped in, and this is the sin she shares with the ironically named Frank.

During the 1880s, Schreiner carried out a concerted reading and critique of then-current work on prostitution, as well as becoming personally involved with a number of prostitute women and in discussing the existence and nature of prostitution with friends and colleagues, including in the Men and Women's Club. Her developing analysis focused on the social causes and consequences of prostitution, not only for women who sold their sexual services to men, but also regarding its inter-personal implications for the way that men in general think about women in general.

In Woman and Labour, published in 1911, Schreiner remained concerned with what she saw as the fundamental way that prostitution underpinned women's other inequalities. Her portrayal of marriage in FMTM deals with far more than sexual trust and betrayal at an individual level, for it is concerned with the structural relationships engendered by the financial dependence of one person upon another, in prostitution but also within marriage, and the corruptions stemming from this that affect both partners. This is paralleled by the book's account of the hidden, denied but omnipresent existence of white men's exertion of sexual services from black women, also a mutually corrupting relationship, and one that divides black and white women and prevents realisation of the similarities of their sexual and economic exploitation.

In the early chapters of *FMTM*, it seems as though the two sisters enter entirely different trajectories in their lives: the naively simple and dependent Bertie is seduced, then gossiped about and progressively driven out of 'polite' society, first into being a 'kept woman' and then into common prostitution; while the educated, clever and independent Rebekah marries 'well' and has children. However, as the plot unfolds, Rebekah comes to realise that her husband's infidelities are more fundamental than merely sexual ones and that in a wider moral sense he is 'not worthy of her'. She becomes aware that her sexual desire for and enthrallment with Frank has kept her from this knowledge, and continues to bind her to him even after she gains it. Because of Frank's unworthiness, it is Rebekah's sexual dependence and not her financial one that constitutes her moral fall: her marriage is one of prostitution by another name.

There are deeper ironies even than this. Rebekah appears to be clearly the novel's hero, the person who has moral credibility and gains more, who reaches for sexual and racial equality, and who rejects the competitive message of Darwinian thinking. But the very moment of Rebekah's full flood of high-minded anti-Darwinian debate with herself is also the very moment when her sister Bertie is being cast out of polite society by malicious gossip and thereby revealed as one of the unfit who will not survive. Rebekah's long soliloquy in her study is abruptly interrupted by the slamming of a door; Bertie has run from a dance in tears at malicious gossip about her, to hide in her sister's home; but Rebekah listens, hears only silence, and continues quite unaware. The savage irony is clear. What is less clear is whether Rebekah's later patronage of black people – expressed initially in a story she tells to her sons, and then through her relationship with Sartjie, the daughter Frank had unknowingly fathered during his illicit sexual involvement with a black woman servant in their household – is intended to be part of the ironically critical gaze that Schreiner casts over the pretensions of her protagonist or not. The unnamed woman thoroughly despises Rebekah and makes no attempt to conceal this, and so the likelihood is that Schreiner did intend every bit of both the irony and the criticism. My view is that Rebekah started out as a more conventional 'hero of her own life' but that, as Schreiner's political sensibilities developed and changed, so episodes such as these were re-worked. Consequently they bear the imprint of both 'earlier heroism' and 'later irony', and this unsettles any definite or fixed attribution of 'the meaning' of *FMTM* in a moral sense, and so of its protagonist too.

As I commented earlier, *FMTM* is, with some exceptions, a seriously underrated novel.[185] The prevailing evaluations of it derive from a conventional realist idea of what 'a novel' is – a novel should have a clear temporal narrative, central characters that the reader and author identify with, and an ending that follows logically from prior events. By these standards, *FMTM* is troublesome and flawed. But seen as the product of a different and experimental writing project which sought to centre ideas about social morality and to 'mix writing genres' in doing so, it is a considerably more attractive book. Because of its developing ironies upon ironies throughout the text, successive re-readings of *FMTM* reveal more and more of Schreiner's subtle purposes. As a feminist polemic on marriage and conventional moral hypocrisy, and on the social injustices buried within Darwinist assumptions, it provides a fascinating and sustained fictional commentary. And as a swingeing dig at the massive pretensions of white liberals, it is unparalleled among Schreiner's literary contemporaries. Surely now, when postmodernist and deconstructionist ideas about 'the text' supposedly rule the intellectual roosts, the time has come for a serious re-look at Schreiner's novel and an attempt to see its 'flaws' in a different light?

And Now –

Writing 'a conclusion' to the discussion of Olive Schreiner's writings and ideas provided in this chapter is not an appropriate way to end it. This is in part because of the range and complexity of her writings. It is more importantly due to the groundedness of what Schreiner wrote, and her receptiveness to the specific. That is, her writing was keenly responsive to the particular times, places, persons and events that engaged her ideas and her creative sensibilities as well as her emotions. I shall, though, stand back from the ideas in particular pieces of Schreiner's writing, to comment on her analytic approach as a whole at the end of Chapter 4 and also in Chapter 5, considering what kind of social theory and what body of ideas she produced and what her work as a whole, as an 'oeuvre', adds up to.

As I noted at the start of this chapter, however dispassionate my intentions in outlining Schreiner's ideas and their inscription in particular pieces of writing, I have inevitably presented these through the framework of my own point of view and interpretational approach. In Chapter 4 I look at a number of important interpretations of Schreiner's work, and I shall also make explicit the underpinnings of my own.

Notes

1   Many of Schreiner's writings have been re-published over the last decade or so. For those still out of print, 'good libraries' will either already have or can obtain copies. A sensible guide to 'plots and characters' is provided by Clayton 1997, although readers should note that this does not discuss either Schreiner's letters or "The Dawn of Civilisation".

2   OS to Betty Molteno, ?3 October 1896, UCT Schreiner.

3   *Thoughts* pp.83-5.

4   The phrase, the 'real and the ideal', recurs in Schreiner's work; it is also the title of Schopenhauer's philosophical thesis, one of the books in Schreiner's collection now in the Cradock Public Library in the Eastern Cape. When she read this in England in the 1880s, she was amazed at the similarities between his ideas therein and her own. Schreiner fairly frequently referred to herself as 'a man', I think doing so in the same determined (or perhaps bloody-minded) spirit that she continued to use the word 'God', to rehabilitate it, to infuse it with her own holistic meanings.

5 She made a number of swingeing criticisms of the pretend realist conventions of realism in literature. With regard to her own writing, for the use of ribbed and plain styles of writing, see OS to Havelock Ellis, 8 August 1884, Draznin 1992, pp.124-5; and for the use of 'buffers', see OS to Havelock Ellis, 12 April 1886, Draznin 1992, p.412.

6 OS to Will Schreiner 17 July 1913, UCT Schreiner.

7 This is how Virginia Woolf (1925/1979) described her.

8 Some of Schreiner's correspondents foiled his intentions.

9 Cronwright-Schreiner 1924b, Rive 1987, Draznin 1992.

10 For Schreiner's rejection of 'biographising', see Cronwright-Schreiner 1924a pp.295-300.

11 The appearance of the second volume was prevented by his death.

12 Rive 1987, p.viii.

13 The notes were compiled or completed after Rive's death, so he is not responsible for this.

14 Rather, that part of it archived in the HRC. It had been assumed no other Schreiner/Ellis letters survive, although two additional sets have recently been added to the NELM Schreiner collection.

15 This is not (usually) negligence on the part of researchers but due to Schreiner's notoriously bad handwriting. Cronwright-Schreiner sees this as a product of her 'personality'. Her 'basic' handwriting was actually very good, but she often wrote lying down, she nearly always wrote at full pelt, and her eyesight grew worse; the result is sometimes monumental problems in transcription.

16 Dating many letters has involved considerable detective work by Draznin.

17 With this in mind, I am extremely grateful to the UK's ESRC for funding me to prepare a new edition of Schreiner letters.

18 Schreiner corresponded with Kent, who had reviewed An African Farm, both about this novel and about writing more generally; see here HRC Schreiner Uncat 2 November 1883, 11 December 1883. Ellis also provided critical comments about "New Rush"; see Havelock Ellis to OS, 8 July 1884, Draznin 1992 pp.82-84.

19 In spite of its New Rush/Kimberley 'birthplace', An African Farm is set in a South Africa before the discovery of diamonds – the children on the farm, for instance, come across a curious blue stone which the reader, with hindsight, is likely to realise is actually a large diamond.

20 Destroyed by Cronwright-Schreiner, apart from a few pages to illustrate handwriting changes and provide extracts for use in posthumous publications. Schreiner kept a diary and a journal for most of her adult life, so the loss is incomparable.

21 Cronwright-Schreiner 1924a, p.187.

22 The manuscript of Undine, in the NELM Schreiner collection, is pristine. Cronwright-Schreiner thought her grammar and punctuation faulty; her original reads better than his changes, which are either more stilted or else based on misunderstanding the meaning of passages.

23 Undine lives on a farm in the karoo, goes to England after her parents and brother Frank die, rejects a sexual overture from her married Cousin Jonathan, who tells the icily 'correct' Albert Blair, who Undine loves, she has been 'untrue', so Blair rejects her. She marries Blair's father to give Albert her marriage settlement to pay debts, but he marries a wealthy woman immediately before, so her sacrifice is wasted. When her venial husband and sickly baby die, she gives up her fortune, returns to Africa, becomes destitute then earns her living ironing. She realises that a nearby dying man is Albert Blair; her death from fever follows his.

24   For an interesting discussion of the Mignon figure and the re/appearances of this queer little girl, see Carolyn Steedman's (1995) *Strange Dislocations*.

25   Initially Schreiner was given only a one-off payment for rights over it for a number of years; thereafter financial problems led her to accept exploitative amounts and low royalty rates for a number of years; in addition, pirated editions in the USA (not then adhering to international notions of copyright) sold enormously but not to her financial benefit. Still, by the time of her death, with her other publications, it provided a good annual income, an income which Cronwright-Schreiner received thereafter. As well as *An African Farm*, her books of allegories and *Trooper Peter* sold in very large numbers in successive editions and many translations; and her political essays and pamphlets also sold enormously internationally as well as within South Africa. Contrary to Cronwright-Schreiner's insistence that he supported her (1924a p.362), there is strong archival evidence to suggest that for lengthy periods of time it was the other way about.

26   Edward Aveling, at the time Eleanor Marx's comrade rather than lover, reviewed it in 1883, raising all the issues that later generations of reviewers and commentators have also invoked; Clayton 1983 (pp.67-9) reprints his and various other contemporary reviews.

27   Willie Bertram (until his death in 1878, Schreiner intended to dedicate *An African Farm* to him) had also recommended she read Ralph Waldo Emerson's *Essays*. These had a great effect on her, and also helped her mother Rebecca during the period when she converted to Catholicism after Gottlob's death. The 'Ralph', like Waldo's name, was for Emerson. Waldo's surname, Farber, means iron in German; Schreiner's early letters mention her wanting to be 'hard', not open to being hurt, and the 'Iron' may relate to this; thus she had commented that while at Lelie Kloof in 1878 she was hard and analytical (Cronwright-Schreiner 1924a p.144). It is important to note that the pseudonym was less a disguise and more part of the allegorical framing of the novel.

28   Blenkins had smashed Waldo's model sheep-shearing machine after tricking him into thinking he admired it; it might have been the battery to his emotions rather than his body that broke his will.

29   See Matz 1909.

30   Brown 1937.

31   OS to Adela Villiers Smith, nd October 1909, *The Letters*, pp.290-1.

32   OS to Betty Molteno, 20 August 1896, 1 October 1896, UCT Schreiner.

33   OS to Havelock Ellis, 12 July 1884, HRC Schreiner, Draznin 1992, pp.92-94.

34   In "Workers", for instance, "And that spirit said yes and flew to the other side of the mountain" becomes "And that spirit flew away"; SAL Schreiner 1.4.

35   Cronwright-Schreiner's "Introduction" and "A note on the genesis of the book" in *FMTM* briefly quotes one of Schreiner's journals, that she had made up her mind "to write 'A Small Bit of Mimosa' and 'Wrecked' in one" (p.7).

36   She moved into the Kilburn convent in April 1886 and the Harrow one in July, leaving this latter in October 1886.

37   Agreed in conversations and letters with Ernest Rhys, who wanted it to appear in the 'Camelot Classics' series he edited for the publisher Walter Scott.

38   NELM Schreiner SMD 30.12.a. Schreiner 1994; Burdett 1994.

39   Visiting her sick mother in Grahamstown just after returning from England, Schreiner had lost a tin trunk containing allegories, other writings and personal possessions; see OS to Ettie Stakesby Lewis, nd November 1889, UCT Schreiner.

40   OS to Havelock Ellis, 2 November 1888, Rive 1987 p.142.

41   I *do* view this story in allegorical terms, for the conversation is clearly not a literal one and mentions of it elsewhere suggest Schreiner saw it as one of those epiphanous 'moments', like the death of Ellie.

42   Schreiner 1994 p.190, her emphasis.

43   Schreiner 1994 p.192.

44   OS to Karl Pearson, 26 October 1886, Rive 1987 pp.111-2; also OS to Isaline Philpot, 18 February 1888, Rive 1987 p.136.

45   See OS to Ernest Rhys, early 1888 and Sept/Oct 1888; to William Dircks early 1888; to Havelock Ellis 2 November 1888; Rive 1987 pp.136-7, 141-3.

46   OS to Havelock Ellis, 2 February 1889; HRC Schreiner, Draznin 1992 pp.447-8.

47   OS to Havelock Ellis, 25 April 1890, HRC Schreiner, Draznin 1992 p.460. The woman in "The Buddhist Priest's Wife" rejects the 'interiority' of love with the man, for a life of exteriority abroad.

48   *Thoughts* p.15.

49   For instance, the full text of Schreiner's speech to the women's congress at Somerset East in October 1900 (which was originally published in the *Eastern Province Herald* of 22 October 1900) is reprinted as Appendix C in *The Letters* and makes very powerful reading; its effect on a highly charged audience can be imagined.

50   Very different estimations, for instance, are provided by Beeton (1974 p.53), Burdett (1994b p.225) and Horton (1995 p.77).

51   *Thoughts* p.48, 49.

52   *Thoughts* p.49.

53   She had great admiration for the rulers of some of these states and was immensely pleased when they out-manoeuvered imperialist and capitalist interests. See here Parsons 1998 for the background.

54   This period of enormous moves of people in Southern Africa is known as the mfecane, a period of turmoil and warfare. Debates have concerned whether Zulu imperialism was a cause, or whether creation of the imposed order of the Zulu state was a result. See Hamilton 1998 for an interesting commentary.

55   *Thoughts* p.59, my emphasis.

56   *Thoughts* p.182.

57   *Thoughts* p.110.

58   *Thoughts* pp.113, 114-5, p.116.

59   *Thoughts* pp.125-6. Her comments about 'miscegenation' in this passage draws on then-current thinking that mixed race peoples were more fertile than the 'out of place' white colonists, who would eventually die out.

60   Thus: "no element in our complex South African situation is under so deep an obligation to any other as is the white man to the half-caste. The obligation to cultivate him and aid him ... appears to me morally imperative, and, if possible, more so than in the case of the pure bred natives", in *Thoughts* p.352.

61 *Thoughts* p.268. Her analysis here and as it developed in *The Political Situation* and *Closer Union* is very similar to that of David Yudelman (1984), that the 'shape' of South African capitalism over this period (and well after it) was one in which: (a) there was a marked concentration and homogeneity of non-indigenous capital resulting from the impact of mining (diamonds, gold and coal) which was not assimilated into political or other national elites; (b) the working class was starkly divided on 'race' lines, with whites in accommodation with both capital and the white state, and blacks as internal migrants living in conditions making their regulation and control easier; and (c) a state formation dominated by Afrikaner interests and highly resistant to infiltration by capital.

62 The substance of her public letter to striking Johannesburg shopworkers in 1905; Cronwright-Schreiner 1924b, Appendix D.

63 *Thoughts* p.309.

64 *Thoughts* p.274.

65 *Thoughts* p.310, 311.

66 For a heavily laundered version of its writing, see *The Life*. Jan Smuts, at that point a strong supporter of Rhodes and his imperial dream, was deputed to give a formal public response shortly after.

67 *The Political Situation* pp.9-20.

68 Edgar Walton, editor of the *Eastern Province Herald* in Port Elizabeth, had put these arguments to Merriman in a vain attempt to persuade him of the need for the liberals to organise as a party in late 1893; see Rotberg 1988 p.452. Schreiner's argument about the role of the Bond and its political organisation is in *The Political Situation* pp.21-30. Regarding Rhodes and 'squaring', a perhaps apocryphal story runs that, in talking to Charles Dilke about solutions to 'the Irish problem', Dilke had commented about the opposition of the Pope to the strategy they were discussing; so then, responded Rhodes, we will square the Pope.

69 *The Political Situation* p.79.

70 *The Political Situation* pp.86-131.

71 *The Political Situation* pp.108-9.

72 *The Political Situation* pp.97-8.

73 *The Political Situation* pp.31-36.

74 As John Mackenzie, a highly important presence in Southern Africa and leader of the London Missionary Society until just before his death in 1898, commented: "I have had special & reliable information from Matabeleland; & the facts will, I think, astonish the ordinary English reader. Having the telegraphic wire ever ready to back them up, the Company has got to occupy a position to which it would appear it has not the slightest title, judging from what it has actually done. Its native policy has been a complete failure, & a disgrace to Great Britain. It was almost inconceivable that the long-oppressed Mashonas should have sided with their oppressors, the Matabele, rather than with the white men, who, it was supposed, were their friends & protectors. I was for weeks here refusing to believe that the Mashona had also risen; till at last the evidence was undeniable. While our general native policy was such that the Mashona preferred to fight along with the Matabele rather than assist the white men, in Matabeleland the Company undoubtedly established forced labour as a permanent institution. Incredible, you say; nevertheless, the fact. The Company has lowered us far below the Transvaal boers as to the treatment of the [incomplete and breaks off at this point]"; John Mackenzie to Mr Oates, 7 October 1897, Wits John Mackenzie Papers A75/8: 2764.

75   OS to Betty Molteno, 20 August 1896, UCT Schreiner, Rive 1987 p.288 (with a slightly different transcription from mine); and OS to Betty Molteno, nd. July 1896, UCT Schreiner, Rive 1987 p.287. See also OS to Betty Molteno, 30 Sept 1896, 21 October 1896, UCT Schreiner, Rive 1987 pp.288, 290, 293; OS to Rev G.W. Cross nd Aug 1896, Rive 1987 p.289.

76   This was removed from the second edition by the publisher. In later South African editions it was 'tipped in' loose, so that according to the whims of censorship under apartheid it could be removed or included.

77   OS to Will Schreiner 15 March 1897, UCT Schreiner; OS to Betty Molteno 21 October 1896 UCT Schreiner.

78   "There is a tree, known as the hanging tree ... Hither the doomed men were conveyed. On the ropes being fastened to their necks, they were made to climb along an overhanging branch, and thence were pushed or compelled to jump ...", from Sykes 1897, pp.77-8.

79   Readers' reports on *Trooper Peter* for Fisher Unwin, HRC Schreiner Uncatalogued Papers, Correspondence with T. Fisher Unwin 1887-1911.

80   Blackwood's *Edinburgh Magazine*, April 1897.

81   It received a very large number of reviews; the large majority of these were very positive.

82   Stanley 2000b.

83   Schreiner rejected this chocolate box Europeanised version of Jesus. Cronwright-Schreiner (1924a p.7) notes that "She said she always pictured him as a dark little Jew, with flashing eyes and a hooked nose"; her letters also invoke this view of him.

84   *Trooper Peter* p. 121.

85   *Trooper Peter* p. 53, p. 54.

86   OS to John X. Merriman, 3 April 1897, SAL Merriman, Rive 1987 p. 308.

87   Strictly speaking, with the Transvaal; however, it had an offensive and defensive alliance with the Free State.

88   In August 1899, Smuts on behalf of the Transvaal government offered a 5 year residency retrospective franchise for the uitlanders; this was refused. The Transvaal presented an ultimatum to Britain on 9 October when British troops began massing near its frontier; when it expired on 11 October, the South African War began.

89   *An English South African's View* p.4. It sold 3,500 copies in the first five days after publication; see OS to Fan Schreiner, 26 July 1899, UCT Schreiner, Rive 1987 p.371.

90   Reprinted in Rive 1987 p. 387.

91   *An English South African's View* p. 27.

92   *An English South African's View* pp. 36–7.

93   See Yudelman 1984 on this.

94   *An English South African's View* pp. 49–64.

95   *An English South African's View* p. 56.

96   *An English South African's View* p. 87.

97   *An English South African's View* pp. 89–90.

98   OS to Will Schreiner, 14 September 1899, UCT Schreiner, Rive 1987 pp. 378-9.

99   OS to Will Schreiner, 10 May 1908, UCT Schreiner.

100   *Thoughts* p. 57.

101   *Thoughts* pp. 271–2, 348.

102   *Thoughts* pp.336, 340–1.

103   *Thoughts* p. 340–1.

104   *Thoughts* p. 343.

105   *Closer Union* pp. 8–9.

106   The classical liberal view.

107   *Closer Union* p. 15.

108   *Closer Union* p. 18.

109   *Closer Union* pp. 42–55, p. 42.

110   Considering how accurate many of her 'predictions' were and her awareness of how
      radically the war had affected Afrikaner thinking, it is curious that Schreiner under-read
      the signs of developing Afrikaner nationalism until 1912-3.

111   *Closer Union* pp.43-4. She is deliberately using a worst instincts/best interests argument
      here.

112   *Closer Union* p.45.

113   *Closer Union* p.47.

114   *Closer Union* pp.49–50.

115   *Closer Union* p.51.

116   *Closer Union* pp.53–4.

117   *Closer Union* pp.54–5.

118   *Closer Union* p.51.

119   *Closer Union* p.54.

120   OS to J. Henderson, 26 December 1911, Cory MS 14.847, my emphasis.

121   See Emily Hobhouse's letters to Rachel Isabella Steyn of 30 October 1913 and 5
      November 1913, Van Reenen 1984 pp.395–7. See also Stanley 2000c.

122   OS to Betty Molteno 12 Nov 1920, UCT Schreiner.

123   *W&L* p.283.

124   It has been suggested that Gilman's book not only influenced Schreiner's analysis in
      Woman and Labour but also provided the idea of parasitism (Harris 1993). This is
      incorrect. The term parasitism isn't actually used by Gilman, while Schreiner's analytic
      framework, including the term of sex parasitism, is contained in her "The Woman
      Question", published in the USA in early 1899, while the basic idea of parasitism appears
      regarding 'the labour problem' in the 1896 published *The Political Situation* as well as in
      an essay by her now published in *Thoughts*, but originally published in the USA in the
      early 1890s. While Gilman was in London around publication of her book, Schreiner was
      in South Africa confined under martial law and not allowed to receive new reading
      material by post. There is no sign that the analysis in "The Woman Question" essay had
      changed in anything other than minor respects when incorporated into *W&L*. As Larry
      Ceplair (1991 p.13) has noted, there is considerable evidence that Gilman read all of
      Olive Schreiner's work; however, there is no evidence Schreiner read Gilman's book until

later. In addition, while Schreiner gave the term a particular analytic twist, it was used by many other contemporary commentators and so 'belongs' neither to her nor to Gilman.

125 Burdett 2001 sees Schreiner's analysis of parasitism as a means of targeting and criticising Pearson's eugenicism. Perhaps this was an element within it, but she clearly had much bigger analytical fish to fry than Pearson.

126 The terms she uses, regarding 'the age of muscular force' and 'the age of nervous force' are drawn from John Stuart Mill's work, which she admired, but were also part of the conceptual armoury of the day and 'belong' neither to her nor to him.

127 *W&L* p.22.

128 *W&L* p.23.

129 *W&L* p.24.

130 *W&L* p.13.

131 *W&L* p.16.

132 Reprinted in Barash 1987.

133 Cronwright-Schreiner's *The Life* treats Schreiner's account as a lie or fantasy covering the fact that the 'sex book' had never been written; the archive evidence supports Schreiner rather than him.

134 *W&L* pp.40, 42. On Schreiner completing her 'little book on the woman question', see OS to Mimmie Murray, nd 1911, NELM 2001.24, Mrs Murray Letters.

135 *W&L* pp.48-9.

136 *W&L* p.50.

137 *W&L* p.67.

138 *W&L* pp.115, 114.

139 *W&L* p.,116.

140 *W&L* pp.98–101.

141 *W&L* p.281.

142 *W&L* pp.82-3, footnote 1; pp.103-4. To emphasise again: for Schreiner 'civilised' was often used an insult implying increased inequality and injustice, and 'primitive' thus was a positive comment.

143 *W&L* pp.125–6; see also 122–50.

144 *W&L* pp.135.

145 *W&L* p.167.

146 *W&L* pp.168, 169, 170.

147 *W&L* p.176.

148 *W&L* p.178.

149 *W&L* p.185.

150 *W&L* p.223.

151 *W&L* pp.27–8.

152 *W&L* pp.256–8.

153 *W&L* p.260.

154 For example, OS to Betty Molteno 20 April 1907, Schreiner UCT.

155 But see Cynthia Enloe's (1983, 1989, 2000) longstanding and extremely astute analysis of the military machine as a crucial component in inter/national economies.

156 Appendix I, *The Life* p.401.

157 For Schreiner's war allegories, see for instance "Eighteen-Ninety-Nine", "The Cry of South Africa", "Seeds A-Growing", "The Great Heart of England" and "Who Knocks At the Door" in Schreiner's *Stories, Dreams and Allegories*; and of course also *Trooper Peter*.

158 *Stories* pp.53, 54, 55.

159 *Stories* p.145.

160 *Stories* pp.146.

161 *Stories* pp.148-9.

162 In *Stories*.

163 *Stories* p.142.

164 See for example OS to Edward Carpenter, nd 1915, NELM Schreiner SMD 20.32.r.

165 OS to Havelock Ellis, 16 October 1914 *The Letters* p.340; OS to Havelock Ellis, nd but 24 October 1915, HRC Schreiner, Draznin 1992 p.495; OS to Betty Molteno, ?30 April 1915, Schreiner UCT.

166 OS to Edward Carpenter 16 March 1916, NELM Schreiner SMD 30.32 u.

167 Appendix H, *The Letters* p.399.

168 Appendix H, *The Letters* p.399.

169 Appendix I, *The Letters* p.400.

170 Appendix I, *The Letters* p.401.

171 SAL Schreiner MS 1.6, and HRC Schreiner MS 1 – 4. "The Dawn" is edited from Part 3 of the SAL manuscript and introduction. The four other Parts have corrections, overlaps and gaps. On a cover note on the typescript Cronwright-Schreiner had made, he notes that "This MS, with her own corrections, was handed to me ... in August 1920 ...", and he ignores the rest of the manuscript. It is not possible from the archival evidence to tell what Schreiner thought was the status of this version. Interpretational problems are increased when the HRC manuscript is considered. This is a fuller manuscript and bears a closer relationship to "The Dawn", with its first two sections having the same title and part numbers as the published version. The HRC version has also been corrected by Will Schreiner and also in a hand that might be Cronwright-Schreiner's, or might be Olive Schreiner's neatest, or might be some else's altogether.

172 "The Dawn" p.913.

173 "The Dawn" p.912.

174 "The Dawn" p.914.

175 "The Dawn" p.914.

176 "The Dawn of Civilisation", part 3, HRC Schreiner.

177 "The Dawn of Civilisation", part 3, HRC Schreiner.

178 "The Dawn of Civilisation", part 4, HRC Schreiner.

179 OS to Havelock Ellis, 16 May 1884, Draznin 1992 pp.52-3; and 21 November, Draznin 1992 pp.223-4.

180 There are drafts of three chapters in the Schreiner HRC collection, although these are early versions given to Havelock Ellis. Cronwright-Schreiner definitely 'did things' with the title. 'From man to man' is a phrase Schreiner had taken from one of John Morley's writings, and to his knowledge she had only ever referred to the book by this title; however, he comments that a typescript of 1911 used the title 'The Camel Thorn' (a large shrubby tree), although this was crossed out and replaced with 'Perhaps Only', a phrase the child in the Prelude uses and indicates wonderment at the (uncertain) nature of things, and is now its sub-title.

181 His diaries (NELM Schreiner SMD 30.1.a – g) show he spent some weeks carrying out this work but unfortunately provide no details, only his exasperation at Schreiner's deficiencies and also those of their mutual friend Anna Purcell, who typed the final manuscript.

182 My detailed comparison of the manuscript (in the NELM Schreiner collection) and the published version of *Undine* shows that the changes Cronwright-Schreiner made were minimal, although in a few cases they did alter the sense of what Schreiner had written.

183 These dates are pieced together from archive sources, mainly Schreiner's letters.

184 *FMTM* pp.19–29. It is also a recurring feature of how 'great writers' are seen; see Leader 1996.

185 For two notable exceptions, see Berkman 1989; Heilmann 1995.

Chapter 4

Interpretations

Will the Real Olive Schreiner Please Stand Up?

A number of sharply diverging interpretations of Olive Schreiner and her work exist[1] – indeed, it sometimes seems there might be two or three women who happen to share the same name but have different lives and characters! The co-existence of these reveals more about disagreements between political and analytical viewpoints than about Schreiner and her writing,[2] and should be approached in this light. The first interpretation I look at in this chapter presents its knowledge as incontrovertible, and it was constructed around controlling how Olive Schreiner was publicly perceived. Some subsequent accounts have been equally keen to prove a particular viewpoint, including concerning Freudian ideas about infant conflicts and adult neuroticism, or social Darwinism as the main characteristic of Schreiner's life and thought, as with two of the interpretations I go on to discuss. Of course there are also interpretations of Schreiner and her work which are illuminatingly responsive to complexities and alternative ways of thinking about them, and I discuss a number of these too.

Adopting a judgemental approach to Schreiner and/or her work[3] is as prevalent as it is because there are things about this area of scholarly activity which encourage people to demonstrate that their political and/or scholarly credentials are in order. The first is that Olive Schreiner wrote in the context of imperialism, racism and the origins of the apartheid state in South Africa, so that she is sometimes seen as an emblematic 'white South African' and tainted by everything this has come to mean. The second is that the things she was centrally concerned with analysing – capitalism, imperialism, 'race' and racism, the oppression of women – remain ethically and politically extremely important, and people feel drawn to particular 'sides' in writing about them. And the third is that feminist scholarship in particular has tried not to be seen as 'cultist' or as unduly praising of Schreiner and, as a consequence of appeasing anti-feminist criticisms, it has (over-)emphasised problems and flaws in her and her work.

This chapter discusses the key interpretations of Schreiner's life and writing because few present-day readers come to Schreiner's work 'cold', but instead do so via accounts which draw on one or more of the major interpretations that exist. It is therefore important to unpack these, looking closely at 'knowledge' about Olive Schreiner, who claims to possess it and with what degree of certainty. Ultimately, I do not find any of the existing interpretations completely convincing, not because the motifs they discern in Schreiner's work cannot be found in her published writings or unpublished letters, but because there is so much else about her life, her writing and her thinking that does not fit them. Thus the motivation for writing my own. My arguments are of course equally to be seen as part of this process of knowledge claims-making, and I conclude the chapter with an outline of my own interpretation and its whys and wherefores.

Rather than discussing these interpretations in the chronological order of their publication (as I did with Schreiner's own writings), I do so by grouping them in a more thematic way. I start by looking at those which take a basically biographical approach (Cronwright-Schreiner; Friedmann; First and Scott; Schoeman); then move on to those that interpret Schreiner's work specifically in relation to ideas about 'race' (Gordimer; Barash; Burdett); and finish with those that seek to place Schreiner and her work within a broader social and intellectual context (Berkman; McClintock; myself).

The Damaged Genius

The first published biography of Olive Schreiner was written by her estranged husband, and so it is hardly surprising strong emotions are discernible on its pages. There are many 'widow's biographies' and these are usually (and sometimes unfairly) seen as hagiography – 'the great man' reverentially presented as flawless and saintly. A widower's biography like Cronwright-Schreiner's *The Life of Olive Schreiner* is much more rare. Although apparently hagiographic and containing many insistencies about her 'genius', it carries out an efficient hatchet-job by insisting on Schreiner's peculiarities, weaknesses and failures. In fact Cronwright-Schreiner's stance is hyper-critical, obsessively concerned with the in/accuracy of often insignificant statements about events and people many years earlier in Schreiner's life, and repeatedly insistent that he is completely correct about absolutely everything.[4] The result was known to Schreiner's family and friends as 'Cronwright's novel'.

Most of Schreiner's family and friends refused to help with *The Life* because they knew she had not wanted a biography to be written, and so they saw Cronwright-Schreiner's book as a betrayal. Many of them also disliked him and experienced him on a range from humourless and pig-headed to intolerable. Olive Renier, the adopted daughter of Schreiner's close friend Alice Corthorn, proposed that Cronwright-Schreiner's's biography was an act of retaliation – "In the end he had his turn. He wrote her life and edited her letters, according to his view of what posterity might be allowed to know about her".[5] Olive Schreiner's niece, Lyndall ('Dot') Gregg, was more concerned with the result than his motive, emphasising the one-sided impression his biography gives and that its readers "may not realise how strong was her sense of the ridiculous, but we listened ... with constant delight to all her funny stories".[6] She also referred to Cronwright-Schreiner as her aunt's husband or as Mr Cronwright, never as her uncle, and she concluded wryly but scrupulously that "The husbands of famous women are not perhaps always their most generous biographers, and this is a strange book, which may, temporarily, have damaged her fame ... [but] its author did, in his own way, value the prophetic genius, deep sincerity, and great tenderness of heart of his famous wife".[7] Karel Schoeman's assessment, made with hindsight, is the stronger one that Cronwright-Schreiner's biography was deliberate revenge.[8]

Cronwright-Schreiner presents Olive Schreiner as a damaged genius, barely capable of surviving without constant protection and support. She was a 'divine child' and, like other geniuses, characterised "by physical mannerisms, by strange emotional manifestations, and by unexpected limitations of the intellect in fields where its superb quality is not operative ... the incalculable power and illumination of the one throwing into more glaring contrast the comparative inequalities and limitations of the others".[9] He repeatedly insists that she was "so strange and incredible" that he would not have believed such a person could exist before he met her. He refers to "Olive's power ... her extraordinary intensity ... her serious, direct, merciless intelligence ... the blaze of eye and explosive energy ... the ringing vibrant tones when Olive was aroused", and he concludes "There was something almost awesomely elemental" about her.[10] He also presents her as a deeply damaged person with great flaws in her character.

In doing so, Cronwright-Schreiner insists over and over that Olive Schreiner's own contrary voice is not to be believed. He insists that she exaggerated to the point of lying, making what she said always completely unreliable; and if she imagined something had happened, then, regardless of 'the facts' totally obvious to everyone else, she behaved as if her imaginings were true.[11] His loud insistences occur to the point where it is apparent that 'the gentleman doth protest too much'. In addition, there is extra-textual information which confounds the 'portrait' provided, and also textual material is tucked away within *The Life* which also suggests his claims are actually shaky. One example is that Schreiner said that she had 'no schooling' and emphasised how differently her brothers were treated, while Cronwright-Schreiner insists this was wrong and makes a great deal of her having briefly attended some classes taught by Theo and Ettie in Cradock when she was thirteen. He thereby entirely misses her point, that her brothers had been sent to schools and colleges while her education was *ad hoc*, domestic and entirely 'by the way'. A second example is that Schreiner said she had an incapacitating heart complaint and its seriousness had been confirmed by specialists, while Cronwright-Schreiner insists this was a fantasy that 'real' specialists found no evidence of and only quacks did. He thereby ignores the inconvenient fact that all her siblings died from the same heart condition their father had died from,[12] that the 'quacks' were equally reputable medics, and also that the post-mortem she arranged to be carried out after her death confirmed both the reality of the heart condition and its cumulatively disabling effects.[13]

For *The Life*, the source of these and other 'flaws' is Olive Schreiner's 'genius' related to her childhood. Cronwright-Schreiner characterises her father as lovingly kind and gentle and her mother as an emotionally denuded martinet; and in religious terms the entire family apart from Olive is presented as narrowly bigoted. Thus he describes her puritanical older siblings Theo and Ettie verbally hounding her over a period of years, ending only in late adolescence when she 'faced down' Theo and his religious persecution, with the repentant Ettie later writing a number of letters expressing her shame at this. However, as I noted in Chapter 2, the character of Otto in *An African Farm* may be a re-worked version of her father Gottlob, but this is certainly not a sentimentalised 'portrait' but rather an indictment of intellectual naivety. From her young womanhood on, Schreiner became very close to her mother and recognised the considerable strains of her (rather than her unworldly and childlike husband) having had the responsibility for bringing up their large number of children in conditions of frequent danger and (relative to many other whites) penury.[14] She also became very close to Ettie, in some ways closer than to her younger brother Will. This is not to say that Schreiner did not write on a number occasions about the confinements and punishments of her childhood and the lack of loving attention from her mother, and also remember with anger her treatment from Theo and Ettie. But it is to suggest that she developed a balanced view of the circumstances in which these things had occurred and had forgiven if not forgotten.

Cronwright-Schreiner also makes sweeping claims about Schreiner's failings as a writer, insisting that, in spite of her great gifts and total support from him, her life was characterised by a continuing failure to write.[15] Certainly he acknowledges her international fame, her independence of mind, and the importance of *An African Farm* for many readers, himself included. But alongside this he advances a host of criticisms. He insists that she wrote hardly anything, and in particular the 'big book' to earn them a large sum of money never materialised. He also insists that her claim that the long-planned 'sex book' was destroyed during the South African War was another lie, stating categorically that the book never existed and so could not have been destroyed. Her claim, he states, was simply a tale to cover the fact that she had not written it.

When Cronwright-Schreiner's claims are compared with what Schreiner actually did write, two things are striking. The first is the quantity of what she wrote, often in difficult personal and political circumstances, and the second is the great international as well as national influence many of her writings had. This is not 'failure' as most people understand it, and what is remarkable is less that Cronwright-Schreiner should have characterised it as such, and more that so many people have believed him. Specifically regarding the 'sex book', the weight of evidence is against Cronwright-Schreiner's contention that it never existed. There is the circumstantial evidence that he did not know about various other writing until after Schreiner's death, including the complete novel *Undine* and the completed but 'vanished' novel "New Rush"; also the contents of *Woman and Labour* are similar to the plan for the sex book which Schreiner had sent to Karl Pearson many years before;[16] and in addition he misrepresents what Schreiner claimed, which was that a part of the sex book had been destroyed, not all of it. Thus even from the circumstantial evidence, "Cronwright's evidence is so contradictory as to be worthless";[17] in addition, there is also archival evidence that suggests that Cronwright-Schreiner had in fact acknowledged the existence and destruction of the book at the time of the looting.[18]

The account provided by Cronwright-Schreiner continues to be influential in even present-day interpretations of Olive Schreiner and her work, because many of his shaky contentions and deliberate misrepresentations have over the years become 'common knowledge' now divorced from their origin in his bionovel and/or bowdlerised letters. This process had its origins in the 1950s, when a psychoanalytic study of Schreiner and her novels by Marion Friedmann, *Olive Schreiner: A Study in Latent Meanings*, was published. This was influential in South Africa, where it was published, and also more widely because referenced by subsequent writers on Schreiner. Friendmann's study draws extensively on Cronwright-Schreiner's work, which it treats as though a primary source. It is useful to look at how Friedmann draws together various of his 'descriptions' to construct what she presents as Schreiner's failure as a writer due to her neuroticism, caused by her damaged childhood and infancy. Friedmann does this in particular by reading the novels 'as biographical fact', then reading backwards and forwards between them and Cronwright-Schreiner's account.

Friedmann's "Introductory Note" states that Schreiner was "preoccupied with painful experience", being damaged, self-punishing and "hag-ridden".[19] Her study starts with *Undine*, dismissed as "undeniably poor stuff", and focusing on the women in it, for "The book is hag-ridden by what we might call the older-woman figure ...".[20] These older women are predominantly mothers, and Friedmann proposes that "The noteworthy features of *Undine* are repeated in *An African Farm*. The wretched childhood; the painful religious experiences; the strong sense of guilt that rejection of the Deity brought; mental and physical torments inflicted on the weak; stupidity and sadism accompanying religious fervour ....".[21] She sees *From Man to Man* continuing the same basic theme, for "The two central characters are made to suffer ... To the Hags' gallery we may add almost all the minor female characters in the novel"; and she confidently insists that "If this brief account of its 460 pages gives the reader the impression that this is a poor novel, that impression is not far off the truth".[22]

Friedmann claims the "constant revision" of Schreiner's last novel occurred because Schreiner "felt compelled ... an impulse that 'drives' her on", and this idea of 'compulsion' is linked to Friedmann's broader argument, that "The main theme is the theme of punishment, and the offender seems to be a child ... Olive could have comforted those frightened children, protected those tortured young women ... Instead she frustrated and punished them ... I ask the reader to accept the suggestion she was punishing herself".[23] For Friedmann, this resulted from Schreiner wrestling with problems caused by her supposedly damaged childhood: neurotic behaviour, chronic depression, attacks of acute grief, thoughts of suicide, unsatisfactory relationships with other people, particularly women, and being 'latently homosexual'.[24]

Friedmann links the 'punishment' she sees constantly re-imposed on children in Schreiner's novels to Schreiner's asthma, which she sees caused by an "unsatisfactory parent-child relationship"[25] between Schreiner and her (surprise, surprise) mother. Amalgamating Schreiner's fiction with Cronwright-Schreiner's *The Life* and *The Letters*, Friedmann concludes that "Rebecca was harsh and unloving to her family ..." and there is "little doubt" she is the source of the sinister hags and harridans in Schreiner's novels.[26] Friedmann then links this to Schreiner's purportedly 'markedly ambivalent' relationships with women, to the 'old harridans' who are landladies, and the statement (taken out of context) that "'My mother has never been a mother to me'".[27] She concludes that Schreiner was a maladjusted child, and that her childhood behaviour and especially her rejection of a God should be traced to even earlier events. This is then connected with her oddest statement, that "One cannot ignore the strange *mouth* behaviour of Olive's characters", for the denouement of Friedmann's argument is that "the origin of this difficulty lay in the infantile feeding situation".[28]

"There is no doubt", Friedmann claims, that all of Schreiner's writing was "to express herself, for herself, and to her self alone".[29] She is unequivocal that: "The woman and the work were one. Olive was what she was largely as a result of the unfortunate relationship which existed between herself and her mother from the earliest years".[30] Friedmann categorically dismisses Schreiner's writing, concluding that "Perhaps Olive failed so often as a writer not because she was narrowed down to a vision, but because that vision could not be communicated to others. It began and ended with herself".[31] 'So if Schreiner's work and life are such failures then why bother?' is the question that readers of Friedmann's period-piece may well ask.

It is difficult now to take Friedmann's arguments seriously, not because she is a Freudian or interested in psychoanalysis, but because she is such a wretchedly flat-footed butcher of psychoanalytic orthodoxies of the 1950s. On one level her book is merely a period-piece, a curious example of a teleological cod-Freudian argument and little more. However, like Cronwright-Schreiner's work, on which Friedmann is so dependent, some of her unevidenced and sometimes quite outrageous contentions have been re-cycled in later scholarship as though fact: X references Friedmann; Y references X and also Friedmann; and then A and B reference only X and Y; and so on.

The Asthmatic Personality

Olive Schreiner by Ruth First and Ann Scott, published in 1980, was the first present-day account of Schreiner's life and work to be based on primary sources and original research, and it has had considerable impact. It resulted from a collaboration between Ruth First, a South African Marxist and political exile with predominantly political interests, and Ann Scott, a UK feminist whose particular interest was the 'language of personal life'. As the authors comment, "Throughout our five years' work together we have tried hard neither to restrict each other's special interests nor to allow these to distort the main themes we set ourselves to explore".[32] These 'special interests' also result in different emphases in the book, so that at times ideas about 'the woman and her inner life', as compared with 'her works and politics and contexts', for me never quite meet in its pages.

Olive Schreiner was written under the great difficulty of Ruth First being banned from re-entering South Africa and so prevented from having direct access to its archive sources. Nevertheless, academic and archival networks managed to subvert this to the extent that copies of many relevant documents were dispatched to her. This aspect of the biography, grounded in archive materials, in my view stands up remarkably well against more recent scholarship. What has worn less well is the particular version of psychoanalytic ideas used for interpreting Schreiner's 'personal life' and her asthma, which, for this reader at least, is the source of the dated feel to parts of the book.[33] Overall, it was (and is) a 'very good read' and provided what was at the time of publication much new information. In doing so, it substantially undercut some of Cronwright-Schreiner's claims about Schreiner, including his suppression of evidence and silencing of important persons and contrary views.

Karel Schoeman describes *Olive Schreiner* as "far the best of the limited number of biographies ... [but] much stronger on analysis than on factual data ... First and Scott contented themselves with referring largely to Cronwright-Schreiner's *Life* of 1924, which ... is virtually useless ...".[34] This is I think an over-statement, for First and Scott made good use of the then-available archive materials to provide a good deal of new information about Schreiner's life as well as a new analysis of Schreiner's writings. But it is certainly true that First and Scott take on trust a good deal of Cronwright-Schreiner's work as the basis of important aspects of their account. This is a deliberate feature of their working methods, it should be pointed out:

> *Cronwright was not only concerned to build a monument to her as a writer, but also, by destroying much of the material to which he had access, to perpetuate a view of Olive acceptable to himself ... But whatever its omissions, of course, Cronwright-Schreiner's Life remains indispensable as a biographical source. In that it does provide unequalled access to original material we have drawn on it ... using it most extensively for her own account of her childhood. We have relied more on his edited collection of her Letters, though these too were carefully selected.[35]*

The result is that, in dealing with Schreiner's childhood and the period she worked as a governess, First and Scott write that most "information about this period in Olive's life, including quotations ... and others' recollections of her, can be found in *Life*, Ch 2 ... and Ch 3."[36]. They also state that "Where verbal recollection of her as a child is involved, we have relied more on others' statements than on hers, since she was given to exaggeration and getting her dates wrong",[37] with this referenced to Cronwright-Schreiner's claim. One result is that a reader who comes across many of Cronwright-Schreiner's contentions sees these as corroborated by the later work of First and Scott, whereas they have merely uncritically repeated them. Another result is that, in what is a feminist or (given Ruth First's identification as a Marxist) a proto-feminist account, Schreiner appears almost as denuded of female friendships and feminist political networks as in Cronwright-Schreiner's work.

It is not surprising that First and Scott should have assumed that useful factual material could be found in Cronwright-Schreiner's work, for they were the first to recognise that some of his editorial activities were highly suspect. What is surprising is that they accepted many of his blatantly dismissive comments about Olive Schreiner's character or personality. First and Scott also positively evaluate Friedmann's work, describing it as "the most coherent" of the then-existing biographical studies, and suggest that "she is obviously right to describe Olive as neurotic".[38] They use Friendmann's account of Schreiner's personality as corroboration of their view of Schreiner's troubled mothering: "The child is in an intolerable situation in which the hated mother is also the loved mother of infancy ... Her aggression towards Rebecca was redirected towards an object easily identifiable with her";[39] and they, as well as Friedmann, treat this as the source of Schreiner's rejection of Christianity and disbelief in any god.

The main impact of Cronwright-Schreiner's and Friedmann's work on First and Scott, however, concerns their view of Schreiner's asthma, treating hers as in effect an 'asthmatic personality'. They see Schreiner's asthma as the expression of conflicts about power and control and the contradictions thus wrought in her life, treating it as the psychosomatic product of damaging mother/child relations arising from conflicts over in/dependence. The dynamic of Schreiner's life is accordingly presented as a swing between frenetic but often unproductive activity, and periodic neurotic retreats into asthma. Even at the time of writing, such a view of asthma was outmoded; now it seems extraordinary.

First and Scott's work, as I noted, has stood the test of time well regarding its primary historical research; there are two particular aspects of this I want to comment on. Firstly, First and Scott chart Schreiner's developing analysis of the interconnections of 'race', labour and imperialism that produced the South African War and point out that hers was the most clear-sighted account to be produced contemporaneously. Therefore, although they conclude Rosa Luxemburg produced a 'better' analysis, they also emphasise that this was written more than a decade after the event while Schreiner's was produced in the thick of it. Surprisingly little work has been carried out on this aspect of Schreiner's work; and I have found their account a still useful starting point in relation to Schreiner's ideas about the war and what produced it. Secondly, they provide an interesting discussion of the schism between Olive Schreiner and Cronwright-Schreiner which existed by 1912 and the impact this had on his misleading account of Schreiner's resignation as Vice-President of the Women's Enfranchisement League. Even now, little attention has been given to the political background to this or to their deteriorating relationship and its impact on *The Life* and *The Letters*; consequently, I have found First and Scott's discussion a useful starting point here too.

First and Scott's *Olive Schreiner* remains, twenty-five years after publication, a still useful overview of Schreiner's life and writing, testifying to the considerable strengths of their work. It is also notable that the book contains very different estimations of the woman and of her work – that Schreiner's writings are interesting and largely laudable, while her life is characterised by neuroticism and failure. Few readers can have finished the book without having been struck by the divorce it presents between the perceived successes of Schreiner's work and her apparently miserably failed life. What First and Scott's *Olive Schreiner* ascribes to a divorce within Olive Schreiner herself, I see instead as the product of the divergent 'special interests' of its authors. However, other commentators too have discerned a 'fatal flaw' as characterising Schreiner's life and work, and Karel Schoeman's version of this leads him to be considerably less appreciative of Schreiner's writing than First and Scott.

Some Fatal Emotional Flaw

In the 1991 English-language version of Karel Schoeman's *Olive Schreiner: A Woman in South Africa 1855–1881*, he describes his book as a biography in the 'life and times' tradition, 'recreating' Schreiner's life by locating it within the social context of South Africa during the period he is concerned with.[40] The same characterisation – 'life and times', and 'recreation' – can also be made of Schoeman's *Only an Anguish to Live Here: Olive Schreiner and the Anglo-Boer War 1899-1902*, published in 1992.[41] To these two concerns can be added a third, for Schoeman sees the present-day feminist interest in Olive Schreiner as one that 'reduces' her and presents his biography as a 'counterbalance' to this.[42]

Karel Schoeman's two books 'add up' to the currently most detailed account of Olive Schreiner's life over the periods he deals with. In this sense they are exemplary and they make an extremely important contribution to Schreiner scholarship, Through painstaking archival work, Schoeman has pieced together an account which provides much new information and corrects some erroneous contentions about Schreiner's life. My discussion recognises Schoeman's many detailed factual contributions and excellent scholarship and sees his two books as crucial reading on Schreiner; it takes off from this, to focus on some of the interpretational issues which Schoeman's approach gives rise to.

Schoeman describes Schreiner as "a minor nineteenth-century woman novelist",[43] a description which is of course evaluatively loaded: not only a minor, but a minor woman, novelist; the genre she wrote in is confined to the novel; and her work is implicitly evaluated against an interpretation which conceives the novel in specifically narrative terms. Schoeman also sees Schreiner as "more than just a novelist … and more than just an early feminist … She was also a complex, gifted and extremely interesting personality in her own right", and he suggests she was "a remarkable personality who greatly impressed her contemporaries" and was the progenitor of South African writing.[44] Nonetheless, in his judgement Schreiner failed to realise her potential, because of her lack of education and odd childhood, but also "beyond that some fatal emotional flaw which doomed her to be always searching and striving, energetically but aimlessly, but with little tenacity and without developing any strongly pronounced sense of purpose".[45]

Schoeman's view of this 'emotional flaw' person leads him to find Schreiner wanting against a 'norm' I think more that of a machine than a person, concluding that "it is perhaps her life itself which is of importance rather than any actual achievements".[46] This 'fatal flaw', Schoeman argues, meant she was unable to transcend her autobiography, with this being the source of her failure as a creative artist: she could not 'create', only stay immersed within the limitations set by her own experience. Although Schoeman acknowledges that in general it is dangerous to treat elements in a creative work as autobiographical, nonetheless he proposes that in relation to Olive Schreiner "this is a relatively minor hazard, since her stories and novels reveal, only too often, the limits of her creative imagination and her inability to transform the substantial autobiographical elements in her fiction into a new fictional entity".[47] Schoeman also comments that he doesn't like Schreiner's novels "on literary grounds" and thinks that her "literary creativity was limited".[48] His discussion, however, focuses predominantly on biographical matters and he fails to specify what specifically literary grounds he might be referring to.

For Schoeman, Schreiner's 'flaw' is related to two linked factors. One is that "her evidence must be handled with caution" because she exaggerated: thus she wasn't nine when her sister Ellie died but ten years and five months, she didn't receive as many as fifty strokes of the cane, she wasn't eleven when she left home but thirteen.[49] Schoeman, like Cronwright-Schreiner before him, fails to recognise that memory works for most people less as a series of specific dates, more as broad lines of events cohering around a particular year or age which then acts as a symbolic marker for these. The other is the existence of what Schoeman sees as autobiographical elements which are not 'transformed' in Schreiner's novels, with this confirming what he calls her "intense subjectivity".[50] How Schoeman assesses what is 'transformed' and what is not is nowhere explained, although he does suggest that Schreiner's didacticism led her to lose control of her writing, an argument he makes about both *An African Farm* and *From Man to Man*. Thus 'Times and Seasons' in *An African Farm* is seen as an autobiographical intrusion which "bears no relation to any of the characters in the rest of the book", while neither the theorising nor the 'sermonising' in *FMTM* " ...is integral or essential to the plot, instead they impede the flow of the narrative".[51]

Schoeman has a highly conventional narrative view of 'the novel', then, and it is Schreiner's transgressions of this putative norm he reacts strongly against. His overall evaluation is that "Olive's lack of literary models may be partly to blame ... together with her failure or inability to ask for advice or criticism ... More serious handicaps, however, were her egotism, and her intense emotional involvement with her work, which prevented her from adopting the detachment and gaining the perspective necessary for artistic creativity".[52] For him, Schreiner reached her peak with *An African Farm*, with its promise never fulfilled in later work. Schoeman also suggests that "*African Farm* was in fact all Olive was capable of as a creative artist, and that it realised her full potential in this direction. Her later career suggests very strongly that she was not truly a novelist or even a creative artist, but had turned to fiction purely for lack of alternatives".[53] The Schreiner family relished a story about a man trying to sell a horse; his honesty compelled him to adumbrate its many faults, but nonetheless he concluded by saying it was still 'a damn fine horse', and this became a family catch-phrase. Schoeman's account is very much in the 'damn fine horse' vein and would have produced much wry laughter from the Schreiners.

Archival sources are not coterminous with 'life' and never provide complete representations of 'the past', including because there is always the possibility that new sources might turn up or some existing ones might have been overlooked. Schoeman provides a number of what seem like 'certain facts' about Schreiner, to stand against her own presumptively 'faulty' ones. But archival evidence exists which casts a different light on a number of these, two of which I want briefly to discuss.

Firstly, Schoeman discusses Schreiner's relationship with Julius Gau, when she briefly lived in Dordrecht from August 1871 until August 1872 as governess to the children of the Reverend Zadoc Robinson, and then in the household of Gau and his sister. Schoeman writes about this in "we do not know, but ..."[54] terms. He conjectures that Robinson probably made sexual overtures to Schreiner so that she fled to the Gau household; Miss Gau's illness meant she was conveniently 'out of the way', and so Julius Gau, Schoeman supposes, almost certainly seduced Schreiner. Because of an eating disorder Schreiner's periods then stopped, and Schoeman also supposes that gossip about a possible pregnancy then hounded her and she left Dordrecht hurriedly, driven out.[55] For Schoeman, Schreiner merely imagined there was some formal commitment between her and Gau, and he further supposes it was the removal of the scare of a possible pregnancy that led Julius Gau to withdraw from her life.[56]

Against this, archived letters written contemporaneously by Schreiner to her married sisters Katie Findlay and Alice Hemming, and from their mother to

Katie Findlay, tell a very different story.[57] An increasing number of people in Dordrecht became ill in early 1872 with a 'fever' local people identified as typhoid, and Miss Gau was so ill as to be likely to die. Many similar cases had occurred, there were no nurses to be hired, and so Schreiner left the Robinsons to look after her friend.[58] Miss Gau became first a little better, then much worse but, although many other people died, she slowly recovered. Julius Gau and Olive Schreiner became unofficially engaged; the upwardly mobile and socially fastidious Gau didn't want his wife-to-be to have a job at all, let alone work as a lowly governess; and so, rather than have her go to another governessing job, Gau took Schreiner to her parents' home in Hertzog in August 1872, where she was to stay until their marriage. Gau met her parents, the engagement was announced to them, and he returned to Dordrecht. Nothing is definitely known about how and why the engagement ended, but some time later Schreiner received a letter which greatly upset her and Gau married an older richer woman, a widow, in 1874.[59] Schoeman's exciting tale of seduction, gossip and pregnancy is actually conjecture and there is little evidence to support it, while there is strong archival evidence of the more humdrum events of a serious illness and then an engagement between a lowly governess and an upwardly mobile businessman being broken off, with him marrying a widow with money soon after.

Secondly, Schoeman claims that, when Will Schreiner became Prime Minister of the Cape just before the war in 1899, he 'withdrew' from his sister because her exaggerations and unrealistic sense of self-importance were a political liability to him.[60] But the archival record of the continuing letters between Will and Olive Schreiner suggests something rather different, as does the emphasis given to her political acumen by Will Schreiner's biographer.[61] Both Will and Olive Schreiner were well aware of the embarrassing circumstances Will was in, as a Prime Minister of the Cape not only with a wife who was sister to Frank Reitz, formerly President of the Free State who had become State Secretary of the Transvaal, but also a sister who was a leading figure in the peace movement. In fact the archive letters show that the 'withdrawing' was on actually Olive Schreiner's part, not on Will's, for she deliberately stopped talking and writing to him about politics until the war was well underway so as not to compromise his loyalties.

Schoeman uses Emily Hobhouse's comments about Olive Schreiner as those of an 'objective witness' and he concludes, in Hobhouse's words, that " ...'Her powerful imagination, lacking its normal outlet in the continued writing of novel or romance, preyed upon common life and one soon found she mixed imagination with fact until it was not clear which was which' ...".[62] The archival evidence here, however, shows that Emily Hobhouse was by no means dispassionate about Schreiner at the time of writing this, and that South African feminists were ambivalent about Hobhouse.[63] Hobhouse had been a powerful defender of the Boer women and children in British concentration camps during the South African War and was much respected by Schreiner and other feminists for this. She was also imperious and insensitive; and so, for instance, in letters between Betty Molteno and Alice Greene they comment that, while powerfulness was something Hobhouse and Schreiner shared, there were crucial differences in Schreiner's sense of humour, ability to laugh at herself and keen sensitivity to others.[64] Hobhouse's criticisms derive from Schreiner's public refusal to speak to her when, a professed pacifist, she had supported Smuts when he led South Africa into the 1914–1918 War and joined the Allied war cabinet. While Hobhouse presents this as Schreiner being petty and childish, archive letters indicate it was a matter of serious principle in which Schreiner publicly 'cut' her erstwhile friend, not because Hobhouse had reneged on her principles, but because she was unable to recognise that other people might be legitimately disappointed or angry with her about this.[65]

Schoeman's intention to 'recreate' Schreiner's life and times represents an approach that Philip Abrams criticised as 'resurrectionalism' – the idea there can be certain knowledge of the past, which can be recreated and 'brought back to life' by good research.[66] Schoeman's view is that part of the necessity for this is because feminist scholarship on Schreiner 'reduces' her and so a 'counterbalance' is required because Schreiner has been turned into a 'feminist icon', a cult figure. I am puzzled by this, for the growing interest in Schreiner is shared by both feminists and non-feminists, is a popular as well as an academic one, and it mixes stringent criticism with its appreciation of her writing. Consequently precisely what Schoeman is supplying a 'counterbalance' to remains mysterious, for there is little evidence of the 'iconising' he expresses such concern about. Indeed, there is a strong strand in current interpretation which positions Schreiner and her writing as problematic or even racist, of which Nadine Gordimer's discussion is a case in point.

In the Prison-House of Colonialism

In 1980, Nadine Gordimer published a review of First and Scott's *Olive Schreiner* which has had a considerable impact on Schreiner scholarship, being reprinted in a number of collections, referenced widely, and some of its arguments influential in shaping subsequent re-readings of Schreiner's work.[67] Gordimer is a highly esteemed Nobel prize-winning South African novelist whose work has interestingly engaged with the 'place' of the white liberal in a political and existential sense, along with other public themes of South African society. Her review mixes compliments, some of them rather back-handed, about First and Scott's book with a considerable critique of Schreiner and her work. She places Schreiner's work within the 'prison-house of colonialism' and, as part of this, sees her as advancing a personal and egocentric agenda (feminism) of no relevance at all to the 'actual problem' ('race') of South Africa.

Commenting that Schreiner has been badly served by earlier biographers, Gordimer sees First and Scott as combining Schreiner's own mixture of feminism and political sense: they "make a superb combination and one is curious about how they overcame the tremendous differences between their two ideological approaches".[68] Gordimer understands 'feminism' and 'politics' as quite distinct, indeed she sees Schreiner's feminism as rooting her to colonial ties with a European 'home', because she interprets feminism as something specifically concerned with the position of women within a European context (a characterisation Schreiner would have flatly rejected). And in opposition to First and Scott's view that Schreiner's reputation as a writer suffers because of her social and political commentary, for Gordimer this is the source of the problem, seeing Schreiner as "the broken-winged albatross of white liberal thinking".[69]

For Gordimer, Schreiner's allegiance to Europe as the 'world of ideas' was related to the fact that an appropriate culture 'at home' for her writing (and that of other English-speaking South African writers) was not being created. Gordimer sees this as "a culture whose base would be the indigenous black culture interpenetrating with imported European cultural forms ...", so that "the works they had written ... were solitary contradictions of the way ... life was being conceptualised, politically, socially and morally".[70] Gordimer reluctantly acknowledges that, while Schreiner was in Britain, "I suppose one must allow she had a right to concern herself with a generic, universal predicament: that of her sex", but this is immediately followed by her insistence that "the fact is that in South Africa, then as now, feminism is regarded by people whose thinking on race, class and colour Schreiner anticipated, as a question of no relevance to the actual problem of the country – which is to free the black majority from white rule".[71] Gordimer's conclusion is that "Schreiner seems not to have seen that her wronged sense of self, as a woman, that her liberation, was a secondary matter ... Ironically, here at least she shared the most persistent characteristic of her fellow colonials (discounting the priorities of the real entities around here) ...".[72]

Schreiner was in Gordimer's view crucially hampered by fighting against ways of thinking which imprisoned her. Only once, Gordimer proposes, did she find a literary form to carry her 'advanced perceptions', in *An African Farm*; otherwise she developed the "preachy, nasal singsong of a sermon" to express her political vision.[73] For Gordimer, then, rather than writing 'tracts and pamphlets' and dissipating her energies, Schreiner should instead have crafted her creative imagination in the service of her "fierce and proud convictions, and her political and human insight".[74] However, she proposes that the 'prison-house of colonialism', and Schreiner's supposed neuroticism and "tortured, heightened sense of being", prevented her from doing this.[75]

How to respond to Nadine Gordimer's powerfully condemnatory critique? Karin Wagner has proposed that the history of Gordimer as a writer is one of "the submerged guilts, fears and repressions of a white consciousness Gordimer's vision has been shaped by".[76] While this is too dismissive as well as too neat and tidy, certainly Gordimer is very aware of the self-justifications of liberal politics; and in criticising some white South African writers for not being political enough, she has also emphasised that in doing this she is castigating herself.[77] This is one element in my response to her comments on Schreiner, then, that through these she is commenting more about white South African writing of the 1970s than she is about Schreiner and her work. This includes her own perceived deficiencies and 'egocentric' values, for if any present-day English-speaking South African writer has explored the place of white women in relation to the conundrums of liberal politics in the apartheid society, it is Nadine Gordimer.

My other response concerns what I conjecture might have been deliberately provocative remarks Gordimer was making about the separation of feminism and politics and the unaffordable luxury of the former. Ruth First, earlier a highly politically involved white radical rather than liberal in South Africa, was a political exile when the Schreiner book written with Ann Scott; and Schreiner herself lived in Europe for long periods as well as being seen by Gordimer to treat Europe and not Africa as 'the world of ideas'. Nadine Gordimer, however, stayed 'at home' and grappled with the political and other complexities of being that strange creature, 'a white liberal South African'. At the time that Gordimer wrote her review, Ruth First's choices and her allegiance with European feminism through her collaboration with Ann Scott on *Olive Schreiner* might have seemed the easier option (she was later killed by a letter-bomb planted by the South African security services). It seems to me it was white liberal guilt that led Gordimer to perceive 'no relevance to the actual problem' in Schreiner's concerns, separating starkly 'race' from sex/gender and other sources of inequality in a way that, thankfully, the ANC resisted. A 'more radical than thou' stance is one white liberals seem particularly prone to, projecting onto Schreiner and her work the issues and problems of Gordimer's own time and circumstances, and this surfaces in other Schreiner interpretations as well.

The Social Darwinist

Both Carol Barash[78] and Carolyn Burdett[79] are concerned with re-reading 'the work' of Olive Schreiner rather than 'the life', and both perceive a strong social Darwinism characterising the approach taken to 'race' matters in it. There are, however, important differences as well as similarities between their approaches, differences which, as my discussion will suggest, have considerably widened over time and as Burdett's work has developed. Still, I think that enough common ground exists around the earlier shared concern with social Darwinism for their Schreiner interpretations to be legitimately looked at in a 'comparing and contrasting' kind of way.

Carol Barash's discussion is very clear that social Darwinism not only characterises Schreiner's writing, but is also embodied in her as a person. For Barash, the key terms are 'virile womanhood' and 'master race', which she uses to invoke "Schreiner's incantatory Darwinian rhetoric".[80] Her critique in fact has its own incantatory ring, proclaiming that:

> *Crossing Darwin's models of racial determinism and female sexual selection creates a heterosexual determinism that glorifies motherhood without changing the world into which women and men bear children. Darwin's ideals, based on warfare and domination, are not antipathetic but inextricably linked to Schreiner's belief in timeless maternal values. Schreiner was incapable of tolerating a world which was rent into shards of pain and conflict. But the price of her belief in unity was often a capitulation to the patterns of white male dominance, a need to experience power from the point of view of patriarchy's reproductive needs.*[81]

Barash's insistencies remove from sight the anti-Darwinist and anti-maternalist currents in Schreiner's work, with the result being a starkly clear version of Schreiner's thought which maps only uneasily onto Schreiner's actual writings. Thus Barash couples Schreiner's feminism to maternalism to racism and almost without taking breath she concludes that "Schreiner's use of maternal ideology, her feminism, is fundamentally and unmistakably racist. I suggest that we think of Schreiner as a woman who embodied radically conflicting ideological and narrative positions".[82] These are very strong claims. However, 'maternal ideology' is in fact not a defining feature of Schreiner's work. As discussed in Chapter 3, she actually rejected biologically determinist ideas about sex differences in general as well as about motherhood in particular, and her arguments about this are clearly made. Also the 'evidence' for Barash reading Schreiner's feminism as 'fundamentally and unmistakably' racist derives from her view that social Darwinism characterises Schreiner's work. That is, social Darwinism is defined as including essentialist and racist views about 'race', and therefore if Schreiner's work is social Darwinist then, *ergo*, it is both essentialist and also racist. Barash's whole argument is founded on the assertion of Schreiner's social Darwinism; once this is disputed, then the edifice crashes to the ground.

Carolyn Burdett's work on Schreiner's writing is also concerned with matters of 'race' and her interpretation similarly perceives social Darwinism as a strong feature of it. However, there are some interesting and important differences between Barash's tub-thumping insistences and Burdett's developing approach and it is useful to explore these as well as the earlier overlaps.

In looking at the interconnections between Schreiner's draft "Wollstonecraft Introduction", her 'sex book', and the short story "The Buddhist Priest's Wife", Burdett sees Schreiner's argument in the first of these as a "sketchy and crude evolutionary narrative which relies upon the racist figuring of African womanhood to speak an unmediated 'truth'"[83]. She also proposes that "*If, as I have claimed*, Schreiner's attempt to write an introduction to Wollstonecraft's *A Vindication* ... can be read as a submerged history of the writing of *Woman and Labour, then it is clear* that that text ... is certainly limited in a way that Schreiner could not acknowledge, by the terms of the evolutionary science which she employed".[84] Burdett's argument here rests on her extremely dubious 'if, as I have claimed, then it is clear ...' contention. Indeed, she proceeds as though the 'if ...' is not merely a claim she is making, but instead an 'as ...' ; that is, as though this is certain rather than contentious and arguable. Burdett extrapolates from Schreiner's inclusion of an African woman's remarks about men's violence to women,[85] to characterise Schreiner's approach as social Darwinist without considering whether this is appropriate, if her ideas changed, or her explicit rejection of such views in published writings (and as suggested in Chapter 3, the Wollstonecraft fragment is likely to be a very early draft which was discarded by her). At the same time, Burdett also interestingly comments on the issues faced by Schreiner in attempting to assimilate a non-western heritage within her feminist analysis, something surprisingly rarely discussed. The 'Africaness' of Schreiner's work is more usually ignored, with Africa seen as an exotic location, rather than the source of much of her thinking about politics and the relationship between society and landscape, so Burdett's comments here are particularly to be welcomed.

As Chapter 3 proposed, it is important to recognise the development of Schreiner's ideas over time and, as a review article by Burdett of Schreiner's *Trooper Peter Halket of Mashonaland* and *Thoughts on South Africa* points out, looking in detail at Schreiner's writings from 1890 on shows that her ideas changed considerably.[86] Burdett points out that "the project of re-reading opens up the possibility of a more productive understanding in that it sees her 'failure' as articulate of something important about the impasse of aesthetics and politics".[87] But this begs the question of whether Schreiner's work *was* a failure, not only for those present-day readers who, like me and unlike Burdett, reject a notion of 'literary propriety' which "inevitably involves a legislative process in which certain laws are laid down as to what a literary work should be",[88] but also for Schreiner's contemporaries.

In her review article, Burdett sees the plot of *Trooper Peter* as concerned with the fall but also the redemption of "the British soldier hero".[89] She also proposes that the book's accusations against imperialism and Rhodes failed: because Rhodes did not sue Schreiner following its publication;[90] and because, although it separated British humanitarianism from its imperialist practices, the parliamentary Committee of Inquiry Rhodes appeared before was premised on their inseparability. Burdett's view here is that "Schreiner's text attempts to appeal to the possibility of a benevolent, humanistic colonisation (via its Christian rhetoric ...)".[91] For me, this entirely misses Schreiner's point; what Burdett sees as a book "clogged and compromised by the particularized narrative of Peter's reminiscences", I see as using this as a device which is crucial to its savagely ironic purposes. In a later discussion of *Trooper Peter*, the evolution of Burdett's thinking about 'race' matters in Schreiner's work continues, and in this she points out not only that "In *Trooper Peter*, the case against imperial policy in South Africa transports the stuff of metropolitan emancipation debates onto the African veld", but also that "Schreiner's readers must be made to feel the violence all round ... in a colonial context".[92]

Burdett deals most directly with Schreiner's views about 'race' in her comments on *Thoughts*, proposing that "its contents might indicate why it has been so unattractive to a modern readership", which she suggests is because "on the face of it, the essays are a panegyric to the Boer ...".[93] In fact, royalties statements show that *Thoughts* was 'unattractive' from its publication on,[94] and its relative lack of popularity is probably connected more with the reading audience Schreiner's work had in America and Europe, particularly after 1920, where she was typically seen narrowly, as a novelist only.

As Burdett notes, by the time the South African War ended Schreiner's views about 'race' had changed, to incorporate her increasing awareness of Africans as agents rather than victims and her realisation that the political union of whites would lead to an even greater repression of black people. Burdett also interestingly argues that *Thoughts* should not be read as an apologia containing Schreiner's 'improved' politics, for part of its interest "lies in the way in which Schreiner *positions* herself as narrator"[95] – that is, as the writer of a personal document, as the narrator of how her 'insular prejudice and racial pride' changed, and as making reparation for her critique of the Boers in *An African Farm*.

Burdett contentiously claims that "*Thoughts* contains some of Schreiner's most disturbingly essentializing and naturalizing accounts of South Africa ... a rhetoric of maternity ... a use of the crudest elements of nineteenth-century racism ... and the worst sort of appeal to a prelapsarian healthy economy where

Afrikaner colonization and dispossession of African land is naturalized against the artificial ravages of modern capitalism".[96] My re-reading of *Thoughts* in Chapter 3 differs substantially from Burdett's, and I leave readers of *Thoughts* to conclude as to which is the more appropriate. Nonetheless, I certainly agree with Burdett that Schreiner's notion of Englishness in South Africa cannot accommodate her image of Boer pastoralism, "and it is in this sort of self-troubling that much of the interest of the text lies".[97] Indeed, for me this book is all 'self-troubling', to use Burdett's phrase, for its concerns are precisely those aspects of South African's peoples and politics that the returning Schreiner found puzzling or problematic.

A comparison of Carol Barash's insistence on Schreiner's 'fundamental and unmistakable' racism and the hold of social Darwinism over her thinking about 'race', and the marked shift in Carolyn Burdett's approach towards highlighting Schreiner's 'self-troubling' position as an author attempting to assimilate contradictory heritages, suggests they have very different views of what social Darwinism and its ramifications consist in. Barash finds evidence of Schreiner's social Darwinism everywhere in her writing and sees Schreiner 'as a woman' as well as her work embodying social Darwinism and therefore racism. For Burdett, however, Schreiner's social Darwinism is not only composed, but is at the same time undercut, in her writing; consequently Burdett sees the relationship between text, mind and life in a considerably more complex way. For Burdett, neither the form nor the content of Schreiner's writing are treated as inert products of a fixed mind and fixed beliefs, but instead changing because of the circumstances Schreiner was located in and how she responded to these.

Another way of summarising the difference between the positions of Carol Barash and Carolyn Burdett can be found in Burdett's statement that, "while it is easy enough to identify and condemn the racism of Schreiner's texts, it is a more difficult and painful task to follow her fantasmatic imaging of the colonial scene and her own place, as a white woman, within it".[98] While Carol Barash simplifies and condemns, it is this 'more difficult and painful task', and also the considerably more interesting one, that Carolyn Burdett has attempted. The fruits of this are very evident in Burdett's *Olive Schreiner and the Progress of Feminism*, a book which explores Schreiner's published work (but not her letters or other archive papers) around not only her complex ideas about 'progress' but also concerning imperialism and race:

> *Part of Schreiner's power as a thinker and writer ... lies in the fact that she became a critic of progress who never abandoned her commitment to it, nor her determination to make arguments and stories that might persuade others of what she saw as its palpable failings and its potential good ... she is a truly radical writer who forged her way into mainstream metropolitan debate with writing which always also tells an irreducibly particular colonial history.*[99]

Exploring this agenda takes Burdett in an extremely interesting way across Schreiner's published work, offering new accounts and analytical insights which in general do not appear in her earlier interpretations. Thus, for example, her re-readings of "Eighteen-Ninety-Nine" and various of the essays in *Thoughts on South Africa* herein are nuanced and very aware of the political context Schreiner was writing it and her argument is often compelling. This book moves Burdett's analysis out of the 'social Darwinism' framework that bedevilled her earlier interpretations and into an approach which has considerably more in common with those that I discuss in the rest of this chapter.

Carolyn Burdett argues that it is 'easy enough' to find and condemn racism in Schreiner's writings. However, other interpreters have found that, once a 'presentist' re-reading is surrendered and attention directed towards the historical and ideational context in which Schreiner's writings were written and read, then interpreting them is a considerably more difficult business than this suggests. It is this broad context of the development of ideas in the later nineteenth and early twentieth centuries and Schreiner's place within it that Joyce Avrech Berkman's work on Schreiner explores.

The Healing Imagination

The key arguments and broad ideas in Joyce Avrech Berkman's *The Healing Imagination of Olive Schreiner: Beyond South African Colonialism*, published in 1989, are interestingly prefigured in her *Olive Schreiner: Feminism on the Frontier*. This was published ten years before *The Healing Imagination*, in 1979 and at a point when other Schreiner scholarship looked extremely crude by comparison. In it, Berkman discussed the ways in which Schreiner's work not only provided a sustained critique of social Darwinism, but was also innovative in deploying different forms of writing, things most Schreiner scholars are only now beginning to recognise. *The Healing Imagination* took up these and other key aspects of Schreiner's work in an interpretation which remains, over a decade after its publication, still the most considerable exposition of Schreiner's social thought and its place in, and its departures from, the pantheon of the ideas of the late nineteenth and early twentieth centuries.

In *The Healing Imagination*, Berkman describes her approach in the following way:

> Of course, Schreiner's life experiences bear relevance to any analysis of her 'abstract opinions' and artistic activity. What follows is an interpretation of her work as permeated by a unique thematic pattern, one that also characterized her life and its interconnections with the broader social and cultural movements of her time. The pattern urged her to heal both her own and society's ills and, as a corresponding process, to reconceive the relations between spiritual and material reality. In this striving she ran counter to the dominant Victorian outlook of her peers.[100]

As well as describing this 'healing' pattern as recurrently surfacing in Schreiner's work, Berkman also comments that Schreiner rejected binary distinctions. Indeed, she goes so far as to suggest that Schreiner's opposition to the "hierarchical ranking of cultures" and the "symbolic structures of colonialism", together with her promotion of more "organic democratic communities", gives her work an intent closely akin to present-day feminist deconstructionism.[101]

Berkman rejects the usual emphasis on Schreiner as a (flawed) writer of fiction, instead seeing her as a social theorist who produced highly innovative work, not only in her developing ideas but also through her use of mixed genres of writing to express them. I am in full agreement with this and also with Berkman's "What draws me to Schreiner's fiction is less its literary significance – the concern of most Schreiner critics – than the nature of her fertile intellect as it grappled with perplexing issues and overstepped the boundaries of genre".[102] Berkman shows that Schreiner was immersed within the domain assumptions of her time and also questioned and transcended various of these. This is a particular strength of Berkman's work as an intellectual biography, for it resists individualising Schreiner's concerns at the same time as insisting on the distinctiveness of her work. Before moving on to discuss some of the particularly interesting aspects of Berkman's interpretation, there are two caveats about its general approach I want to note.

Berkman's view of Schreiner as a kind of late nineteenth century feminist deconstructionist leads the analysis here to verge on the ahistorical. Certainly Schreiner frequently strove to bring together ideas conventionally dichotomised in contemporary modes of thinking and expression. However, she was not so unique in this as Berkman implies, and many other radical figures of the time, some well-known and others now less so, responded similarly.[103] The result is I think that she over-states the binary obsessions of the Victorian zeitgeist and under-emphasises the powerful under-currents in contemporary discourses which cross-cut these and underpinned a range of radical positions. In relation not only to social Darwinism, but also to imperialism and pacifism, for instance, Schreiner's work is certainly innovative, as Berkman fully recognises, but it was also produced out of a shared framework of ideas postulated, debated and developed by overlapping collectivities of freethinkers, socialists, feminists, liberals ...

Berkman's description of Schreiner's work around the 'healing imagination' motif of her title bears a largely tangential relationship to the rest of her book. Perhaps this is an over-literal comment, but in neither my re-reading of Schreiner's writings, nor in Berkman's discussion over the eight chapters of *The Healing Imagination*, is the 'unique thematic pattern' she perceives very observable. Insofar as it 'recurrently surfaces' and 'permeates', this is mainly through Berkman's comments at the beginnings and ends of chapters rather than in the details of her analysis of Schreiner's work. And while Schreiner's rejection of binary ways of thinking is certainly apparent, in her allegorical writing in particular, Berkman scrupulously points up the other aspects of Schreiner's writing which retain the imprint of more conventional dichotomous ways of thinking. Also connected with this 'healing' motif, it seems to me that Schreiner's typical response to inter-personal conflict was actually rapid disengagement if conflict erupted, and a refusal to engage in situations where it might,[104] and to 'refuse to engage' is not necessarily to 'attempt to heal'. Schreiner's adult response seems more about refusing to compete, behaving 'well', and removing herself when she felt unable to. Certainly more principled statements about disengagement as an alternative to anger and aggression can be found – for example, in "The Sunlight Lay Across My Bed", where the anger felt by the narrator burns and kills the flowers in heaven, and in Schreiner's discussion of her pacifism in relation to conscientious objection. But regarding impersonal and abstract matters, Schreiner had no reservations at all about publicly advancing her own ideas and views and opposing with zest those she disagreed with.

Three aspects of Berkman's work are in my view particularly insightful and important and I want to point up her analysis of these. These concern Schreiner's critique and reworking of social Darwinism, analysis of empire and imperialism, and discussion of the origins of aggression and war.

Berkman rightly emphasises that using 'social Darwinism' to characterise Schreiner's critique of Darwinist ideas is a misnomer, and instead she describes Schreiner's position as a revisionist one.[105] Her ensuing discussion of Schreiner's acceptance of then-prevailing Whigish – and Marxist/socialist – ideas about progress while also rejecting biological determinism and refusing to romanticise the past is extremely interesting. Berkman points out that Schreiner rejects the idea that biology, whether in relation to 'race' or gender or human reproduction, has a determining social effect; and she is one of very few commentators to have noticed the distinctiveness of Schreiner's position here. My view, as I discuss in Chapter 5, is that Schreiner's approach in fact more radically departed from social Darwinism and from biologism than even Berkman proposes.

Berkman argues that Schreiner used 'scientific' terms to indicate 'race' groupings in southern Africa because she saw these as neutral ones, rather than taking the present pejorative meaning of terms such as 'Hottentot', 'Kaffir' and 'Bushmen' as evidence of Schreiner's social Darwinism or racism; I am sure this is exactly right and Berkman's approach to this is a welcome antidote to ahistorical condemnations of Schreiner's terminology.[106] More problematically, Berkman sees Schreiner's use of these terms as the remaining small fraction of Victoriana in her largely deconstructionist thinking;[107] and here I think that Berkman's ascription of a thematic unity to Schreiner's work leaves her unable to explain its internal disjunctures and contradictions except as 'leftovers'. The result is an evening-out of Schreiner's sometimes confusing comments about evolution, civilisation and 'race', of which her use of these 'scientific' terms is one aspect. I am very aware of the difficulties involved here in figuring out just what Schreiner's views on 'race' were; and I proposed in Chapter 3 that a chronological approach to Schreiner's writing and ideas, while more 'bitty', helps prevent an over-unified interpretation of Schreiner's thinking.

Berkman's discussion of Schreiner's analysis of empire and imperialism is particularly convincing. Berkman notes that Schreiner's critique of social Darwinism underpins her analysis of empire and imperialism and this inscribes a change from her earlier thinking.[108] She argues that until around 1890 Schreiner saw England as the protector of vulnerable peoples around the world, a largely beneficent presence saving people from more predatory powers and sometimes from themselves.[109] But then this romanticised view changed, mainly because of Schreiner's growing awareness of the expansionism that propelled Rhodes and his associates in southern Africa, but also through her concerns about the British imperialist presence in Ireland and India as well.

Interestingly, however, alongside this insightful discussion Berkman's account largely collapses 'colonialism' into 'imperialism'. In spite of *The Healing Imagination*'s sub-title, 'Beyond South African Colonialism', it focuses on

Schreiner's analysis of *imperialism* and does not get to grips with her very different position with regard to *colonialism*. Certainly Berkman notes that for Schreiner "the materially deprived and vulnerable are the Undines, Lyndalls, and Waldos of the world"; and consequently, while the "score of Hottentot and Kaffir servants ... come forth with shrewd observations on the ways of white people", Schreiner nevertheless "neglects to depict adequately ... their constrained, vulnerable, and ill-rewarded working and living situations".[110] Berkman interprets this as another vestigial 'loose end' in Schreiner's thinking: "the shadowy treatment of household help is disappointing, reflecting the vestiges of classism and racism in her imagination".[111] In contrast, I think it derives from two deep-seated aspects of how Schreiner saw the world.

In the Cape Colony of Schreiner's childhood and young womanhood, white people of her class and lower – like Undine surviving in Kimberley by ironing clothes – could do very similar kinds of work to the black 'free' labourers there. But while black people might be known and liked or sometimes loved, there was still a social and communicative gulf between them and the white settlers in the Cape which would have prevented Schreiner from 'pressing her fingers up against them' as characters in her novels, figures in the landscape of her mind.[112] Also, not surprisingly in view of her position as both African and white, Schreiner had a considerably more positive response to colonialism than to imperialism so long as certain kinds of conditions with regard to the treatment of African peoples were met. Most Schreiner scholars in fact fail to recognise that imperialism and colonialism are not coterminous; and I shall return to the elided relationship between them later in this chapter and also in Chapter 5.

Berkman's discussion of Schreiner's developing ideas about aggression and warfare is extremely insightful and is one of the few to have used the archival manuscript source of "The Dawn of Civilisation".[113] She notes that Schreiner seemingly departed from her 'usual' anti-biological determinist stance in relation to war, by insisting that "There is, perhaps, no woman ... who could look down upon a battlefield covered with slain, but the thought would arise in her, 'So many mothers' sons! ...' ... No woman who is a woman says of a human body, 'It is nothing!'".[114] I understand this as in fact a highly polemical rhetorical statement made for a particular purpose, rather than one that reflects Schreiner's views in any simple way. But even if it did reflect them when originally written, Schreiner's views on such matters certainly changed thereafter. As Berkman suggests, the sometimes militantly pro-war responses of many women to the 1914–1918 War led Schreiner to develop the argument pursued in "The Dawn of Civilisation", that men and women equally share aggression as a quality which is 'left over' from an earlier phase of human social life but do so in gendered ways.

Berkman points out that "The Dawn of Civilisation" is a largely unexplored part of Schreiner's work, and this remains true even now, for insofar as readers are familiar with it, this is the highly truncated version published posthumously by Cronwright-Schreiner.[115] In contrast, Berkman's discussion rightly assigns to this work an important place in understanding Schreiner's changing thinking. As I noted in Chapter 3, two rather different manuscript versions of "The Dawn of Civilisation" exist, while the Wollstonecraft fragment is likely to be a discarded version superseded by later one/s, and also there are still extant earlier versions of some parts of *From Man to Man*.[116] It is not unusual, then, that a number of differing written versions of Schreiner's thinking could coexist; consequently discerning the 'real' version of work not published in her lifetime requires imposing a closure over her thinking which it actually might not have reached.

Berkman comments on 'lapses, 'loose ends' and 'vestiges' in Schreiner's work, the 'scattered' nature of much of her thinking, its often 'frustratingly sketchy' character, and the fact that it is not 'systematically' formulated.[117] Indeed, on occasion she provides this systematisation for Schreiner, as with "Schreiner's feminism involved a tripartite transformation process ... To be sure, Schreiner never set forth her commitment to this triple goal systematically", and "Schreiner, admittedly, did not use the term androgyny, but this was precisely what her description of the new woman and the new man connoted".[118] Berkman laments, as indeed I have frequently done myself, the lack of a systematically expounded overview of Schreiner's social theory in one of her writings. Schreiner, however, was not a systematic social theorist in the way Berkman would like her to be, but rather one who was responsive to 'the times', and I return to this point in Chapter 5.

Joyce Berkman's interpretation of Schreiner's work places it extremely insightfully in its social and historical context, and it remains at the cutting edge of Schreiner scholarship as the major exploration of Schreiner's ideas to date. It is still the key work exploring Schreiner's intellectual biography. Anne McClintock's interpretation is similarly concerned with ideas, specifically those underpinning and shaping imperialism and commodity capitalism, and it too provides an illuminating discussion of Schreiner's work.

Distinguished by a Paradox

Anne McClintock's (1995) *Imperial Leather: Race, Gender and Sexuality in the Colonial Contest* provides a very interesting contribution to the feminist analysis of the conjunction of gender, 'race' and imperialism, proposing that "Schreiner took the contradictions of colonialism and women's situation under colonialism to the very edge of historical transformation", but that limits were built into her analysis.[119] The framework of McClintock's analysis is her concern with the 'governing themes' of western imperialism as refracted by the transitions of white male power through the bodies and lives of colonised women, the emergent global order of cultural knowledge, and the imperial command of commodity capital. Imperialism, McClintock rightly emphasises, did not take place 'somewhere else', for industrial markets 'at home' and the imperial enterprise 'abroad' were closely related within the development of capitalism.

McClintock comments on the concealed but crucial relationship of gender, 'race' and imperialism. The already gendered dynamics of colonised cultures were 'contorted' by imperialism, but the prior different social, economic, sexual, positions of men and women indigenes meant that colonialism had different gendered outcomes. And colonial women were barred from formal power and so ambiguously placed, but also ambiguously complicit, within colonialism. She concludes that "race, gender and class are not distinct realms of experience ... Rather, they come into existence in and through relation to each other – if in contradictory and conflictual ways ... This, then, is the triangulated theme that animates the chapters that follow: the intimate relations between imperial power and resistance; money and sexuality; race and gender".[120]

McClintock sees imperialism as a contradictory and ambiguous project which binary analytic terms, such as coloniser/colonised, self/other, dominance/ resistance, metropolis/colony, colonial/postcolonial, cannot adequately account for. Her attention is therefore directed to "the myriad forms of both imperial and anti-imperial agency ... mediated through institutions of power: the family, the media, the law, armies, nationalist movements and so on ... people's experience of desire and rage, memory and power, community and revolt are inflected and mediated by the institutions through which they find their meaning – and which they, in turn, transform".[121] In this, McClintock insists on the indivisibility of psychoanalysis and history as both indispensable ways of analysing imperial power, and she presents her analysis as an attempt "to rethink the circulation of notions that can be observed between the family, sexuality and fantasy (the traditional realm of psychoanalysis) and the categories of labor, money and the market (the traditional realm of political and economic history)".[122]

Anne McClintock's ideas in *Imperial Leather* are argued with verve, and her broad framework is an appealing one, for it holds out the promise of having it all, analytically speaking. However, there are two important analytical problems here. The first is introduced through the terms used to conceptualise the political and economic formations McClintock is dealing with. The second derives from the way her concern with psychoanalysis and history – with fantasy and desire on the one hand, and labour and the market on the other – leads her to structure the analysis in the rest of the book.

The first problem derives from McClintock's use of 'imperialism' and 'colonialism' as synonyms apart from briefly indicating the existence of some differences. On a formal level, McClintock certainly recognises that imperialism was 'contradictory and ambiguous'. However, one of the key contradictions over Schreiner's life-time concerned the developing conflict of interests between the English-speaking and Boer colonists in the Cape Colony as well as in the other settler states, versus the imperial expansionist presence of Britain in southern Africa. This is largely unseen in McClintock's account, which focuses on imperialism and sees colonialism as a dependent excretion, rather than an increasingly independent entity in its own right which had some sharp differences of interest with the imperial power.

Schreiner did not treat either the British colonies or the English-speaking colonialists[123] as a sub-set of the imperial presence. In spite of this, indeed because of this, her analysis of the illegitimate presence and practices of imperialism marches hand in hand with seeing white colonists and black peoples in southern Africa competing for what she sees as previously 'empty land'. In effect, Schreiner sees blacks and whites as present on equal (and equally blood-thirsty) terms, until expansionism backed by the use by of mechanised weapons of warfare (explosives and the Maxim gun) gave greater power, because greater force, to the white settlers.[124] Disentangling Schreiner's critique of imperialism, her 'scientific' view of empty lands, and her elision of colonialism, and then relating these to her changing analysis of 'race' and labour, is important in coming to grips with the strengths and weaknesses of her analysis, and I return to this in Chapter 5.

The second problem is that McClintock's wish not to separate 'home' and 'abroad', and psychoanalysis and history, paradoxically results in a book with two fairly separate 'parts', one concerned with 'fantasy and desire' at home, and the other, linked by a discussion of the 'saga of soap', concerned with labour, money and the market abroad. This stems from the slip between McClintock's opening discussion of terms, and the 'actual events' of the past later in the book, noted as the feminising of the land, the invention of colonial domesticity, the massive reordering of land and labour, and resistance to these.[125] McClintock's preliminary discussion of these things encourages the reader to suppose what follows will be concerned with the sharp end of colonialism and imperialism: with how the colonists legitimated their presence, the often illegal and bloody activities of the Chartered Company, the uitlander miners and their appropriation of land and expropriation of labour from black people, the role of speculation and finance, the imperial government and its policies, and the sometimes genocidal activities of imperial forces and their henchmen. But McClintock discusses these only at a remove, through the discussion of soap as the symbol of commodity capital, the writings of Rider Haggard in relation to colonial discourse, and Olive Schreiner's writings concerning the limits McClintock perceives to her feminist critique. There are no private armies, bankers and financiers, Boer trekker-farmers, wars with African peoples, pain and suffering, acts of genocide, bloody deaths, in McClintock's account. And while there is nothing 'wrong' in focusing on writers and their publications, this was not what I had expected from the discussion at the start.

That being said, McClintock's discussion of Olive Schreiner's writing is an interesting and nuanced one. Overall, McClintock's view is that "Olive Schreiner's life was distinguished by a paradox", for, "though a daughter of empire, she devoted her life and writings to championing the dispossessed ... Migrating restlessly between colonial South Africa and fin-de-siècle Britain ... At odds with her imperial world, she was at times the most colonial of writers" and her writing embedded this paradox by being "crisscrossed by contradiction".[126] For McClintock, Olive Schreiner reinvented her identity – composed by gender rebellion, a fierce need for autonomy, guilt for her transgressions against her mother and family and accompanying self-punishment. However, McClintock sees her as ultimately unable to resolve these dilemmas and sees them surfacing in what is presented as Schreiner's multiple phobias and obsessions.[127] McClintock sees Schreiner using language as a kind of magic to solicit her mother's approval, but, because this was also the medium of her transgression, it also progressively distanced her as an exile within.

From the outset, McClintock proposes, 'race' formed an acutely ambiguous dimension of Schreiner's rebellion and "The most troubling presence of these imbalances appears in her work on the racial doubling of the mother figure".[128] Thus she sees Schreiner portraying goodness around a highly romanticised notion of nature that is both feminized and white, while displacing any portrayal of a powerful/angry mother onto African female servants, as with 'Old Ayah' (who is actually an Indian woman)[129] in the Prelude, "The Child's Day", to From Man to Man. For McClintock's, there are two related problematic aspects of this.

One is that " ... it was to the shadowy presence of African women in the household that Schreiner owed whatever fragile sense of privilege she had. Yet this presence was paradoxical ... As a white child, she held potential racial power over the African workers in the home; but these women possessed a secret and appalling power to judge and punish her".[130] The other is that McClintock sees black women as present in Schreiner's writings 'almost without exception' as servants and so serving (literally) as boundary markers, at windows, doors and walls, and by mediating the social traffic between the whites 'at home' on farmsteads and the Africans 'outside' the domestic world of the farm and the farmhouse and its denizens. McClintock sees Schreiner's later writing as highly sympathetic to black people, but views her novels, written earlier, as giving "her African characters no agency beyond the colonial narrative",[131] thus reducing them to 'forbidding ciphers'.

McClintock notes the barely suppressed anger that Schreiner's writing ascribes to black people, but fails to recognise that Schreiner's representation of angry, powerful and resentful African and Indian servants might be more accurate than her own insistence that white children had power over them (this is not to deny the power of adults and the strange shifts that 'former children' go through regarding their adult relationship to black people). Schreiner is both deliberate and consistent in her depiction of the constellation of power relations in the small worlds of South African farming homesteads and city life. In her novels, servants establish allegiances with whoever is perceived as holding most domestic power: with Tant' Sannie in An African Farm and not Otto; with old Ayah rather than the diffident removed parents in "A Child's Day"; with Frank rather than Rebekah in From Man to Man. In addition, the white child protagonists are perceived by all the adults concerned to be subservient to Indian and African as well as white authority figures – there is nothing 'secret' about this.

However, the true boundary-markers in Schreiner's novels are not the 'upper' domestic servants that McClintock focuses on. These are rather the considerably more seditious figures of the female as well as male farm workers, who silently appear and disappear at the farmhouses at dawn, leave their farming work when they are not supposed to and vanish into the veld, take gifts with no show of gratitude whatsoever, and derisorily mock their supposed 'betters' in ways that barely mask contempt. McClintock sees the reduction of Africans to domestic figures as a form of racism and fails to appreciate that Schreiner and other white women in southern Africa of the time (and the majority of white men too) didn't, indeed couldn't, know Africans outside of domestic settings: 'separate spheres' is an accurate description of relations between white and black people when Schreiner first drafted her novels in the 1870s. As Schreiner's "Preface" to An African Farm emphasises, she was determined to dip her pen in greys: to write what she knew about, and not romances; and the depiction of Africans as 'heroes of their own lives' would have been a romance, lying outside of anything that Schreiner could have had knowledge of at that time. But by the time Schreiner came to write her short stories "Dream life and real life" and "My adventures at the Cape by Paulinsky Smith", around 1881 and 1882, her critique of the position of children in relation to adults, and the arrogance and stupidity of British imperial masculinity, had already sharpened and was to develop further in her political essays of the 1890s.

For McClintock, Schreiner's inability to 'own' her anger with her mother led to displacement and disavowal in her writing,[132] a claim I find very debatable. The mothers in *Undine* and *An African Farm* are absent because dead: killed off, one might say, by the author; and killing someone you are angry with does not actually seem to be a 'displacement'. Of the living mothers, the 'little mother' of "The Child's Day" is engrossed with her new-born child, ignores its dead twin, and neglects her anxious small daughter, while in *From Man to Man* the mother betrays her younger daughter Bertie through her wilful naivety; and shining a light on insensitivity and betrayal does not really seem to be 'disavowal'. McClintock's suggestion that Schreiner named her feminist 'heroine' Rebekah in *FMTM* after her mother as part of her displacement and disavowal fails to perceive the extreme irony here. Her mother intensely disapproved of uncouth Boer farmers, had beaten Schreiner as a child for using a single Boer word, insisted on strictly 'proper' behaviour in her daughters, and thought her husband and children cared too much for black people. But 'Rebekah' is the Afrikaans version of her name, she is the child of Boer farmers and later a city-dweller, and she becomes a feminist struggling to be anti-racist.[133] 'Rebekah' is a public overturning of all the values Schreiner's mother stood for.

McClintock positions Schreiner and her work as a part of contemporary analyses of international political events, rather than seeing her as just 'a woman writing'. In doing so, she recognises the impact Schreiner's writing had contemporaneously, and that Schreiner was 'out of the ordinary' as a commentator in grappling with fundamental political issues when few others did so. McClintock's interpretation both appreciates the importance of the particular in Schreiner's writing, and links this to the general ideas and arguments Schreiner developed. She also recognises that Schreiner's thinking changed, became more open, more radical, and is alive to the fact that the existence of flaws in Schreiner's thinking does not mean it should be dismissed or its power and purpose denied or denigrated. Inevitably, there are divergences of opinion and understanding between McClintock's approach and my own as well as many areas of agreement. This indicates that 'point of view' does indeed make a difference, as does my archival research on the unpublished letters and other primary source materials, for how Schreiner's ideas and writings are interpreted. And so I now move on to discuss my own approach to Schreiner and her work.

Or, A Woman of Her Time

My own approach has so far remained largely implicit, located in those aspects of Schreiner's life and writings I have picked out as salient or downplayed, and in my discussions of other people's interpretations. There are three broad themes that underpin my approach which I hope make it distinctive.

Firstly, I insist that no 'real Olive Schreiner' can be found by any commentator: for every point of interpretational certainty about her, another equally plausible argument can be found, for she was a complicated and sometimes contradictory person, and of course (like all of us) her ideas changed over time. Rather than searching for 'fatal flaws' of the social Darwinist/ maternalist kind, my approach is grounded in my particular take on social theory and my long-term research interest in the feminists and socialists of the last fin de siècle rather than a claim about what kind of person she 'really' was. Secondly, I am concerned with Schreiner's writings as a whole, looking at these as an 'oeuvre' and basing my re-reading of them on extensive work on the archived primary sources as well as her published writings. As part of this, I reject evaluating her ideas and analyses by reference to (often very shaky) 'ad feminam' assumptions about what kind of woman she was. I very much agree with Schreiner that it's her ideas that matter and I endeavour to treat them in a serious and attentive way. And thirdly, like Schreiner herself, I eschew the 'neatness' approach to understanding the relationship between lives and writings, perceiving this as a variant on the 'stage method'; and I reject it for 'the method of the life we all lead'. I am sure that Schreiner was right about this and that taking seriously her emphasis on the 'method of life' points up the ways in which her ethics, politics and aesthetics come together around her ideas about 'writing, as such'. In the remainder of the chapter, I flesh these points out, while Chapter 5 outlines what I see as the key features of Olive Schreiner's social theory and responds to some questions about how to interpret and evaluate her work overall.

My focus, then, is concerned with Olive Schreiner's ideas and writings and the contexts these were produced in and it sees 'the life' as subordinate to this. Of course, I have a view of what Olive Schreiner was like, as well as an interpretation of her writings. If asked to describe Olive Schreiner by the proverbial 'stranger on a train', I'd start with 'the more I know the less I'm sure'; after this, words I'd use would include insightful, opinionated, prescient, argumentative, self-willed, amusing, generous, ironical, kind, self-doubting. But I really don't know if I would have liked her or not, and anyway this doesn't seem very relevant to my interest in her work, nor appropriate given the difficulties in gaining any sense of 'the person themselves' from the archival record.

Schreiner's work interests me enormously. I like much of her published writing a great deal, especially its artful rejection of conventional ideas about genre boundaries and distinctions. Her archived letters seem to me often startlingly prescient and are always interesting even in the minutiae they contain. At times I am embarrassed or furious about the views of 'race' she sometimes expresses, even though I know she changed and always did her best, while her assumptions about heterosexuality and marriage as often jar and annoy me. Alongside this, I try to keep firmly in mind that Olive Schreiner is not 'one of us' in fancy dress, that she is indeed a woman of another age, of another mindset. Criticising her for not being a late twentieth century politically correct person, and 'discovering' that she wrote some sometimes objectionable things, is just plain daft and I do my best to resist both of these.

At the back of some interpretations of Olive Schreiner is a concern with the 'inner woman' in a psychological or psychoanalytic sense, rather than with her and/or her writings located in her times. Such an ahistorical and asocial emphasis on an 'inner' notion of self seems to me to result in unhelpful reductionism. My approach to subjectivity is a sociological one: I conceptualise it as inter-subjectivity, conceiving this in social, relational and material terms, and seeing the idea of an 'inner' self as itself a social construction with which one can agree or, in my case, disagree. I am very willing to find a psychoanalytically-based account of Schreiner's life, writings and the construction of the 'Schreiner archive' interesting and helpful. However, no one so far has satisfactorily used psychoanalytic ideas to do this in the way that, for example, Jacqueline Rose has done so superbly with regard to the Sylvia Plath archive.[134]

As it was ideas that mattered to Olive Schreiner and the biography of the person who wrote them not one whit, I feel strongly her own ideas should not be explained away by reference to psychology, or to biography, or to 'ad feminam' judgements of an 'I don't approve of Olive Schreiner so her ideas are no good' kind. The 'biographical imperative' of searching out minute portions of her life of a preferably scandalously sexual nature preoccupies some present-day Schreiner scholarship.[135] Outside of such prurience, the biographical certainly has an important place in informing the work by illuminating the context in which someone's ideas developed, changed and had meaning. This is precisely why my approach has proceeded by looking at Schreiner's life in connection with her ideas and the context in which both were located, and then discussed the main ideas in her writings as a topic in their own right.

As my work on Schreiner has developed, I have become increasingly interested in the structure of her writings, the ways she went about crafting and writing them, and particularly the relationship between the expression of her ideas and the different genres she wrote in. For Schreiner, matters of genre and writing are also matters of principle, while her aesthetics are less about questions of ethics than they *are* her ethics; or, rather, her ethics and her aesthetics are each constitutive of the other. Both operate within Schreiner's 'creative' work as much as in her 'polemical' and 'analytical' writings; they take shape around her view of the relationship between people and society and her hopes for 'the good life'; and thus encompass her politics.

The aesthetic trumpet-call Schreiner sounded in the "Preface" to An African Farm acts not only as a way of understanding the production of Schreiner's work, but also as a useful means of thinking about the shifts within it. The metaphor of 'the method of life' retains a sense of there being a whole, but it also recognises the fragmentary nature of this and insists that, although there may be an overall pattern, this is difficult to perceive. From a point of view that requires narrative coherence and also a triumphal development from, as it were, chrysalis into butterfly, Schreiner's work and her social theory will seem fragmentary, even disorganised. However, looked at through the lens of 'the method of life', it appears as a set of grounded responses to particular events, contexts and circumstances made at different times and for different purposes, rather than being conceived as 'a theory' in the formal sense of a programmatic account of ideas intended as a cohesive whole, a point I return to in Chapter 5.

While there are some constancies in Schreiner's analytic concerns and ways of working, I want to avoid giving the impression that she had a fixed 'point of view': over some fifty years of thinking, writing and theorising, her ideas and analyses inevitably changed, sometimes markedly so. For instance, in relation to Schreiner's views on ethics and war, her thinking moved from emphasising materiality and people's ability to make choices which could radically change the world, to seeing some aspects of social life, particularly regarding aggression, as so deep-seated as to resist volitional change. It was in order to recognise such developments that I outlined Schreiner's writings chronologically in Chapter 3, because this immediately introduces the idea of changes occurring over time. And in thinking about Schreiner's work like this, I noted that she herself indicated a broad shift in its emphasis, from a focus on interiority and the interpersonal and analysing the structural within this, to a focus on exteriority with the structural being the key site for her analytic attention. This change I think does indeed mark Schreiner's work and there *is* a shift from 'interiority' to 'exteriority'. Doubtless many influences underpinned this, including her return to South Africa, the increasing visibility of the massive structural changes occurring there, and the events leading up to the South African War. Whatever, after her return Schreiner maintained this attention to exteriority and the structural to the end of her life, including through the books, published letters and political essays she published on a variety of world and South African political matters.

As her unpublished letters in particular suggest, Schreiner's analysis of capitalism, imperialism, autocracy and what would now be termed patriarchy continued developing. In doing so, unusually for social theorists and more typically for political activists, she continued 'to think forward' about where things were going, where events might be leading, and how best to respond to this. I continue to be struck by Schreiner's political acumen. In Chapter 1, I noted her comments to Jan Smuts about how South Africa was likely to develop if he didn't 'see far enough'– and later developments amply proved her right. Another example of her prescience concerns her comments on the scale and technical ferocity of weaponry and warfare, magnified by the speed and efficiency of new developments in communications, displayed in the 1914–1918 War, and her insistence that international politics had fundamentally and irrevocably changed as a consequence. And even in 1914, when the war had only just started, while her letters supported the idea of the 'League of Nations' she also suggested it was doomed to failure as an answer to war, because the likely peace settlement would cause resentments, and because it would act more in the interests of some nations than others; and she thought that an even more terrible conflagration would eventually result. Very few people indeed could 'see far enough' about these things in 1914, and her foresight here is remarkable.

Schreiner was intensely interested in the political opposition to autocracies, and greatly admired political radicals in Ireland, India and Russia. Relatedly, she saw the development in South Africa after 1910 of what later became apartheid as both predicated upon the particular local form of capitalist exploitation of labour crossed with gender, and also part and parcel of an attempt to stop these wider revolutionary changes from happening in South Africa. Here she emphasised the interconnectedness of the social and the political, frequently contrasting this with, and at times against, government, and against what would now be referred to as the state, especially in its autocratic and imperial forms. A phrase Schreiner often used was 'bring up your rears', by which she meant that it is ethically important for the most oppressed and exploited to be raised, or to raise themselves, to an equal level with everyone else. Without this, she thought that sooner or later there would be a literal day of reckoning, and thus her conviction in the 1890s of the inevitability of revolutionary uprisings in Russia, Ireland and India, and then, from 1910 on, regarding a future uprising of black people in South Africa. Oppression and exploitation will rebound, she argues, not on the oppressors and exploiters themselves, but on future and 'innocent' generations who will have 'inherited the earth', morally speaking, and will reap the whirlwind as a consequence.

There are strong utopian currents in Schreiner's writings, concerned as they are with 'might be' and 'ought to be', although they can even more appropriately be seen as a political analysis which has a keen eye on the future and how to move from 'now' forward to 'then'. For Schreiner, 'what would come after' – how policy effected now in the present could affect then in the future – is always part of the analytic frame. In her earlier work she rejected economistic, religious and other systems of thought which saw large-scale social change occurring outside human agency, or which treated 'idealism' and 'realism' as mutually-exclusive, and she analysed 'exteriority' and structures from within an 'interiority' frame of human agency and will. In her work from 1889 on, her focus turned firmly towards 'exteriority', seeing 'interiority' through its lens, although still insisting that human agency and the power of ideas remained an essential part of the motor-force of change.

Schreiner's approach is concerned with the *longue durée* of deep-seated fundamental change in the social fabric, although hers is neither a social Darwinist nor a Whiggish approach to this. She thought that social change often moved humanity backwards in a political and ethical sense, something she felt strongly concerning the value accorded women's domestic and paid labour. And while she thought that social movements were 'thrown up' by the processes of social change, she also thought they could then direct its trajectory. Insofar as Schreiner gave credence to any kind of determinism, this was to economics, and thus her analyses of race and sex parasitism – although even here she insisted that the nature, direction and extent of change was socially produced and could be re/directed by organised social movements.

Schreiner's support for self-determination, democracy and freedom from autocracy 'abroad', was combined with her rejection of anti-semitism and racist policies and her espousal of democracy and federalism 'at home'. These convictions coexisted with a set of assumptions about 'race' matters that seem highly 'Victorian', including her liberalism, her use of 'scientific' terms, and her assumption of 'empty lands' in South Africa and Australasia. But Schreiner's ideas about sex and 'race' are at the same time startlingly 'modern' regarding her insistence on the socially constructed plasticity of 'race' and sex characteristics, and the complex interconnections of 'race' with gender and class inequalities. And even where Schreiner's ideas on 'race' matters were very much 'of her time', they were in the vanguard of radical thinking. Consequently present-day accounts which assign to her a social Darwinist position on 'race' misrepresent her thinking by divorcing it from her times and the ideas and viewpoints then-current, over-dichotomise the 'Victorian' and the 'modern', and also fail to see the more radical ideas developed in various of her writings.

Olive Schreiner was not a 'shrinking violet' sort of woman, and she was usually resolute and steadfast in her ability to confront unpalatable social facts that most other people simply refused to see. Consequently I am fascinated by the elision of colonialism in her analysis, for this is surely the key to her persistent failure to see black Africans as other than 'children' until later in her life. But why and how did this persist in the thinking of a woman otherwise so radical and far-sighted? This is I think related to the social situation – and the ontological shakiness – of white settler populations, a characteristic that strikes me as shared by the white populations of the settler societies of Australasia and Canada as well as southern Africa. That is, once the fact that southern Africa was not 'empty' but actually belonged is conceded, then where, if anywhere, do the white settlers and those who are their present-day heirs belong? They are in fact not 'in between', as Schreiner had argued in *An English South African's View of the Situation*, but are actually outside of both African and European societies and, ontologically speaking, they belong nowhere.

In arguing what I have, am I actually contradicting the view with which I began this chapter? am I implying there is a 'real Olive Schreiner' and I have possession of her? There are some good reasons why I don't think so. Firstly, what I have outlined here is an argument, made from Schreiner's writings and the primary sources. I think it is a good argument and I want to make it persuasively, but at the same time I also accept its permeability by new information and ideas. Secondly, I am much more interested in crafting a broad workable approach than in advancing 'an interpretation' in the narrow sense; I recognise the provisionality and 'for now' quality of what I have argued and am happy to change my mind in the face of new archival evidence. Thirdly, I fully accept the areas of agreement and overlaps with the work of other Schreiner scholars and I am very pleased that a more nuanced and appreciative interpretation of Schreiner's work is growing apace. At the same time, I continue to think my account is distinctive in resting on an extensive, indeed getting on for exhaustive, use of archival sources.

What these things add up to is that, for me, Olive Schreiner was very much 'a woman of her time'. She was not a deconstructionist; or a racist; or an anti-racist; she did not live within or by our terms and ideas and values; she belongs to that other country of the past where they did things differently, thought about them differently. As a young woman on the colonial frontier, there was no running water, sewers, roads, gas, electricity, telegraph, cars, repeating guns, high explosives. She lived her life through a period of massive social, economic and political change; as a child and young woman, international capitalism, democracy and secular society did not exist; and over her life-time the meanings of 'Africa', 'labour', 'capitalism', 'woman', 'family', 'race' and 'imperialism' all underwent fundamental changes.

What, more precisely, do I mean by this idea of Olive Schreiner being 'a woman of her time'? is there anything more to this than 'life has changed'? 'Her time' in fact includes some very different times – between Schreiner's childhood and youth, and her middle age, some extraordinary changes took place during the period of her adult womanhood, so that 'being a woman' encompassed very different possibilities at the beginning and at the end of her life. In an 1894 review, the journalist and editor W.T. Stead referred to Olive Schreiner as 'the Modern Woman par excellence', a comment which captures both the 'newness' of the modern and also the 'oldness' of the social context that the 'modern woman' lived within.

Olive Schreiner seems to me to embody the idea of the 'New Woman' of the last fin de siècle. And along with many other New Women, Schreiner was self-determining, economically independent and independent-minded; and yet she also sought sisterhood, comradeship and an equal and free sexual union. She was questioning and questing, rejected received orthodoxies and threw off religion; yet her freethinking also sought a systematic ethics and politics to provide an alternative world-view. In all of this she was deeply serious, although not in her delight in humour and ability to poke fun at her own and other people's seriousness, conceiving it a social duty to have purposefulness in life. She was engaged in breaking the mould, but still held its pieces in her hands; and her contradictions in doing so were those of the times and shared with other people similarly engaged in questioning, seeking and endeavouring to live alternatives. In these things too, she was both a woman of her time and at the same time a 'Modern Woman par excellence'.

Like other New Women, Olive Schreiner inhabited discourses that would later be characterised as being mutually-exclusive, as binaries – materialism and symbolism, conservatism and radicalism, anti-imperialism and colonialism – but which were lived out as over-lapping complexities. And, like them, she tried to do her best with the means at her disposal. In her case, this meant using her ability to think analytically and to write reflectively about such matters. The result is a distinctive, interesting and still strikingly innovative body of writing and of social theory that deserves a wider present-day readership.

Notes

1 See Stanley 2000a, 2001a, 2001b, for discussions.

2 As Clayton 1983 (p.15) commented; this is still so.

3 Burdett (2001 p.150) refers to 'effort-free hindsight', a phrase that nicely captures the dynamics involved.

4 See Chapter 7 in Stanley 1992.

5 Renier 1984 p.10.

6 Gregg 1955 p.71.

7 Gregg 1957 p.16.

8 Schoeman 1992 p. 34.

9 Cronwright-Schreiner 1924a p.34.

10 Cronwright-Schreiner 1924a pp.vii, 22, 23.

11 A demonstration of the 'claim not certain fact' nature of Cronwright-Schreiner's insistences is provided by the manuscript of part of Chapter 1 of The Life omitted at Unwin's suggestion. This relates the story of Theo and Will finding a large but flawed diamond, which Theo named 'the Faith Diamond' because he promised to use money from selling it for 'God's works' (he did). The manuscript notes that 'old Mrs Schreiner' told the story of it being found and Theo teasing Ettie; it adds "Her version shouldn't be taken literally ...", but this has been crossed out, presumably because he remembered it wasn't Olive's story but her mother's. See NELM Schreiner SMD 30.40.g.

12 All the siblings were agonisingly incapacitated by and then died from the same heart condition.

13 See Chapter 2.

14   See here Schreiner's letters to her dying sister Ettie. Schreiner refers to her love for her mother and that she acted as a propelling force in her life. See especially OS to Ettie Stakesby Lewis, 12 November 1903, UCT Schreiner-Hemming BC1080.

15   Schreiner's niece Katie Stuart commented, "He was the evil genius of her life – who killed her genius by his ambitions for her and his planning for her to write. Could you? could I? write a word if someone was ceaselessly planning, arranging and cajoling us to do so? and then blindly disappointed because we couldn't!" (Katie Stuart to Ruth Alexander, 4 December 1924, SAL Schreiner MSC26 5.1.1).

16   OS to Karl Pearson, 10 September 1886, Pearson London, Rive 1987 pp.103-5. Cronwright-Schreiner denies the overlaps and similarities, unable to conceive that analytic themes might be written about polemically or allegorically.

17   First and Scott 1980 p. 268.

18   See for instance First and Scott 1980 p.267-8 and their footnote 9 p.362. See also OS to Betty Molteno, 21 September 1900 UCT Schreiner; Mrs Jane Fisher Unwin to Rosalind Vaughan Nash (nèe Nightingale), 1 Nov 1900, SAL Schreiner MSC 26, 8.2.3a.

19   Friedmann 1955 p.1.

20   Friedmann 1955 pp.1, 3.

21   Friedmann 1955 p.14.

22   Friedmann 1955 p.14.

23   Friedmann 1955 pp. 14, 15, 17.

24   Friedmann 1955 pp. 21-33.

25   Friedmann 1955 p.24.

26   Friedmann 1955 p.41.

27   Friedmann 1955 p.31.

28   Friedmann 1955 p. 54, her emphasis.

29   Friedmann 1955 p.17.

30   Friedmann 1955 p.54.

31   Friedmann 1955 p.63.

32   First and Scott 1980 p.11.

33   Compare, for instance, with the subtleties of Rose 1991 and Young-Bruehl 1998.

34   Schoeman 1991 p.vi.

35   First and Scott 1980 p.20.

36   First and Scott 1980 p.344.

37   First and Scott 1980 p.344.

38   First and Scott 1980 p.22.

39   First and Scott 1980 p.53.

40   Interestingly, Schoeman's introduction notes the absence of such a tradition in Afrikaans and that the 1989 Afrikaans text was read as a kind of fictional narrative about a factual person and factual events in her life.

41   Schoeman 1992.

42   Schoeman 1991 p.v, vi; 1992 p.78.

43   Schoeman 1991, p.v.

44   Schoeman 1991 p.v; 1992 p.216, 217.

45   Schoeman 1992 p.217.

46   Schoeman 1991 p.217

47   Schoeman 1991 p.70.

48   Schoeman 1991 pp.v, 71.

49   Schoeman 1991 pp.56, 113, 142, 168-9.

50   Schoeman 1991 p.56.

51   Schoeman 1991 p.73 and pp.389-90.

52   Schoeman 1991 p.412.

53   Shoeman 1991 p.413.

54   Schoeman 1991 p.232.

55   In fact her mother wrote to her daughter Katie that "I am expecting Olive as soon as
      Miss Gau can spare her" (undated letter but 1872, Wits Findlay A1199: 1101), so her
      leaving Dordrecht was fully expected.

56   Schoeman 1991 pp.226-34.

57   See OS to Katie Findlay 6 April 1972, ? August 1872, 18 August 1872, Wits Findlay
      A1199: 1098, 1118, 1124; and OS to Alice Hemming, nd, and 8 May Wednesday no year,
      archived as 1872, UCT Schreiner-Hemming. See also Rebecca Schreiner to Katie Findlay,
      6 October 1872, Wits Findlay A1199: 1131, for family conjectures as to 'what to do for
      the best' to help Olive over it.

58   This was not for the dramatic reason proposed by Schoeman, but the sadder and more
      mundane one that the Robinsons' young daughter Aggie had died and Schreiner didn't
      want to be paid for a job that no longer existed; see here OS to Katie Findlay, 6 April
      1872, Wits Findlay A1199: 1098.

59   OS to Havelock Ellis, 26 November 1884, HRC Schreiner, Draznin 1992 pp.229-30.
      Schreiner told Ellis that the scene in which Undine receives a letter from Albert Blair
      breaking their engagement was based on Gau writing to her.

60   Schoeman 1992 p.72.

61   Walker 1937.

62   Schoeman 1991 pp.71-2.

63   See references to Hobhouse in a range of letters from Schreiner, Betty Molteno and
      Alice Greene from 1902 to 1913 in the UCT Schreiner collection.

64   For Schreiner's view, see for instance OS to Will Schreiner, 26 Oct 1913 and ? November
      1913, see also Alice Greene to OS, 28 January 1914 and 29 January 1914; and Alice
      Greene to Betty Molteno 23 Nov 1913 and nd 1918; all UCT Schreiner.

65   See Emily Hobhouse to May Murray Parker, 18 Sept 1918, SAL Schreiner.

66   Abrams 1982.

67   I quote from the reprint in Clayton 1983.

68   Gordimer 1983 p.95.

69   Gordimer 1983 p.96.

70   Gordimer 1983 p.97.

71   Gordimer 1983 p.97. A view not shared by many black South Africans or the ANC, as the twenty years since her review was written have shown.

72   Gordimer 1983 pp.97-8.

73   Gordimer 1983 p.96.

74   Gordimer 1983 p.98.

75   Gordimer 1983 p.98.

76   Wagner 1994 p.56.

77   Peck 1997 pp.139-54.

78   Barash 1986, 1987.

79   Burdett 1992, 1994a.

80   Barash 1986 p. 333.

81   Barash 1986 p. 339.

82   Barash 1987 p. 19.

83   Burdett 1992 p.111.

84   Burdett 1992 p.113, my emphases.

85   Burdett 1994a.

86   Burdett 1994b. Carolyn Burdett's ideas about Schreiner's work have also changed markedly. Her 1999 re-reading is rather different, as I note later.

87   Burdett 1994b p.222.

88   Burdett 1994b p.222.

89   Burdett 1994b p.222-3.

90   This is true. However, as discussed in Chapter 2, Cornwall, a henchman of Rhodes, sued Cronwright for libel regarding an intemperate letter published in a newspaper, in November 1897 and won.

91   Burdett 1994b p.224.

92   Burdett 1999 p.43.

93   Burdett 1994b p.225.

94   Royalties and sales statements for the 1920s are in NELM Schreiner SMD 30.37.a-n.

95   Burdett 1994b p.226.

96   Burdett 1994b p.227.

97   Burdett 1994b p.227.

98   Burdett 1992 p.119.

99   Burdett 2001 p.7.

100 Berkman 1989 p.4.

101 Berkman 1989 p.6.

102 Berkman 1989 p.7.

103 Maccoby 1938, 1953; Porter 1968; Maynard 1993.

104 In Chapter 2, I noted this regarding her family relationships; I think it later characterised her marriage as well.

105 Berkman 1989 pp.73-99.

106 The political fortunes of the term 'Bushmen', for instance, have involved it being 'scientific', then rejected as racist and replaced with 'San', but then this latter term seen as offensive to many of the people so-called, with 'Bushmen' now coming back into 'correct' usage.

107 Berkman 1989 p.85.

108 Berkman 1984 pp.100-124.

109 I see these statements as politically performative ones, a way of encouraging this result rather than description. Schreiner was always very well informed about the shadier side of Empire and never so naïve as this implies.

110 Berkman 1989 p.165.

111 Berkman 1989 pp.165, 164. I shall return to this in discussing McClintock's interpretation.

112 Used about Thomas Hardy's *A Pair of Blue Eyes*; OS to Havelock Ellis, 28 March 1884, Draznin 1992 pp.38-40.

113 Berkman used the HRC Schreiner manuscript.

114 *Woman and Labour* pp.175-6.

115 In the *Nation & Atheneum* in 1921 and also in Schreiner's *Stories, Dreams and Allegories* from the 1924 second edition on.

116 HRC Schreiner Manuscripts.

117 Comments in Berkman 1989 pp.46, 85, 87, 126, 160, 164, 198.

118 Berkman 1989 pp.126 and 141.

119 McClintock 1995 p.295.

120 McClintock 1995 p.5.

121 McClintock 1995, p.15.

122 McClintock 1995, p.8.

123 English-speaking colonists might live in the Transvaal or the Orange Free State, as well as in the Cape Colony or Natal.

124 This is an important reason why Schreiner is less than fully critical of the Boer trekker-farmers, seeing them as pastoralists hardly different in their way of life or their degree of connection with 'the modern world' from African peoples.

125 McClintock 1995 p.28.

126 McClintock 1995 pp. 258-9.

127 McClintock 1995 pp.259-67. She includes Schreiner's supposedly 'hysterical protest' at her confinement as female, with asthma resulting. 'Obsession' is mentioned frequently in the second part of *Imperial Leather*, with the reiteration linking this to the discussion of 'fantasy, desire and difference' in the first part.

128 McClintock 1995 p.267.

129 McClintock's use of 'black' derives from the politics of 'race' in the USA, and in my view fails to speak to the very different configurations of 'race' in a specifically South African context. Old Ayah's place in the colour hierarchy, as well as the domestic hierarchy, is an important component of her power-base.

130 McClintock 1995 p.267.

131 McClintock 1995 p.271.

132 McClintock 1995, pp.268-70.

133 I adduce Rebekah being Boer from her name, and because as a child she had a tin box with Queen Victoria's head on it and in several letters Schreiner comments about Boer country girls in her youth collecting these.

134 Rose 1991.

135 See Bradford 1995, building on Schoeman's similar claim.

Chapter 5

When The Curtain Falls…
Olive Schreiner's Social Theory
Reconsidered

Introduction

This chapter considers what kind of social theory and what kind of feminist theory Olive Schreiner produced. In doing so, it stands back from the details of particular pieces of writing, it ignores conventional distinctions between 'theory' and other kinds of writing, and it focuses on what Schreiner accomplished rather than what she failed to do. It responds to some of the questions that have been raised about Schreiner's work, concerning the essentialism, racism, social Darwinism and other disreputable 'isms' sometimes perceived in it. And it also addresses some wider questions about the 'fate' of Schreiner's writing, particularly the gulf between its contemporary fame and significance and its present-day estimation. It concludes with a final valedictory comment.

In contemporary intellectual life, 'theory' has become almost coterminous with the highly formalised, programmatic and abstract variant usually referred to as 'social theory'.[1] There are, however, other kinds of theory, more open, grounded and provisional than the now dominant or 'canonical' kind. It is important to recognise the existence of different kinds of theory, and that the version currently dominant has not always been so, not least because until recently the vast majority of theory written by women, including by feminists, was not of the social theory variant. The idea of theory used here in thinking about the successes and failures of Olive Schreiner's work is of the more open, less formalised (and less formulaic) kind. This encompasses thinking through an issue or problem, gathering relevant evidence about it, reflecting thoughtfully on this and the problem itself, commenting analytically about issues that arise, and drawing some conclusions about these matters, and I use the term 'reflective analytical theory' to characterise it.

As Olive Schreiner put it in the "Preface" to An African Farm, "The canons of criticism that bear upon the one cut cruelly upon the other". Thus when her work is thought about using the social theory model, Schreiner wrote 'theory' only in Woman and Labour and the related articles, and barely (or badly) even then; but when thought about in relation to the reflectively analytical model, she wrote little but theory. The social theory model provides what I think is an inappropriately narrow, prescriptive and proscriptive means of thinking about the ideas and analyses that Olive Schreiner produced, then; consequently I situate her work very much within the reflective analytical tradition.[2]

There is certainly a greater 'might have been' about her work, given Olive Schreiner's persistent and disabling ill-health and its increasing inroads on her productive energies; and certainly the shadows and echoes of the never written, the written but vanished, and the written but unfinished, are discernible among her archive papers. However, the focus in this chapter is on what Schreiner *did* write and *did* produce; and my view is that, looked at as a body of work, as an 'oeuvre', it adds up to something extremely interesting and also rather impressive.

What Kind of Feminist Theory Did Olive Schreiner Write?

I have of course already written a good deal about Olive Schreiner's ideas earlier in this book and I don't want to repeat what has already been discussed in previous chapters. Some of the important continuities in Schreiner's thinking over time and also areas of significant change have been indicated, while additional ones may have been discerned by readers, and so there is no need to labour these points either. Instead, I want to draw these things together and look at what it adds up to and what kind of theoretical and analytical contribution it makes, what kind of feminist theory and what kind of social theory it is.[3] In doing so, Schreiner's own terms or phrases are used as headings to summarise the key ideas she was concerned with.

The method of the life we all lead[4]

'Writing, as such' was a central activity for Schreiner from her teenage years on, and even before this she was engrossed by many of the activities she associated with writing. She saw the creative processes involved in a holistic way, around giving material form to the original allegorical conception she had experienced. As a consequence, she had a very structural approach to plot and narrative, rejecting what she saw as false realism and its pretend descriptions and supposed realistic narratives which tidied up life, making it 'believable' by subordinating it to the conventions. Comments Schreiner made in letters about her writing are interestingly suggestive about the processes in which ideas came and she then formed and expressed them; the surviving extracts from her diaries and journals suggest it is likely she 'wrote about writing' in these too, so there are additional grounds for lamenting their destruction.

Schreiner's approach to genre, plot, narrative, characterisation and time is expressed in the 'ethics of aesthetics' formed by the "Preface" to An African Farm. Her aesthetics was also concerned with what writers were for. Writing was a thing in itself, something she valued immensely; but she also valued it because it sought to represent human experiences in ways that could make people think, while later she became explicitly concerned with writing as a means of encouraging people to *act* as well. Writing had a social purpose and writers had ethical duties; for Schreiner, they were neither above nor beyond such responsibilities.

Her structural approach to writing makes Schreiner very unusual if not unique in her time – for instance, other feminist writers who were contemporaries were drawn to the short story because of its episodic rather than narrative concerns,[5] although I can think of no feminist contemporary with such an innovative approach to genre and so determined a rejection of realism.[6] This marks Schreiner's 'political' writings as well as her 'fictional' ones; indeed, this distinction breaks down around her writing from very early on. What Schreiner's contemporaries more widely saw as peculiar if powerful conventional work (of either a fictional or a factual kind) now comes into view as interesting attempts by her to find alternative representational means to those of the then-prevailing narrow conventions. And oddly, even some present-day poststructuralist re-readings have succumbed to interpreting Schreiner according to largely realist conventions. Against this, I look forward in the future to some re-readings of Schreiner's work that are as structurally-focused and as challenging to realist convention as her writing.

A striving and a striving and an ending in nothing[7]

The phrase 'a striving and a striving and an ending in nothing' from *An African Farm* recurs in Schreiner's letters, and, together with the metaphor of the toiling dung-beetle underpinning it, it had great significance for her. 'Pessimism', Carpenter's term, is one way of describing Schreiner's insistent gaze on the unpredictability of life, although I think this ignores the seriousness of her thinking about 'the method of life'. While some people lead cocooned lives, many more turn their eyes away from the bleakness of life as experienced by whole sections of the population, indeed by the entire populations of some countries; however, Olive Schreiner did neither. And at a personal level, 'the best laid plans' of people are subject to the whims of others, illnesses, sudden changes of circumstance. Consequently, for Schreiner living had to be an end in itself, for no planned conclusion to it can be guaranteed and there is no after-life in which the things gone wrong will come right; thus her conviction (for instance, in the "Times and Seasons" opening to Part II of *An African Farm* and also in her critique of gossip in *FMTM*) of the need for ethics as the basic fabric of social as well as individual life.

But there is considerably more to Schreiner's thoughts on ethics than this. For her, social structure, the external world, impinged on people regardless of their individual aptitudes and characters. Individuals alone cannot surmount this, but, acting together, people's attempts to do so will accumulate, gradually but inevitably changing things. Schreiner was also clear about the importance of childhood experiences in affecting aptitudes and character. Childhood for Schreiner is a kind of world within the world and children are highly vulnerable, including in ways not immediately apparent. Therein ticking clocks tick away lives and resound with morality and mortality, unthinking behaviour by adults shapes children's inner sense of self and will, and both impact on what a child can become within the social constraints of their time.

Schreiner did not see what a person is as the product of 'inner' aptitudes, or indeed of the 'outer' social mores, howsoever these may constrain what they can do. Instead she had both a 'plastic' and constructionist view of people as social beings (it is what happens to people that shapes their self and will); and also an awareness of the importance as well as the limitations of social structure (while the social framework of sanctioned possibilities legislates the parameters, nonetheless self-determination still exists). Thus Waldo is damaged and will-less, but in a society in which, as a man, he could easily have become what Lyndall wants and has the will for and strives towards; but her aptitudes and abilities count for little and her individual struggle will fail, simply because she is a woman.

Schreiner's ideas about trust and vulnerability structuring the relations between the powerful and the powerless had a wider reach even than this, as with her 'as we sow so shall we reap' conviction that the conduct of one generation will resound on future ones. Thus I think it neither an accident nor a racial (nor in a simple sense a racist) convention that underpins her use of the 'adult/child' metaphor to read 'race' relations in South Africa, but rather that she was keenly aware, perhaps over-aware, of the effects of betrayals of trust on those who are, or have been made, vulnerable. She was very attentive to the constructed infantalisation and constrained dependency of women, and this informed her analysis of sex parasitism. And increasingly, she applied the same analysis to the equally constrained infantalisation of black Africans, denied human as well as civil and legal rights and treated as merely 'engines of labour' and providers of sexual as well as domestic services.

Times and seasons[8]

The phrase 'times and seasons' is the title of a major 'interruption' within An African Farm concerning the development of morality as a central part of growing up and becoming a person. This is situated at the literal centre of the novel, a book centrally concerned with morality and ethics in the context of the relationship of people to society, to each other, and to themselves. Within this, for Schreiner death takes on a variety of rather different meanings. It is often matter of fact, just what often happens, and so its mundane part in the everyday scheme of things has to be acknowledged. Death sometimes represents a resolution restoring harmony and calm by ending something out of place (as with the death of Undine and the woman in "The Buddhist Priest's Wife"). It can be something to which a person is resistant, representing a defeat because thwarting their will (as with Lyndall until she is too weak to resist). Occasionally it represents the human spirit joining a vast unity beyond individual specificity (perhaps as with Waldo), or as more simply the consequence of 'living the good life' in the face of life's evils (as with Jannita in "Dream Life and Real Life"). But, whatever, it is always there, the great insoluble fact of human life and existence that all ethical, moral and political ideas need to take account of.

One of the important ways it is 'there' regarding the development of Schreiner's ideas about morality and ethics concerns aggression, violence and war, for death on a mass-scale can be almost casually imposed on people as a by-product of other purposes. Thus, for instance, Trooper Peter was conceived around the fact that expansion 'required' the expropriation of land and resources and this in turn required expendable people, their lives accorded little value and their deaths even less.

Seeing the writer as a responsible moral agent within their writing just as much as within their lives, Schreiner felt strongly the relationship between ethical purpose and the power of ideas to traverse time and place. This didn't mean she saw writing as simply didactic, a technology to produce given effects. Indeed, she was very opposed to such a view of 'art' in general, writing in particular, seeing it as a betrayal of its creative origins and thus of 'artistry' as the realisation of the ideal. But she certainly thought there was a more general ethical duty for the writer to engage with 'the times' and not stand aloof from these.

Misty figures ... the rustle of paper passing from hand to hand[9]

Schreiner analysed capitalism as by definition concerned with profit and so 'by nature' exploitative; and this forms both a strong analytic background to her ideas and also a major part of the foreground in her (fictional as well as factual) writing. As well as the general systemic features of social relations within capitalism, Schreiner was concerned with its particular dynamics in an African context, specifically the context of the European 'scramble for Africa'. Thus in her South African essays she saw finance capital – with its international banking houses, laundering of money and 'deals' and its networks of men operating 'behind the scenes' of public life, behind government and politics in particular – as supremely consequential in marking the tenor of public life and morality and also in establishing the organisational structures and particular configurations of 'local capitalism' in South Africa.

For Schreiner this involved not only the mundane corruptions of 'squaring' – cutting deals by paying people off with whatever currency (monetary, sexual, status) they most desired – as masterminded by Rhodes and the way it came to characterise economic and political life in South Africa more generally. These activities happened behind the scenes and the 'misty figures' passed money, power, information, whatever it took, from hand to hand. People and their lives were simply another form of currency in such exchanges.

As a consequence of the depersonalisation that was the effect of such machinations, Schreiner's political essays also emphasise there were structurally much more damaging implications for economic and social organisation. Depersonalisation enabled one whole class of people, because of their 'race', to be seen and treated as merely objects, as 'hands' to carry out tasks with as little reward or civility of treatment as possible, and Schreiner saw this as crucial to South Africa's particular local form of capitalism. Schreiner saw the mind-set of brutalisation as increasingly characterising the parasitic class of whites in South Africa. In prophetic mode, she thought this would eventually engulf the whole society, because there would be a violent conflagration, a revolutionary overturning of the white supremacist racial order.

Imperialism is the euphonious title of a deadly disease[10]

Schreiner's thinking about ethics spanned fundamental existential matters of life and death (as in *Trooper Peter*), through to individual people making decisions about how to conduct themselves in everyday life (as in the allegory "The Woman's Rose"). It was also concerned with what lies between, and thus her analytical concern with different forms of government and state. Schreiner's critique of imperialism and autocracy focused on these as systems of government grounded in relations of exploitation and regulation of people who ought to be but are not free and equal citizens. While imperialism did this 'abroad', autocracy did it 'at home', and both were founded on lack of justice and thus of legitimacy. Schreiner's objections to British imperialism on these grounds led to her fervent support for freedom movements (including for the precursor to the ANC in South Africa when it started); and it also fuelled her feelings about the need for full adult democracy 'at home' and federalism as a safeguard against autocracy as well.

Imperialism in Schreiner's analysis underpinned capitalism's destruction of pastoralism and other socially more productive divisions of labour. As a 'way of life', pastoralism was founded on mutual inter-dependencies, with equal value being accorded to the different divisions within it because each was equally necessary to the others. Schreiner therefore saw it as both 'higher' and also 'more civilised' because involving a greater degree of equality and social justice – she had no truck with the Darwinian-influenced Marxist idea of the 'idiocy' of rural life, and she also firmly rejected seeing technological development as 'progressive' in a social sense.

For Schreiner, imperialism was the 'highest' stage of capitalism as a system, for it made nakedly apparent the ruthless search for profit that drove economic relations and which corrupted all other social relations as well. The symbiosis of capitalism and imperialism lay in the dynamic of expansionism; its defining character for Schreiner was conveyed in a phrase she used in a letter to her brother Will: "crush the native – cheap labour – new mines – the native territories".[11] This was written when she was contemplating what union between the four settler states would mean, for imperialism was in process of being 'translated' in the Union into starkly autocratic relations between subjugated black Africans and an authoritarian white state constitutionally inscribing rights on one side of a colour line and so regulating its 'others'.

It left out one whole field; to me personally, the most important[12]

What is often omitted from analysis of 'the woman question', Olive Schreiner emphasised to Karl Pearson in 1885, was the part played by men in producing the situation of women. In Schreiner's analysis, 'the problem of men' is the root of 'the woman question', for it is this 'one whole field' of men's abuses and exploitations of women which leads to the corruption of the character and will of both. And women are in a sense inferior, Schreiner proposes, but this is the effect and not the problem itself.

Schreiner analysed the part played in conditioning 'women's role' by long-term shifts and changes in the economic sub-structure, the ways in which scientific and other developments affected economic production and social divisions of labour, and accompanying changes in the value accorded to some forms of labour but not others. Her analysis also included men, their behaviours, their expectations and feelings about women, their relationships with other men, and the marital and other relations they structured and enacted. The 'frozen rationality' of men indicated deep emotional damage, but also had deleterious effects on women; male homosociality meant men's prime relations were with other men; and the value accorded women was set by purchase of their sexual services in prostitution and their dependency as well as their domestic labour and sexual services in marriage. The fact that women could be bought sexually was for her the key to how men think of all women, as less than fully human objects to the male subject.

Schreiner saw women as deeply damaged by oppression. The trivial lives that many women led, the under-valued drudgery that characterised most women's daily lot, the role of gossip in keeping other women in line and reducing life to personalities, the jealousies that divided women around competition for male attention, were all phenomena she commented sharply on. But she also retained a very strong sense of commitment to other women, recognised that women were often large-hearted against the grain, and acknowledged that many women wanted a better world in which men weren't damaged either.

For Schreiner, men were not fully human, indeed could not be so until they were fully and equally involved in carrying out social labour, particularly the care of others. Caring in her analytical schema was both highly productive and also humanising in a fundamental sense, because it led to value being accorded to those vulnerable people – the young, the old, the sick – with whom we have relations of trust. And even after she recognised that equal social motherhood would not end aggression and war, she continued to see it as valuable in its own right and as social justice for women.

While men had no structural incentive to change, women did. Schreiner analysed the Woman's Movement, like other world-wide social movements, as produced by deep-seated structural changes occurring to women's economic and social position. But this certainly didn't mean she thought that 'things would change' by themselves. "That vast and restless 'Woman's Movement' which marks our day"[13] was something she thought was crucially necessary to bring about the changes that she and many other women desired, for themselves, but also for 'humanity' as a whole in an ethical sense. And this didn't mean she gave blanket-approval to it or to any other social movement: she remained aware of the problems as well as the great possibilities.

As we sow so shall we reap[14]

Schreiner's later thinking about 'race' drew on some of her ideas about 'the woman question', 'labour' and 'the problem of men', including the importance of militantly active social movements for change. These ideas developed through her recognition of the links between the situations of children and women, and were later reworked around her analysis of relations between black people and 'the problem of whites'. Her initial analysis of 'the native question' had situated this very much in terms of her ideas about 'the labour question', focusing in South Africa on capital's expropriation of land giving access to mineral wealth, and its creation of a cheap proletarianised labour force, the members of which were constrained or compelled to live in compounds. Later, after the South African War, she became much more aware of the marked gendering involved in the reconfiguration of 'race', including the exploitation of black women as domestic labourers and also the economic and other constraints that produced sex work.

Underpinning these structural matters, Schreiner concluded, were endemic prejudices that whites held about black people's lack of value as people, including, as she recognised, by her. Ironically enough, this realisation was brought about by the misogyny of some Indian and black male leaders, who wanted 'uppity white women' barred from political meetings and organisations. The structural similarities between the situations of black and Indian South Africans, and women of all 'races', struck Schreiner with immediacy, as did the comparisons between her attitudes to black people and theirs to women.

Long-term, Schreiner was utterly convinced that things would change, whites would not be 'in charge' forever, and how black people were being treated when she was writing would rebound on the future. Treating people as if they are objects is degrading and it impacts on people's sense of self-worth and will. It also brutalises those who behave like this. Schreiner's prognostication was that South Africa would become a 'sick society' through and through, and that ultimately black people would organise against the autocracy that oppressed them and overthrow it in ways directly comparable to those used by other freedom movements. When writing to Jan Smuts, Schreiner's letters often took on a prophetic tone, and her comment about 'as we sow so shall we reap' comes in a letter in which she insists that Smuts, inheriting prime ministerial control of the government from Louis Botha, had in effect the last chance to pull back from the threshold of major structural changes that would further institutionalise racism in South Africa.

Sex parasitism [15]

Schreiner's analysis of sex parasitism has its origin in her 1896 analysis of parasitism as a defining characteristic of the way that whites lived off value and profit created by the labour of black Africans. In her 1899 analysis of 'the women's labour question', it was given a new twist around her view, expanded in *Woman and Labour*, of the ways that mechanisation was occasioning major structural changes in how labour was organised, carried out, and meaning and value (in both an economic and a social sense) accorded it. There were changes to the amount and kind of labour available, but more consequentially the gendered divisions of social as well as paid labour that existed were being changed as well. For Schreiner, there was another crucial twist here: these new forms of mechanised labour were so productive that, for the first time, one entire section of adult humanity could become parasitic upon another. For her, sex parasitism was not women leaching upon men, but rather men constraining and indeed compelling women's parasitism upon them as a mark of their status and power in the eyes of other men. She saw neither societies nor economies existing in a state of stasis; and, as one class of people could be compelled to remain static under conditions of parasitism, so the gap between the subordinate parasitic group of women and the dominant group of men could widen. A collapse could therefore happen, which Schreiner sees occurring because the system would have a major weakness at its heart that would eventually stultify 'ordinary change'.

Schreiner's account of sex parasitism was not intended as a literal description, but rather pinpointed an underlying tendency and spelled out some of the possible consequences of this. Hers is a warning about possibilities, then. Even more so, in my view its main purpose was to provide a powerful and emotive argument in favour of women having 'labour, and the training that fits us for labour', as *Woman and Labour*'s battle-cry puts it. Schreiner cared passionately about this because she thought there was an ethical social duty to be productive; for her, it was this that made people truly human and justified their lives.

A social labour theory of value[16]

Schreiner's ideas about a 'social labour' theory of value are drawn together around her writings on 'the woman question' from 1899 on. In thinking through her ideas about the different form that the labour question took for women, and then later for black people, she came to re-think her ideas about value. Initially attaching value to 'labour power' as Karl Marx had done, she then took a different tack. Value, she recognised, was progressively, or rather regressively, denied to 'what women did', because deemed to be non-productive or less productive in the narrowly economistic sense by virtue of who carried it out. And when women carried out labour which *was* highly productive, it was not valued as labour, but instead its value was seen as coming from elsewhere, and thus as extraneous to 'labour, as such'.

For Schreiner, in contrast, 'labour' and 'value' were conceived in a more innovative way. She turned the tables on economism by socialising the terms of engagement. That is, she places, analytically speaking, all forms of labour within the framework of social labour as that which gives rise to value. More than this, she conceived as 'productive' as only that labour which could be accorded social value, in part defined around its contribution to social reproduction and in part around an 'appropriate fit' between the means used to carry out a given task and its end. The effects of her analysis are highly radical – much of production in the narrow capitalist and economist sense of rendering profit in financial terms is re-cast as both non-productive and lacking in value in social terms; and much of production in the social sense is defined as labour and thereby accorded new value.

Now with the male sex form, and then with the female[17]

Rather than being 'essentialist', I understand Schreiner's approach as actually a strongly social constructionist one, arguing for the plasticity of biology, which she sees as non-deterministic and taking very different (sometimes diametrically opposed) forms in different species and different human societies. Schreiner rejected not only the supposition that biology might be determining, but she held this view even in relation to reproduction itself. Bodily organs certainly affect who gives birth, but for Schreiner biology entails nothing beyond this. Men's desire for children is as strong as women's, and she thought that both women and men could, and in men's case should, be 'mothers' in the social sense.

Social mothering was the form of labour Schreiner accorded the highest value to, for it enabled the reproduction of society in the social, rather than biological, sense. Involving the care of the most vulnerable, social mothering brings the future into existence. Schreiner was convinced that a fully equal share in social mothering would transform men (as it did Gregory Rose in *An African Farm*), make them 'grow up' and become better kinds of people. And she saw this as crucially necessary if a more just, less violent and exploitative society is ever to exist. Later she came to see aggression as extremely deep-rooted in humanity, a strongly persisting reminder of our animal origins. And while Schreiner emphasises biology here, she perceives women as well as men being aggressive and war-like but in socially-sanctioned and gendered ways, and she also recognises there are men as well as women who are pacifists 'by nature'.

As this indicates, Schreiner had a strongly anti-Darwinian approach to ideas about change and progress in human affairs. She conceived 'evolution', not in the 'survival of the fittest' way, but as periods of rapid change; and for her these were propelled by economic factors, not biological ones, and could be shifted and changed by social movements. She was also insistent that change can take a society, or humanity as a whole, backwards as well as forwards in terms of real 'progress', for this concerns social justice. A further anti-Darwinian element in Schreiner's thinking is her insistence that a truly progressive society will insist on the importance of 'bringing up your rears', of ensuring equality and justice for all, because unless all are equal, society cannot be just. For her, a society that does not do this contains an in-built structural instability, for sooner or later the repressed and the dispossessed will 'return' with a vengeance.

The desire for vulgar domination and empire, which has ensnared us all[18]

Schreiner's comment about 'the desire for domination' which has 'ensnared us all' was made in supporting conscientious objection and pacifism during the 1914–1918 War. Her analysis of war and ethical responses to it proceeded from seeing war as fully part of the social, in two senses.

The first concerns Schreiner's analysis of labour, seeing war and fighting as labour which engaged large numbers of people beyond the 'fighting forces' during times of war, and as 'ordinary labour' in times of peace for members of standing armies and navies and also the large numbers of auxiliary workers whose labour services them. A major part of the economy in times of peace is organised around labour which supports warfare and, as Schreiner points out, this raises immense ethical questions and dilemmas for people like herself, who were pacifists by rooted conviction: how can one withdraw support for something so endemically present throughout the fabric of society as this?

The second involves her view that societies compete, or rather states do and their citizens acquiesce. As capitalism becomes ever better established and organised 'at home', and as its imperialist incarnation competes for the scarce resources of labour, land, minerals and markets as well as strategic concerns 'abroad', so the possibility of conflict and war becomes built into relations between countries on a world-wide scale. This, coupled with mass communications systems and the new technologies for mass destruction being developed, led Schreiner to view warfare as in permanent escalation, leading to what she thought at the end of the 1914–1918 War would be world-wide conflagration of an undreamed of scale and ferocity in the future.

Before the 1914–1918 War, Schreiner had been convinced that warfare was a 'left over' from an earlier time in human development, one which would end once men became truly civilised, truly humanised, through social labour. The events of that war led her to become convinced there was something more deep-seated, more 'animal', about aggression and its relationship to violence and war than she had previously thought, and that both men and women shared this, although it took highly gendered forms.

Small states tell for more in favour of freedom and good government[19]

Schreiner was not only concerned with individuals in society, but also with the role of different forms of governments and states. Her desired baseline was a form of state in which government was elected under conditions of full adult suffrage (which did not exist anywhere when she began to write about it), applied from the beginning to South Africa and even when her thinking on 'race' matters was least fully developed. She was also a strong supporter of proportional representation, because of its contribution to the existence of checks and balances on centralised power within a state.

Schreiner thought that, even outside of autocratic systems, there was a strong tendency for a central power or state to disregard, or at least not prioritise, the rights and freedoms of individuals because it was concerned with managing internal differences and potential external conflicts. Her strong preference, from before she returned to Africa in 1889 and held through to her last writings on war and peace, was thus for a federal relationship between a number of small states, in which different political and other arrangements could coexist, provide choice for citizens and act as exemplars for the other states. This was not least because of her analysis of war itself: the checks and balances built into a federal system in her view made it considerably less likely that the governments of these would be able to wage war on other societies, even if they wanted to.

I often ... wonder what all my work would be like when it is done[20]

Olive Schreiner did not produce a programmatic body of feminist social theory, nor did she set out to construct a systematic theorisation of social life. As a consequence, her analyses are not organised around the need to be systematic, nor are they always contained in something labelled as 'theory', nor is every end neatly tied up so that her ideas could exist as a 'thing', a set-piece of intellectual machinery. Instead, her work was produced in response to the particular, organised around ideas conceived in a context, and could as well be produced in allegory, in a narrative story, or in polemic, as in analytical essay or theoretical discussion. Schreiner's, then, is theory conceived piecemeal because conceived responsively and contextually, and in whatever writing genre she thought most appropriate to the ideas and how best to give expression to them. There are also some good reasons to suppose that she had 'in principle' objections to the programmatic notion of social theory.

Schreiner had initially admired and then recoiled from the aridity of Herbert Spencer's social theory, seeing his work as over-systemic and therefore deterministic and static; she also thought it had no human feeling to it. She rejected the 'objective' rationalism of Karl Pearson for similar reasons, seeing his work (for instance, on ethics) as clever and interesting but lacking emotion, and containing some faulty logic about both women and men. Havelock Ellis' early work she saw as lacking human compassion and commitment, while she thought his later writing was too much about 'ideas' and too little about the time and place of its production; she characterised the many volumes of his 'Studies in Sex Psychology' to Cronwright as embodying an obsessional concern with the pathological. Given these reactions to her contemporaries, not only is

Schreiner's approach to social analysis and theory (not that she would have used these terms) very different from the programmatic versions of social theory in general and feminist theory in particular that are now presently dominant, but there are also good reasons to suppose she would have rejected its scholastic abstractionism, its inwardness of gaze on the work of other theorists, its emotional divorce from real world matters and its failure to engage with political developments concerning these.

For Schreiner, theorising about the world – thinking seriously about events and processes and writing conclusions about this – was not a thing in itself, simply an intellectual activity occurring in a vacuum. Instead she saw theorising in the reflectively analytical sense as a means, as a tool to be used to do things with, and in particular so as to effectively engage with and change aspects of social, economic and political life. Schreiner's theory as a body of work is strongly anti-capitalist, anti-imperialist and anti-authoritarian. It not only critiqued these as systems, but also showed their impact at a grounded and human level, regarding social organisation and relationships, concerning labour and how it is organised and given value, and regarding different forms of state and notions of citizenship, for instance. It also engaged with inter-personal forms of politics as well, including how people have relationships and behave towards each other, how children are treated, how women do or don't gossip about each other and to what consequence, and how sexual relationships are conducted.

The theory that Olive Schreiner produced, like each of its constituent writings, has fault-lines – although, of course, what set of ideas developed over nearly fifty years does not? Sometimes her ideas are muddled, or she fails to see where her analysis might be taking her, or she does not spot disjunctures in her thinking between one piece of work and another; and her work also contains elisions, of which colonialism is the most notable, closely followed by heterosexuality. So how are readers to follow Schreiner's changes of mind over time, given the piecemeal nature of what she wrote, its internal fault-lines, and that some of her ideas appear in unfinished pieces of writing or in private letters? How should readers evaluate the result as an 'oeuvre'? Readers should follow these shifts, I think, in the same spirit, the same frame of mind, that Schreiner produced them – that is, by recognising the importance of the particular, the local, the grounded, in being able analytically to comprehend the general and the global and thus to sensibly theorise about them. As for how to evaluate the result, what it 'adds up to' as a body of work, the most important aspect of this I think is to read her published work in a serious way. That is, it involves reading it from her earliest written novels, through her allegories and essays, the novella, to the posthumous publications, including the three presently published collections of letters. It also involves resisting generalising about Schreiner or her ideas from paragraphs taken from here and there, or from individual pieces of work.

Olive Schreiner produced a set of analytical ideas that add up to more than the sum of the parts, and these constitute 'a theory' of a non-programmatic, mixed genre, contextually-grounded, responsive and reflectively analytical kind. Many of its 'fault-lines', as I've called them, are things that in fact result from its particular strengths, and this too should be kept in mind. That is, because her writing was responsive and grounded in events as these were happening, it doesn't have a 'now I shall theorise about X' quality to it. If X wasn't on the agenda of the things that were happening, then X remained absent from Schreiner's analytical concerns. Also X2 might well differ from X1 and so the disjunctures in Schreiner's thinking about them may indicate real world differences and not just intellectual loose ends. And some of the other fault-lines exist because of Schreiner's refusal to 'know her place', theoretically speaking. She certainly did not stay within the conventional parameters of what was 'fit work for women theorists', around domestic divisions, the family and traditional spheres of women's work. Consequently she produced feminist theory of an unbounded kind, taking all of social, economic and political life as her province. No wonder there are loose ends.

Some 'Was She...?' Questions and Answers

Here I want to consider some of the 'was she...?' questions that have been asked about Olive Schreiner's work and about her political and intellectual values. As the preceding discussion has touched on most of these, my responses will simply draw together and state succinctly my view of these things.

Was she... a misogynist?

No, but she didn't think women were angels either. This question arises because of divorcing the things that Schreiner wrote about women from the contexts in which she wrote them. Along with this, she didn't see women as merely victims of oppression; indeed, she thought that the effects of oppression could be very negative and also produce behaviours which were damaging to other people. Rather than misogyny, I'd say instead that she refused to romanticise oppression, thought it was a dirty and horrible business that affected the oppressed in sometimes appalling ways. For instance, she didn't approve of the massacre of whites by the Ndebele and Shona in 1896, although she appreciated why this happened. She also thought that many women's trivial lives produced people who thought and behaved trivially and sometimes also very destructively, as with gossip and its effects.

Was she... a maternalist?

No, not at all. This comes from misreading passages in Schreiner's writing, particularly in *Woman and Labour* and the essays that preceded it, by taking them out of their argumentative contexts, so that it is assumed that she saw mothering as a biologically determined thing that only women do. I am much more sympathetic to the argument that in fact she over-estimates the importance of caring within social reproduction and as a form of social labour, but I think she does this for both women and men.

Was she... a social Darwinist?

Certainly not. Schreiner wasn't even a 'reform Darwinist', but rather an out and out anti-Darwinist. She had a good deal of admiration for Darwin and his ideas, but she didn't see Darwinism as coterminous with Darwin. She thought of Darwinism as simply an extremely interesting system of thought, not a discovery nor 'absolute fact', and she fundamentally disagreed with its major precepts while agreeing with other aspects.

Was she... a racist?

Perhaps; it depends on what is meant by this. Schreiner was certainly brought up to be prejudiced, and not only about black people. But she didn't want to be, she tried not to be, and in relation to black people she came to see this as an evil which had to be rooted out and ended. The way to do this at a personal level, she thought, was to conduct oneself as though one believed in absolute equality; and at a societal level she thought that the franchise and the form of government or state were also important. She changed her mind radically about some aspects of 'race' over her life-time, moving from liberal patronage, through subsuming 'race' within questions of labour, to seeing racism as deep-seated prejudice and fundamentally wrong, to supporting freedom movements. And even at her most radical on 'race' matters, she never fell into the (also racist) trap of romanticising black people as somehow innately paragons of all the virtues. Consequently I am intrigued as to how her ideas would have developed had her health been better and she had had ten more 'writing years' in her life.

I also think that some white commentators try to prove their radical credentials by criticising others, always others, for racism. They assume that Schreiner, like anyone who is a white South African, must 'by definition' be racist, and so they hunt beneath the surface for examples of racism to 'prove' this. This misreads 'South Africa' over the last hundred years as well as Schreiner herself, and should be seen as contemptuous towards the great complexities of its history and politics, and indeed those of racism to boot.

Was she... an essentialist?

No. In fact Schreiner was a complete social constructionist, to the extent that many people still gasp when they grasp just how radically she dismissed 'biology'. She is sometimes described as essentialist because it exists in a litany with the tags of maternalism and social Darwinism, as in 'she's an essentialist, maternalist social Darwinist' (which seems to be considerably worse than murdering babies). 'Essentialist' has become a convenient way of dismissing ideas and work without having to think too much about them – it acts as an 'ad feminam' judgement that consigns ideas and persons to an intellectual dustbin and is a very slipshod way of dealing with people you think you won't agree with.

And a Few 'Why Did She...?' Ones

Here I want to consider, again very briefly, some questions that follow from my largely positive assessment of Schreiner's ideas and writings, compared with some much more critical evaluations of it by other commentators. In doing so, I fully recognise, as I indicated in Chapter 4, that I am by no means alone in thinking highly of Schreiner's work and that the views stated below are shared by some of the key interpreters of Schreiner's writing.

Why my positive response?

My work proceeds from what Schreiner herself wrote, and it pays attention to the contexts that her ideas and arguments addressed as well as these ideas and arguments themselves. I have also taken no judgement (positive as well as negative) of Schreiner's work or her person made by other people 'on trust' but explored it via the archival evidence. And in working in this way, my reading of the unpublished materials, the primary archive sources, and in particular all the unpublished letters, has inestimably affected the way I think about Schreiner's work. This accounts for many, although not all, of the differences between my assessments and understandings and those of the Schreiner scholars whose interpretations I respond most positively to.

Why the more critical response?

There seem to be five important things, minimally, in producing a more critical response from some commentators, none of which are mutually-exclusive of the others. Some of these commentators just really do not like or agree with Schreiner's approach or ideas. Some commentators have been (unduly) influenced by assessments of Schreiner's work or 'personality' deriving from Cronwright-Schreiner. Some have developed a fetish with 'the text', which has often been small sections of one piece of Schreiner's writing only. Others have adopted the unscholarly habit of generalising from recycled references in secondary literature without investigating original sources (by which I mean Schreiner's published work as well as the archival materials). Also the kind of feminist misogyny that has been ascribed to Schreiner inflects some of the responses to her: people want her to be exemplary and can't forgive her for being flawed; and behind this lurks the fear of being seen as 'cultists' and (gasp, horror) feminists.

Why did she vanish?

As for why Olive Schreiner has 'vanished' from sight as a considerable social commentator and theorist, there is another book in this! The short answer, the only one possible here, glosses like mad over all complexities to list:

- Cronwright-Schreiner 'fixing' the sources as and when he could, thus inhibiting alternative contemporary views and shaping future responses, until the primacy of archival sources was asserted in the work of First and Scott and then Rive;

- massive changes to the zeitgeist of ideas and the language of analytical discourse post-1918;

- the severe retraction of feminism post-1918, its 'loss of memory' concerning its progenitors, and the demise of most of its formerly strong international bonds;

- the 1960s renaissance of feminism around ideas about sexual liberation that for a long while prevented the new scholarship from sensibly comprehending that Schreiner and others of her generation thought differently, lived differently, and that 'the past is another country';

- the compartmentalisation of academic feminism and the dismembering of the Schreiner corpus: limbs to the historians, carcase to the literary lot, entrails to...

A Final Comment

I shall conclude with two comments, in fact. The first of them is mine and, as is fitting, the person who has the last word is Olive Schreiner herself.

My comment is this. With whatever their faults, elisions and sometimes muddles, Olive Schreiner's writings overall represent a major achievement in terms of 'a feminist theorising the world'. Conceived piecemeal, they still ''add up' as a coherent body of ideas and thinking; and looked at together they constitute 'a theory', albeit not of the now seemingly ubiquitous abstract programmatic kind. As an analytical framework, Schreiner's theory takes her to places that the vast majority of present-day feminist theory does not go: it knows its place and it stays well within it, while Olive Schreiner thankfully never did. This is the modest estimate of Olive Schreiner's theoretical achievements as a 'woman of ideas' and as a social theorist. A less modest one says – show me who has done better, who has seen further, among contemporary and present-day feminist theorists than her. And Olive Schreiner's comment is this:

> *I fix my thoughts in the future, even the very far future which is yet so near in the life of the race where so many will reach what we have only dreamed of.*[21]

Notes

1   This is also dominated by networks of male social theorists, who only rarely permit the theory of women to enter the sacred portals of the social theory temple. For discussions which focus on the exclusionarty practices of masculinist social theory, and some of the same characteristics within its feminist variant, see Eadie 2001 and Stanley and Wise 2000 respectively.

2   And see here Stanley 2000e for some more distinctively sociological examples of this approach to theorising.

3   In doing so, I am not picking out absolutely everything; many points referred to earlier will not be commented on here; while a few others – like Schreiner's view that national game reserves should be created in Southern Africa, or her thoughts about the relationship between the state and political architecture – have not been discussed at all.

4   "Preface", *An African Farm*.

5   Showalter 1993, 1997.

6   I can think of examples from the succeeding generation, however.

7   *An African Farm* p.83 and also the epigraph to Part II, p.113.

8   This is the first chapter in Part II of *An African Farm*.

9   *An English South African's View* p.87.

10 *Thoughts* pp.340-1.

11 OS to Will Schreiner, 10 May 1908, UCT Schreiner.

12 OS to Karl Pearson, 12 July 1885, London Pearson, Rive 1988 p.65.

13 *W&L* p.67.

14   Olive Schreiner to Jan Smuts, 28 October 1919, Central Archives Depot Pretoria, copy in SAL Schreiner, Clayton 1983 p.131-2.

15   *W&L.*

16   This is my re-working of two phrases of Schreiner's, on social labour and on value, from *W&L.* ·

17   *W&L* p.185.

18   *The Letters* Appendix 1 p.401.

19   OS to Will Schreiner, 14 Sept 1899, UCT Schreiner, Rive 1988 pp.378-9.

20   "I often – no, I don't, but I did just now – wonder what all my work would be like when it is done. It's funny how one works blindly in the dark, following an instinct, never knowing what one's work will be like. It's not really stranger than when bees make their nests..."; see OS to Havelock Ellis, 14 February 1899, *The Letters* p.155.

21   By 'race' here, Schreiner means 'humanity', the human race. OS to Anna Purcell, and SAL Schreiner 2.9.8.

Appendix
Schreiner Writings and Archive Collections

1. Published Writings

The Story of An African Farm
First published in two volumes in 1883 by Chapman and Hall, London, as *The Story of An African Farm*, A Novel by Ralph Iron. The edition used in this book is an 1892 edition 'by Ralph Iron (Olive Schreiner)' published by Chapman and Hall, London.

Dreams
First published in 1890 by Unwin, London. The edition used in this book is an 'Author's Edition' published in the USA in 1891 by Roberts Brothers, Boston.

Dream Life And Real Life, A Little African Story
First published in 1893 by Unwin, London. The edition used in this book is a reprint by the Academy Press, Chicago, of the 1909 edition by Little, Brown, Boston.

The Political Situation
First published in 1896 by Unwin, London. The first edition of the Unwin book is the version used here, not the original 1895 pamphlet issued by the Cape Times Printing Works for the original reading in Kimberly Town Hall.

Trooper Peter Halket Of Mashonaland
First published in 1897 by Unwin, London. The edition used in this book is the first edition.

'The Woman Question'
Originally published in in two parts in the New York *The Cosmopolitan* in 1899. This essay is reprinted in Barash 1987 pp.65-100.

An English South African's View Of The Situation. Words In Season
Originally published as newspaper articles. First published in book form in 1899 by Hodder and Stoughton, London. The edition used in this book is the first edition.

'A Letter On The Jew'

First published by H. Lieberman, *Cape Town*. Read at a Jewish Territorial Organisation meeting, Cape Town, 1 July 1906 and published in the Cape Times, 2 July 1906. A shortened and edited version was published as an appendix in *The Letters of Olive Schreiner*.

Closer Union

First published in the *Transvaal Leader*, 22 December 1908. Published as a book in 1909 by Fifield, London. A shortened and edited version was published as an appendix in *The Letters of Olive Schreiner*. The version used in this book is the 1909 first edition published by Fifield.

Woman and Labour

First published in 1911 by Unwin, London. The edition used in this book is the first edition.

'Olive Schreiner's Message to those who refuse Military Service for the sake of higher service'

Published in 1916 by the No Conscription Fellowship, Leaflet no 6, London.

'Conscientious Objectors'

Published on 16 March 1916, *Labour Leader*. Reprinted as Appendix H in *The Life*, pp.398-9.

'Letter to a Peace Meeting held under the Auspices of the Union of Democratic Control'

Published as Appendix I in *The Life*, pp.400-1.

"The Dawn of Civilisation"

An edited version of a longer essay also called "The Dawn of Civilisation", published in the *Nation and Antheneum* 26 March 1921. Both this and the two (rather different) archived versions of the manuscript are used and quoted from in this book. The 1921 version was reprinted in *Stories, Dreams and Allegories* from the second edition on.

Thoughts On South Africa

First published in 1923 by Unwin, London. The edition used in this book is a 1976 reprint from the first edition by the Africana Book Society, Johannesburg.

Stories, Dreams and Allegories

First published in 1923 by Unwin, London; the 1924 edition also includes a reprint of the article of "The Dawn of Civilisation". The edition used in this book is the first edition.

From Man To Man; Or, Perhaps Only ...

First published in 1926 by Unwin, London. The edition used in this book is the first edition.

Undine
First published in 1929 by Earnest Benn, London and New York. The edition used in this book is the first edition.

'Diamond Fields'
First published in 1974 edited and introduced by Richard Rive (1974) in *English in Africa* 1, 1, pp.1-28.

'Introduction To The Life Of Mary Wollstonecraft And The Rights Of Woman'
Originally written possibly in 1889, and first published in 1994, edited and introduced by Carolyn Burdett (1994b) in *History Workshop Journal* 37, pp.189-93.

'My First Adventure At The Cape', By Paulinsky Smith (Olive Schreiner)
First published in the *New College Magazine* in 1882; introduced by Helen Bradford (1994) and published in *English in Africa* 21, nos 1&2, pp.21-32.

2. Archive Sources

It sometimes seems as though there is not an archive in the English-speaking world that does not contain a few Schreiner letters. The major collections are outlined below in alphabetical order by country, thus South Africa followed by the UK followed by the USA, and also within country.

Cory Library, Rhodes University, Grahamstown, South Africa.
The Schreiner material held by the Cory Library at Rhodes University consists of two small groups of letters from Olive Schreiner: to the Rev John Cross from the middle and late 1890s containing comments on a number of her writings, Rhodes and the coming war; and to Alf Mattison, a British socialist friend and sometime lover of Edward Carpenter. In addition, there is an important General Missionary Commission collection 'on the so-called black peril', of which Schreiner was a Commission member, which contains a number of her letters.

National English Literary Museum, Grahamstown, South Africa.
NELM was founded to promote the reading and appreciation of all forms of African literature written in English. Its collections are extensive and contain the works of contemporary as well as past African writers in English and are not confined to those of 'literary figures'. Its important Olive Schreiner collection contains typescripts and some manuscripts of Schreiner's writings, as well as various of her surviving journal entries, and a large collection of diaries, notes, letters and other writings by Cronwright-Schreiner. Two important sets of Schreiner letters (to Havelock Ellis, and to Mimmie (Mrs Haldane) Murray have recently been added to the NELM Schreiner holdings.

South Africa Library, Cape Town, South Africa.

The SAL is the national reference library of South Africa, and its Schreiner materials are housed in its Special Collections Department. Its Olive Schreiner and the Olive Schreiner 'Miscellaneous' collections are of particular importance. The Olive Schreiner collection contains a number of Schreiner manuscripts and fragments of manuscripts, typescripts, and proof copies, and also a large numbers of Schreiner letters. The 'Miscellaneous' collection contains all Schreiner material subsequent to the original collection. Related SAL collections include the W.P. Schreiner, Anna Purcell, John X. Merriman, S.C. Cronwright, Betty Tetlow and Karel Schoeman Collections.

University of Cape Town, Archives & Manuscripts Department, Cape Town, South Africa.

The Archives and Manuscripts Department collection of Schreiner material contains the largest single concentration of Schreiner letters. Material written by Schreiner originally contained in other UCT collections have been integrated within the principal Schreiner collection, apart from the letters from Schreiner to her sister Ettie, which remain in the Schreiner-Hemming collection. The Schreiner letters are organised in time periods rather than per correspondent and this gives a very different 'feel' to them, compared with reading individual sets of letters. Major correspondents here include Mary Brown, Jessie Rose Innes, May Murray Parker (a niece of Betty Molteno's), Fan Schreiner, Ettie Stakesby Lewis, Betty Molteno, Will Schreiner. As a collection, the UCT Schreiner letters are deeply embedded in South Africa, its politics, imperialist expansion, the coming of war, and the post-war reconfiguration of politics afterwards.

University of the Witwatersrand, Historical Papers, William Cullen Library, Johannesburg, South Africa.

This archive contains, among other relevant material, a collection of letters sent by Olive Schreiner to her older sister Katie, as well as family letters about her and also photographs, within the Findlay Family Papers.

University of London, The Library, London, UK.

The Karl Pearson Collection in the University of London archive collections contains Pearson's letters, manuscripts and other papers. The collection includes material relating to his involvement in the Men and Women's Club; it contains a group of letters to him from Olive Schreiner which related primarily to the organisation and intellectual concerns of the Club and its members.

City of Sheffield Public Library, Local Studies Unit, Sheffield, UK.

The Edward Carpenter Collection in the Local Studies Unit is a large and comprehensive one, containing letters sent to Carpenter as well as his manuscripts, books and other papers. Carpenter's letter books include a group of letters written to him by Olive Schreiner in the earlier period of their friendship.

Harry Ransome Humanities Research Center, University of Texas at Austin, USA.

The HRC contains a good chunk of the letters, manuscripts and other papers of literary England from the mid-Victorian period onwards. With regard to Olive Schreiner, there are two key collections: the Havelock Ellis collection, which contains letters and others papers sent or given to Ellis by Schreiner; and the Olive Schreiner collection, which contains Schreiner manuscripts and typescripts and also letters sent to her by Ellis. The HRC also holds a large number of related relevant collections, including Edward Carpenter, John Addington Symonds, Arthur Symons and Oscar Wilde collections.

References and Annotated Bibliography

Philip Abrams (1982) *Historical Sociology* Shepston Mallet, Somerset, England: Open Books Publishing Ltd.

Loren Anthony (1999) "Buried narratives: masking the sign of history in *The Story of an African Farm*" *Scrutiny* 2 4, 2, pp.3-13. Uses some of Derrida's ideas, not entirely plausibly, to look at history, time, the past and death in *An African Farm*.

Ann Ardis (1990) *New Women, New Novels: Feminisim and Early Modernism* New Brunswick: Rutgers University Press.

Arai Noriko (1998) "The Japanese New Women and Motherhood: The Japanization of Western Feminism" MA dissertation, Women's Studies Centre, University of Manchester.

Carol Barash (1986) "Virile womanhood: Olive Schreiner's fantasies of a master race" *Women's Studies International Forum* 9, pp.333-40. Starting with "Preferring male to female friendship, considering herself different from other women, and keeping her distance from organized feminism" (p.333), Barash provides a one-dimensional interpretation of Schreiner's writings as an example of social Darwinism and thus racism. Barash's approach is discussed in Chapter 4.

Carol Barash (ed, 1987) *An Olive Schreiner Reader: Writings on Women and South Africa* London: Pandora Press. Extracts from a wide variety of Schreiner's writings, preceded by an 'Introduction' by Barash and an 'Afterword' by Gordimer (1980). The approaches of both Barash and Gordimer are discussed in Chapter 4.

Tina Barsby (1995) *Olive Schreiner An Introduction* NELM Introductions series no. 2, Grahamstown, South Africa: National English Literary Manuscripts. A useful introductory guide with a primarily biographical focus, which also includes discussion of the context of Schreiner's writing.

Gillian Beer (1983) *Darwin's Plots: Evolutionary Narrative in Darwin, George Eliot, and Nineteenth-Century Fiction* London: Routledge & Kegan Paul. An important discussion of Darwin's work and the 'fictive' elements used to presented his ideas. Noting that in Darwin's life-time boundaries between scientific and other ways of writing and thinking hardly existed, so that an 'educated reader' could have immediate access to scientific writing and ideas, she comments "What is remarkable about the mid and late nineteenth century is that instead of ignoring or rebutting attempts to set scientific writing and literature side by side, as is sometimes the case in our own time, both novelists and scientists were very much aware of the potentialities released by the congruities of their methods and ends.... It is perhaps not surprising that the novelists turned to science for confirmation. But the scientists, too, drew upon literary evidence and models, and were aware of the imaginative nature of their enterprise." (p.91). Riveting reading.

Gillian Beer (1989) "Representing women: re-presenting the past" in (eds) Catherine Belsey & Jane Moore *The Feminist Reader* London: Macmillan, pp.63-78. Raises some interesting and difficult issues in a stimulating way.

Ridley Beeton (1974) *Olive Schreiner, A Short Guide to Her Writings* Cape Town: Howard Timmins. Beeton's main concern is to provide an interpretation of Schreiner's writings, but also summarises writings about Schreiner by Uys Krige, Vera Buchannan-Gould, Marion Friedmann, D.L. Hobman, and Johannes Meintjes. Some of Beeton's readings now seem outdated, but his insistence on the importance of Schreiner's writings on South Africa remains needed.

Ridley Beeton (1987) *Facets of Olive Schreiner: A Manuscript Sourcebook* Johannesburg: Donker. Beeton aims to convey, using a wide variety of primary manuscript sources, "a warm, modest, arrogant, angry, loving, erratic and brilliant woman" (p.11). Criticised for some of its transcriptions (a point it makes about earlier work), a very interesting aspect of Beeton's 'sourcebook' approach is that it provides a narrative of his archival work, including his conjectures and reflections as well as his conclusions.

James Belich (1988) *The New Zealand Wars and The Victorian Interpretation of Racial Conflict* Auckland, New Zealand: Penguin.

Mary Benson (1963) *The African Patriots: The Story of the African National Congress of South Africa* London: Faber.

Joyce Avrech Berkman (1979) *Olive Schreiner: Feminism on the Frontier* St Alban's, Vermont: Eden Press. One of the earliest feminist reassessments of Schreiner's life and work, its approach still stands up remarkably well. Berkman's approach is discussed in Chapter 4.

Joyce Avrech Berkman (1989) *The Healing Imagination of Olive Schreiner: Beyond South African Colonialism* Oxford: Plantin Publishers. One of the key interpretations of Schreiner's work, Berkman's book focuses on Schreiner's writings and contextualises Schreiner's work in relation to Victorian ideas. I discuss Berkman's approach in Chapter 4.

Vivian Bickford-Smith (1995) *Ethnic Pride and Racial Prejudice in Victorian Cape Town: Group Identity and Social Practices, 1875–1902* Oxford: Blackwell.

Lucy Bland (1990) "Rational love or spiritual love? The Men and Women's Club of the 1880s" *Women's Studies International Forum* 13, pp. 33-48. An in-depth look at discussions on 'the woman question' and 'the problem of men', including in the organisation and composition of the Men and Women's Club. Interestingly compared with Walkowitz (1986, 1992), Bland focuses on the dynamic of debate as well as its content, and how both underpinned the gendered nature of interaction between Club members, including the 'scientific' way its male members used Darwinist ideas to confirm their 'rational' and 'objective' approach. An extended version appears in Chapter 2 of Bland 1995.

Lucy Bland (1995) *Banishing the Beast: English Feminism & Sexual Morality 1885–1914* Harmondsworth: Penguin. An interesting and analytically important account of English sexual politics between 1885 and 1914, *Banishing the Beast* investigates "the various and contradictory ways in which English feminists discussed and campaigned around issues of sexual morality" (p. xvii) in a way which does not 'homogenize' feminist positions but instead recognises that "Feminist politics were complex, contradictory, and not easily compartmentalised into two opposing camps" (p. xix). It looks at challenges to and reworkings of Darwinist ideas by feminists, and should help move discussion on from the one-dimensional notion of social Darwinism sometimes found in Schreiner commentary.

Helen Bradford (1994) "Introducing Paulinsky Smith" *English in Africa* special issue on 'Revisions' vol 21, nos 1&2, pp.1-20. 'The Husband', as she terms him, stalks the pages of Bradford's Introduction to Schreiner's "My first adventure at the Cape' published in 1882 under the pseudonym of Paulinsky Smith. She proposes that he "suppressed and distorted" (p.4) this and a linked short story to hide Schreiner's supposed affair with Julius Gau in 1872. She astutely comments on Schreiner's story, which "mocks the masculinity and intelligence of a newly arrived Englishman, [and] bears little trace of being written to amuse British schoolboys in an era of ascendant imperialism" (p.5). Bradford's conclusion requires her to ignore the fact that Cronwright's wholesale destruction was not directed at these two stories in particular. It is more likely that Cronwright disliked the 'mocking' (as would befit the author of 'The Koranna Diamond', a deservedly unpublished sub-Rider Haggard adventure story filled with appalling gratuitous violence).

Helen Bradford (1995) "*Olive Schreiner*'s 'series of abortions': fact, fiction and teenage abortion" *Journal of Southern African Studies* 21, 4, pp.623-41. Bradford proposes that when Schreiner lived in Dordrecht in 1872, there was a scandal, "arguably the single most important event transforming an obscure teenager into a world-famous novelist" (p.623). She contends that "Primary sources relating to this period were destroyed; *it is impossible to provide conclusive evidence* of what 'really happened'. *Nevertheless*... the most likely interpretation of events is that Olive Schreiner fell pregnant in 1872, contributed to her own miscarriage, and repeatedly reworked this painful experience in fiction" (p.623, my emphasis). Bradford leaps off from this all-powering 'nevertheless' to ignore the fact that there is no evidence for any of the 'events' outlined, only Schreiner's use in her fiction of the term 'abortion' and two biographical facts: what Schreiner herself described as an eating problem which led to the temporary cessation of her periods; and her later remarks about gossip from her Dordrecht days. *Contra* Bradford, Cronwright destroyed with an even-hand and there is no evidence he took a different approach to anything from this period. Schoeman 1991 contains a similar contention; and I discuss Schoeman's general approach in Chapter 4.

Helen Bradford (1996) "Women, gender and colonialism: rethinking the history of the British Cape Colony and its frontier zones" *Journal of African History* 37 pp.351-70. A very useful critique of the state of historical scholarship on the South African states prior to 1910 and its elision of gender as an important dimension of all aspects of South African society.

Ruth Brandon (1990) *The New Women and the Old Men: Love, Sex and the Woman Question* London: Secker & Warburg. An interesting although idiosyncratic account of Olive Schreiner and her relationship with Havelock Ellis appears in Chapters 1 and 2. Other relationships discussed by Brandon include those between Eleanor Marx and Edward Aveling, Havelock Ellis and Edith Lees, H.G. Wells and various women, Sidney and Beatrice Webb, and Havelock Ellis and Margaret Sanger. There are many inaccuracies in the material on Schreiner and those connected with her, but the book is worth reading if not always believing because it tells a good story and because of the interest of its general theme.

Joseph Bristow (1992) "Introduction" to *The Story of An African Farm* Oxford: Oxford University Press World's Classic, pp.vii-xxix. A lucid and insightful account of Olive Schreiner's narrative techniques in *An African Farm*. Bristow is alive to the influences and success of Schreiner's novel, points out it was more daring about sex than any novel then published, and links Schreiner's narrative inventiveness to the ways she handled this theme in this novel. In dealing with Schreiner's ideas on a larger canvass, Bristow falls into blanket invocations of 'social Darwinism', erroneously insisting that "her social Darwinism is in evidence on many pages of the book" (p.xii). Paradoxically, however, he also notes that "Boldly contending against the sexist biases of the sexual evolutionists", her analysis of 'sex parasitism' in *Woman and Labour* "turned their steadfastly Darwinian rhetoric inside-out to make far-sighted feminist connections between intellectual and manual labour and that other – and often forgotten – 'labour' of bearing children." (p.xxv). One of the most insightful contemporary discussions of *An African Farm* and its part in Schreiner's larger concerns as a writer.

Vera Brittain (1933) *Testament of Youth: An Autobiographical Study of the Years 1900–1925* London: Victor Gollancz.

Mary Brown (1937) "Recollections of Olive Schreiner" in (eds) Angela James and Nina Hills *The Life of Mrs John Brown Including her Recollections of Olive Schreiner* London: John Murray, pp.183-205.

Vera Buchanan-Gould (1948) *Not Without Honour: The Life and Writings of Olive Schreiner* London: Hutchinson. A hagiographic early biography of Schreiner that more often than not alienates by virtue of its superlatives. It is the source of two unproven 'facts' about Schreiner: an 'affair', and her 'renouncement' of Ellis, which derive more from mild fantasy than from 'the record'.

Carolyn Burdett (1992) "Thrown together: Olive Schreiner, writing and politics" in (ed) Kate Campbell *Critical Feminism: Argument in the Discipline* Milton Keynes: Open University Press, pp.107-121. Burdett's argument depends upon an assumed synonymity between Schreiner's 'Introduction' to Wollstonecraft's *A Vindication of the Rights of Woman*, the 'sex book' which Schreiner positions *Woman and Labour* as a part, and her allegorical short story "The Buddhist Priest's Wife". A more satisfactory version appears in her 1994a article, while Burdett's wider approach is discussed in Chapter 4.

Carolyn Burdett (1994a) 'A difficult vindication: Olive Schreiner's Wollstonecraft Introduction' *History Workshop Journal* 37, pp.177-187. An introduction to the fragment of Olive Schreiner's planned introduction to Wollstonecraft's *A Vindication of the Rights of Woman* (which follows in the same issue of *History Workshop Journal*). While there are problems here in assigning to Schreiner (and putatively other women in the Men and Women's Club) what is actually Pearson's social Darwinism, this is a more rounded account of problems faced by Schreiner in attempting to assimilate a non-Western heritage than Burdett 1992. I discuss Burdett's approach in Chapter 4.

Carolyn Burdett (1994b) "Review essay: Olive Schreiner revisited" *English in Africa* special issue on 'Revisions' vol 21, nos 1&2, pp.221-32. An interesting and useful review essay in which Carolyn Burdett reviews reprints of work by Schreiner (*Trooper Peter Halket* and *Thoughts on South Africa*), and two books about Schreiner's work (Vivian 1990 and Berkman 1990). I discuss Burdett's re-readings in the context of her wider interpretive approach in Chapter 4.

Carolyn Burdett (1999) "Love, death and money in Mashonaland" *Kunapipi: Journal of Post-Colonial Writing* 21, 3, pp.36-44. An interesting discussion of *Trooper Peter Halket* in the context of war pamphleteering from Conan Doyle and from W.T. Stead, and it is commented on as part of Burdett's general approach in Chapter 4.

Carolyn Burdett (2001) *Olive Schreiner and the Progress of Feminism: Evolution, Gender, Empire* London: Palgrave. An extremely interesting re-reading of Schreiner's published writings. Social Darwinism no longer appears as a dominant reading of (or imposition on) Schreiner's work, which Burdett locates in the context of contemporary political and literary events and sees as an engagement with, and attempt to push the boundaries of, 'an irreducibly colonial history', by means of Schreiner's critiques of progress, evolution and imperialism. One of Burdett's arguments, looked at in detail in Chapter 2 but falling across other parts of her book, is that Schreiner shaped her ideas and analyses as responses to Pearson's. The result is that Person becomes a Svengali figure in relation to Schreiner's theorizing, presenting Schreiner's work on a narrower and more 'personalised' platform than I think is supportable. But that aside, this is an important account of Schreiner's work. Burdett's approach herein, while a more 'literary' and text-centered one than my own, is also concerned with aspects of the broad context Schreiner was working in. Again, this book is discussed as part of Burdett's developing approach in Chapter 4.

Edward Carpenter (1916) *My Days and Dreams* London: George Allen & Unwin. An oddly constrained account of issues and people in his life for a man professedly so open. Carpenter's friendship with Olive Schreiner is dealt with in one of the two chapters which are a Cook's tour of 'personalities', including Henry Fawcett, William Morris, Henry Hyndman, Henry Salt and Kate Salt, Havelock Ellis and Edith Lees, as well as Schreiner herself. The reader is given no impression of the meaning or relative importance of any of these people in Carpenter's life. His remarks on Schreiner are concerned with her when he first met her and some aspects of her writing, particularly its 'ineradicable pessimism'.

Ellen Miller Casey (1996) "Edging women out? Reviews of women novelists in the *Athenaeum*, 1860-1900" *Victorian Studies* 39, pp.151-73.

Bruce Cauthen (1997) "The myth of divine election and Afrikaner ethnogenesis" in (eds) Geoffey Hosking and George Schopflin *Myths and Nationhood* London: Hurst & Co, pp. 107-31.

Larry Ceplair (ed, 1991) *Charlotte Perkins Gillman: A Non-Fiction Reader* New York: Columbia University Press.

Laura Chrisman (1990) "Allegory, feminist thought and the *Dreams* of Olive Schreiner" *Prose Studies: History, Theory, Criticism* 13, pp. 126-150. Chrisman sees the 1880s as a period of crucial development in Schreiner's work and focuses on Schreiner's *Dreams*, although her Hunter's allegory from *An African Farm* is also discussed. Chrisman reads the concluding passage of an African woman's lament to Schreiner in her " Wollstonecraft Introduction" as a literal event rather than being allegorical. Chrisman argues "Allegory is, like labour itself in Schreiner's theory of value, the activity of freedom, the site of the struggle for the realisation, or freeing, from oppression. But it is a site of freedom that is, in many respects, indistinguishable from oppression... The allegories are not the less important for the impasse they enact, however; it is on the contrary because of their contradictions that they remain significant" (pp. 148-9).

Laura Chrisman (1993) "Colonialism and feminism in Olive Schreiner's 1890s fiction" *English in Africa* 20, pp.25-38. Chrisman examines Schreiner's formal discourse about Empire and white women as commodities and her representations of black women as agents of resistance. Chrisman stresses "those radical and oppositional elements in Schreiner's writing in which her overdetermined implication in the prisonhouse of racist and imperial thinking is interrogated" (p.26), and so by implication (through her use of the term 'prisonhouse'), Chrisman draws on Gordimer 1980. However, her approach at best rejects seeing Schreiner as straightforwardly racist.

Laura Chrisman (1995) "Empire, 'race' and feminism at the *fin de siècle*: the work of George Egerton and Olive Schreiner" in (ed) Sally Ledger & Scott McCracken *Cultural Politics at the Fin de Siècle* Cambridge University Press, Cambridge, pp.45-65. Mainly concerned with the work of Egerton, Chrisman discusses three short stories Schreiner wrote between 1887 and 1892 ("The Woman's Rose", "The Policy in Favour of Protection", and "The Child's Day"). She concludes these are marked by anxieties and ambiguities: "In these texts... black Africa is the point at which identification, for white female subjectivity, stops; it also marks the point where the possibility of metaphor ends, and ideological anxieties about inexorable repressive laws of social and physical determinism receive their most intense expression... white femininity is, for Schreiner, simultaneously inextricable from, and irreducible to, concepts of colonies and empires" (p.62). Hmm.

Cherry Clayton (ed, 1983) *Olive Schreiner* Johannesburg: McGraw-Hill. Cherry Clayton has been an extremely important presence in the 'rediscovery' of Schreiner and her work, and this is a very useful collection. Its contents include: 1. 'Literary background', a series of short largely contemporary pieces about Schreiner and her work by Havelock Ellis, Mary Brown, Edith Lees and Olive Renier among others, 2. 'Contemporary reviews' of Schreiner's main publications, including by Edward Aveling, Canon MacColl, Rider Haggard, Arthur Symons, L.P. Hartley, Hugh Walpole, Virginia Woolf and Nadine Gordimer. 3. 'Journals and Letters', extracts from Schreiner's extant archived journals and a number of letters, some not appearing in any other secondary source. 4. 'Symposium', a collection of articles concerned with Schreiner's work.

Cherry Clayton (1985) "Olive Schreiner: life into fiction" *English in Africa* 12, pp.29-40. Clayton sensibly criticises the assumption that what happened in Schreiner's life can be read from what happens in her fiction. She also insightfully emphasises that many commentators lack "local material and South African contact" (p.31), so that Schreiner's involvement in South Africa is treated as parochial. She concludes that there are "problematic areas in the handling of a colonial woman writer's life, and in basic biographical methodology... related partly to unquestioned assumptions about the relationship between an artist and society, and... the relationship between life and literature" (p.33). Quite.

Cherry Clayton (1989) "Olive Schreiner: paradoxical pioneer" in (ed) Cherry Clayton *Women and Writing in South Africa: A Critical Anthology* Marshaltown, South Africa: Heinemann Southern Africa, pp.42-59. Here Clayton discusses the relationship between Schreiner's work and that of Mary Wollstonecraft and John Stuart Mill, points out Schreiner's greater radicalism, outlines the colonial context of Schreiner's upbringing, provides a critique of *An African Farm*" (p.51), and proposes there is an 'internalised split' in Schreiner's as in other women's writing.

Cherry Clayton (1990) "'A case for the indigenous': Olive Schreiner in South Africa" *South African Historical Journal* 22, pp.184-91. An interesting review of Schoeman's (in English translation, 1991) originally Afrikaans study of Schreiner's life in South Africa from 1855 to 1881, Clayton gives Schoeman his due as a meticulous researcher while noting two problems with his broader approach: his dismissal of the 'worth' of Schreiner's writing while also claiming her importance as a writer in South Africa; and his occasional extrapolations well beyond what his archival evidence supports.

Cherry Clayton (1997) *Olive Schreiner* (Twayne's World Authors Series) New York: Twayne Publishers. Clayton's *Olive Schreiner* provides 'a guide' to Schreiner's major writings with only a subsidiary focus upon her life. It usefully discusses most of Schreiner's major writings, and surprisingly relies rather uncritically on Schoeman's account of Schreiner's early life. Notable omissions are *The Political Situation*, "The Dawn of Civilisation", and Schreiner's letters. A very tightly written book, it gives little away about what Clayton thinks about most of the writings she discusses. This is deeply disappointing, for Clayton is one of the most context-aware and knowleadgeable Schreiner scholars.

C.L. Cline (1970) *The Letters of George Meredith* Oxford: Clarendon Press.

John M. Coetzee (1988) *White Writing: On the Culture of Letters in South Africa* New Haven: Yale University Press.

Jean and John Comaroff (1991) *Of Revelation and Revolution: Christianity and Consciousness in South Africa*, Volume 1 Chicago, University of Chicago Press.

Samuel Cronwright-Schreiner (1924a) *The Life of Olive Schreiner* London: Fisher Unwin. The first biography of Schreiner, it has had great impact on subsequent interpretations of Schreiner's character and work, not least because he frequently destroyed original sources. Its approach is discussed in Chapter 4.

Samuel Cronwright-Schreiner (ed, 1924b) *The Letters of Olive Schreiner 1876-1920* London: Fisher Unwin. Schreiner's letters herein are often heavily bowdlerised and unsympathetically edited; Cronwright-Schreiner also destroyed many original letters. Discussed in Chapter 3, while Cronwright-Schreiner's wider approach is discussed in Chapter 4.

A.R. Cunningham (1973) "The new woman fiction of the 1890s" *Victorian Studies* 17, pp. 177-86.

Arthur Davey (1978) *The British Pro-Boers*, 1877-1902 Cape Town: Tafelberg.

Apollon Davidson & Irina Filatova (1993) "Olive Schreiner: a century in Russia" *English in Africa* 20, pp.39-48. An interesting discussion of Olive Schreiner's popularity in Russia from the 1890s through to the early 1930s. Her work was quickly translated, often without Schreiner's knowledge, with newspapers and magazines also publishing information about her life and her public remarks on different topics.

Apollon Davidson & Irina Filatova (1998) *The Russians and the Anglo-Boer War* Cape Town: Human & Rousseau. An interesting book on what is almost a 'vanished topic', the support by Russians for the Transvaal during the War. A short section confirms that this support "was shaped by one overwhelming influence from South Africa – that of Olive Schreiner" (p.190).

Linda Dowling (1979) "The decadent and the new woman in the 1890s" *Nineteenth Century Fiction* 33, pp. 434-53. An interesting discussion of the fact that both 'the decadent' and the "New Woman' were considered "dangerous avatars of the 'New'" (p.436), and not seen mutually antagonistic figures or principles, it starts with Ernest Dowson's admiration for Schreiner's work and especially for her narrative method.

Claire Draznin (1992) *My Other Self: The Letters of Olive Schreiner and Havelock Ellis 1884 – 1920* New York: P. Lang. A work of exemplary scholarship, containing the letters between Schreiner and Ellis archived in the Humanities Research Center in the USA. Discussed in Chapter 3.

W.E.B. Du Bois (1903/ 1996) *The Souls of Black Folk* Harmondsworth: Penguin Books. A book Olive Schreiner greatly admired. Its chapter "Of the Passing of the First-Born" was one that spoke to her own experience in a particularly direct way.

Saul Dubow (1995) *Scientific Racism in Modern South Africa* Cambridge: Cambridge University Press.

Jo Eadie (2001) "Boy talk: social theory and its discontents" *Sociology* 35, pp.575-82.

Havelock Ellis (1932) *Views and Reviews* London: Desmond Harmsworth.

Havelock Ellis (1940) *My Life* London: Heinemann. Ellis's book is coy about their early relationship and dismissive of Schreiner in middle age. It also elides the growing differences between them, about pacifism and war among other matters. However, it is still crucial reading for its account of Ellis himself and the intellectual and other circles he and Schreiner moved within.

Cynthia Enloe (1983) *Does Khaki Become You? The Militarisation of Women's Lives* London: Pluto Press.

Cynthia Enloe (1989) *Bananas, Beaches & Bases: Making Feminist Sense of International Politics* London: Pandora Press.

Cynthia Enloe (2000) *Maneuvers: The International Politics of Militarizing Women's Lives* Berkeley: University of California Press.

Ruth First and Ann Scott (1980) *Olive Schreiner: A Biography* London: Andre Deutch. This has become the 'standard work' on Olive Schreiner's life, although now in some respects superceded. Using archival materials, it explores the social and political milieu Schreiner moved in, and her South African and political involvements as well as her British and literary ones. Discussed in Chapter 4.

John Fisher (1971) *That Miss Hobhouse, The Life of a Great Feminist* London: Secker & Warburg.

Paul Foot (1982) "New Introduction" to Olive Schreiner *From Man to Man* London: Virago Press, pp.ix-xvii. Foot writes that he "was affected far more by *From Man to Man* than I was by... any other Olive Schreiner work, much though I loved all of it", but he is considerably better at enumerating its faults, which "are very obvious and have been rehearsed often enough by the experts"(p. xvii).

Zelda Friedlander (1967) *Until The Heart Changes: A Garland for Olive Schreiner* Cape Town: Tafelberg-Uitgewers. Composed by 'memories' of Olive Schreiner mainly from people who knew her, with a few from others (like Vera Brittain) who were influenced by her writing. Mixed with insubstantial pieces are some interesting items, including May Murray Parker's 'Letters and pets' memoir, R.F.M. Immelman's 'Olive Schreiner and her brother W.P.' provided through extracts from letters between them, and G.M.C. Cronwright's revelatory 'My uncle Cron'.

Marion Friedmann (1955) *Olive Schreiner, A Study in Latent Meanings* Johannesburg: University of Witwatersrand. A heavily psychoanalytic interpretation of Schreiner's life, seeing her putative ills and peculiarities of writing as the result of her relationship with her mother; it contains some unintentional hilarities. Discussed in Chapter 4.

Mohandas K. Gandhi (1968) *The Collected Works of Mohandas K. Gandhi, vols 8, 29, 41* Delhi: Publications Division, Ministry of Information & Broadcasting of the Government of India.

Sandra Gilbert and Susan Gubar (1988 and 1989) *No Man's Land: The Place of the Woman Writer in the Twentieth Century, Volume 1: The War of the Words, Volume 2: Sexchanges* New Haven: Yale University Press. Volume 1 briefly discusses Schreiner in the context of other 'new women' writers of the early twentieth century, as part of its broader concerns. Chapter 2, 'Home Rule' (pp.47-82), in Volume 2 discusses Schreiner's work (particularly *An African Farm*) with that of Charlotte Perkins Gilman, as the two major feminist polemicists of the turn of the century. Their assessment is the conventional one that "the central problems of this often incoherent work arise from its author's inability to find a plot commensurate with her own and her heroine's desires..." (p. 52), and they ignore any alternative view of what 'a novel' might be.

Charlotte Perkins Gilman (1899) *Women and Economics* (orig. published as Charlotte Perkins Stetson) London: G.M. Putnam's Sons

Nadine Gordimer (1980) "The prison-house of colonialism: Review of First & Scott's *Olive Schreiner*" in the *Times Literary Supplement* 15 August. Reprinted in (ed) Carol Barash *An Olive Schreiner Reader* London: Pandora Press, pp. 221-7; and in Cherry Clayton (ed) *Olive Schreiner* Johannesburg: McGraw-Hill, pp.95-97. An impassioned review that adopts a position fundamentally antithetical to First & Scott's analysis, and indeed to a feminist position more generally. Gordimer's approach is discussed in Chapter 4.

Jane Graves (1978) "Preface" to Olive Schreiner *Woman and Labour* London: Virago Press, pp.3-10. An account of 'the life' of Olive Schreiner is followed by Graves' interpretation of the central motif of *Woman and Labour*: "The basic theme is simple – the utter interdependence of men and woman. A civilisation which impedes the development of one must imperil the fulfillment of the other and in the end destroy itself" (p.9). Graves suggests that few feminist analysts have been so sympathetic to men as Schreiner, which I would re-phrase as Schreiner's recognition of the systemic nature of women's oppression and the damaging effects of this on men themselves.

Stephen Gray (1975) "Schreiner's Trooper at the hanging tree" *English in Africa* 2, pp.23-38 (also published in (ed) Cherry Clayton *Olive Schreiner* Johannesburg: McGraw-Hill, pp.198-209). More than twenty-five years after publication, still the most illuminating discussion of Schreiner's *Trooper Peter Halket*. Gray starts with commenting on Schreiner biocriticism, and points out that discussion of *Trooper Peter* typically sees it as failed propaganda, but that such judgments depend upon treating it as 'a conventional narrative novel' and so "make basic mistakes in literary criticism" (p.26). Gray provides a detailed discussion of the techniques that Schreiner used rather than the conventions she didn't.

Robert Green (1983) 'Stability and flux: the allotropic narrative of *An African Farm*' in (ed) Cherry Clayton *Olive Schreiner* Johannesburg: McGraw-Hill, pp.158-69. An illuminating discussion that proceeds from what Green rightly describes as "the startling modernity of Schreiner's Preface" (p.159) to *The Story of an African Farm*, with its ideas anticipating those more usually associated with high modernism of the 1920s and 1930s. He notes its confident and assured tone and suggests that these ideas were already fully worked out when the Preface was published in the second edition of 1883. As he concludes, once the Preface is taken seriously, then "many of the novel's 'difficulties' suddenly dissolve" (p.162).

Lyndall Gregg (1955) *Memories of Olive Schreiner* London: Chambers. Fascinating reminiscences of Olive Schreiner from one of her favourite nieces, Lyndall Gregg, the former 'Dot' Schreiner, elder daughter of Schreiner's brother Will. Much of what appears herein does not feature in any other source.

Phyllis Grosskurth (1980) *Havelock Ellis* London: Allen Lane. A thought-provoking biography of Havelock Ellis and the circles he moved within. Schreiner is a considerable presence in Grosskurth's earlier chapters; but her asthma is reduced to dosages of bromide and she is seen as over-emotional and unreliable. Grosskurth's discussion of Ellis' involvement in the *Letters* and the *Life* concludes that he bears considerable responsibility for what she describes as "this collection [*The Letters*], which gives such a distorted picture of Olive's life" (p. 299), and a *Life* which provides "a truncated, expurgated version of her life... making no attempt at psychological truth" (p.315). The implications of this assessment for her own account are not considered.

Susan Gubar (1994) "Feminist misogyny: Mary Wollstonecraft and the paradox of 'it takes one to know one'" *Feminist Studies* 20 pp.453-73. A rather odd piece concerned with 'feminist misogyny', starting with Mary Wollstonecraft, to look at what Gubar sees as the wider phenomenon of a 'negative attitude toward femininity and womanhood' by many feminists. Schreiner is lambasted for sex parasitism, which Gubar sees as a literal description, and a woman-hating one; and – in highly 'feminist misogynist' terms – Gubar also writes about *An African Farm* 'obsessing' and Schreiner suffering 'repeated thralldom' to men. It provides a loud example of the phenomenon it criticises, but appears oblivious to this.

Janice Harris (1993) "Feminist representations of wives and work: an 'almost irreconcilable' Edwardian debate" *Women's Studies* 22 pp.309-34. Contrasts three Edwardian feminist theorists on 'wives and work' with a number of grounded investigative pieces of writing. Schreiner's 'sex parasitism' is mistakenly seen as a literal description of the dependency of middle class wives on husbands, and Schreiner is mistakenly seen to have taken this idea from Gilman's writing. The three theory writings are seen as abstract and in a different conceptual universe from the other work discussed; that their rhetoric and argumentativeness was itself a form of political intervention is not considered by Harris.

Mike Hawkins (1997) *Social Darwinism in European and American Thought 1860 – 1945* Cambridge: Cambridge University Press. A very useful overview of debates, controversies and ideas associated with social Darwinism, and essential reading for anyone wanting to think seriously about Schreiner's position vis à vis that of Spencer, Pearson, Perkins Gilman and others.

Anthony Heard (1959) "Olive Schreiner and death" *English Studies in Africa* 2, 1, pp. 110–17. Argues that death pervades Schreiner's thoughts and that her work overall is an attempt to analyse it.

Ann Heilmann (1995) "'Over that bridge built with our bodies the entire human race will pass': A re-reading of Olive Schreiner's *From Man to Man*" *European Journal of Women's Studies* 2, pp.33-50. An interesting article which re-reads *From Man to Man* in the context of feminist criticism of Schreiner's work, noting the very different interpretations that exist of both the writing and the life of Schreiner. It considers elements of plot and characterisation in this novel in the light of "Schreiner's political, artistic and feminist philosophy" (p.35), and thus is also concerned with its lengthy didactic sections in which Rebekah offers expositions of feminist concerns. A sympathetic and insightful discussion of major themes within the novel is provided.

Ann Heilmann (1999) 'Dreams in black and white: women, race and self-sacrifice in Olive Schreiner's allegorical writings' in (eds) Heloise Brown, Madi Gilkes and Ann Kaloski-Naylor *White? Women: Critical Perspectives on Race and Gender* York, UK: Raw Nerve Books, pp.181-99.

D.L. Hobman (1955) *Olive Schreiner, Her Friends and Times* London: Watts & Co. This early biography avoids the interpretational excesses of some books on Schreiner, for instance those by Friedmann (1955) and Meintjes (1965), written around this time. Hobman – who became a feminist as a consequence of reading *Woman and Labour* – made use of material that remained in private hands at the time of writing, although many of her statements remain, annoyingly for today's researcher, unreferenced. Still worth reading for material which does not appear elsewhere.

John A. Hobson (1900) *War In South Africa* London: James Nisbet.

John A. Hobson (1902) *Imperialism: A Study* London: Allen & Unwin.

John A. Hobson (1938/1976) *Confessions of an Economic Heretic* Brighton: Harvester Press.

Myles Holloway (1989) "Thematic and structural organization in Olive Schreiner's *The Story of An African Farm*" *English in Africa* 16, pp.77-89. A useful rebuttal of the 'it's flawed because she can't plot or characterise' realist school of Schreiner criticism. Holloway works from Bahktin's notion of novelistic 'heteroglossia', including 'multiform' style and 'variform' voice, and competing perspectives and 'languages' within a text. For Holloway, heteroglossia is shown in Schreiner's work through her use of 'inserted genres'. Useful.

Richard Holmes (1985) *Footsteps: Adventures of a Romantic Biographer* London: Flamingo.

Susan Horton (1995) *Difficult Women, Artful Lives: Olive Schreiner and Isak Dinesen, In and Out of Africa* Baltimore: John Hopkins University Press. An opinionated and enjoyable book showing just what can be done with ideas strongly felt and passionately pursued. Horton's approach is to "read feminist theory through the lifeworks of Olive Schreiner and Isak Dinesen rather than reading Schreiner and Dinesen through the lens of any feminist theory" (p.28), pointing out that "Each woman's strategies of resistance seem to reveal themselves always and only in the quotidian, and in the 'residue' theory leaves behind: in all those messy particulars of behavior and style; in offhand and especially in parenthetical remarks in letters; in each women's carefully constructed, mutually self-canceling gestures and postures" (p.28). One of the most illuminating of recent discussions of Schreiner's work and a jolly good read.

Yvonne Kapp (1972 and 1976) *Eleanor Marx: Volume 1, Family Life 1855-1883,* and *Volume 2, The Crowded Years 1884 -1898* London: Virago Press. An interesting biography overall, although it provides a partial and unreliable account of the friendship between Olive Schreiner and Eleanor Marx. With no referenced evidence, it portrays Schreiner as a rampant emotionally damaging lesbian, while her need to question mutual friends about the reasons for Marx's suicide is presented as inexplicably prurient, rather than as an understandable need to find out why her friend had killed herself. Phew!

Theresa Kelley (1997) *Reinventing Allegory* Cambridge: Cambridge University Press.

Paula Krebs (1997) "Olive Schreiner's racialization of South Africa" *Victorian Studies* 40 pp.427-44. Focusing on Schreiner's 'personal' essays on South Africa, Krebs provides a valuable discussion of complexities regarding the 'voice' that Schreiner wrote in, her polemical/political purposes, and some of the more problematic things that arose from this. It mistakes Schreiner's use of the word 'evolution' as indicating social Darwinism and doesn't recognize her explicit use of it in a non-Darwinian way. This undercuts part of her argument, but, beyond this, this a very insightful discussion.

Paul Krebs (1999) *Gender, Race and the Writing of Empire: Public Discourse and the Boer War* Cambridge: Cambridge University Press.

Ursula Laredo (1969) "Olive Schreiner" *Journal of Commonwealth Literature* 8:1, pp. 107-24. An early discussion of Schreiner's life and writing which contains useful comments about the lasting impact of Emerson's ideas about the relationship between art and life on Schreiner. Laredo's articulation of the mythology surrounding *From Man to Man* reaches heights with "She was apparently working on the manuscript on the night of her death" (p. 120).

Zachary Leader (1996) *Revision and Romantic Authorship* Oxford: Clarendon Press.

Sally Ledger (1995) "The New Woman and the crisis of Victorianism" in (eds) Sally Ledger & Scott McCracken *Cultural Politics at the Fin de Siècle* Cambridge: Cambridge University Press, pp.22-44. Ledger proposes that "The rise of the New Woman at the fin de siècle was symptomatic of an ongoing challenge to the monolithic ideological certainties of Victorian Britain" (p.22), but concludes that "the New Woman and her advocates were in many respects complicit with residual elements of Victorian ideologies concerning gender roles, sexuality, 'race', empire and social class" (p.41). She also recognises that the 'New Woman' was neither a stable nor an internally consistent category. Interesting, but her discussion with regard to Schreiner contains a good deal of unsubstantiated contention (often from Barash) presented as 'the facts'.

Sally Ledger (1996) *The New Woman: Fiction and Feminism at the Fin de Siècle* Manchester: Manchester University Press. An elaboration of themes in Ledger 1995, pursued through socialism, imperialism, decadence, and an emergent lesbian identity, into the modern city. Her discussion of Schreiner's writing contains useful comment, but is also sometimes flat-footed or incorrect. Thus Ledger suggests that Schreiner as well as other New Woman novelists owed a debt to the 'fictional realism' of Flaubert, Zola and others (p.97, p.194), although Schreiner in fact detested Zola's writing and the literary approach associated with him; she states that in the last analysis Schreiner didn't contest women's maternal role, while Schreiner in fact rejected an essentialist notion of motherhood; and contends that Schreiner "had even gone so far as to defend the Boer's extermination of black Africans, during the early years of settlement" (p.65), a considerable misrepresentation of Schreiner's argument in *Thoughts on South Africa*.

Sally Ledger & Scott McCracken (eds, 1995) *Cultural Politics at the Fin de Siècle* Cambridge: Cambridge University Press. A readable but often annoying collection. The 'Introduction' (pp.1-10) raises, via Gillian Beer's (1989) work, some crucial questions about the relationship between 'historicism' and 'presentism', including regarding the notion of the 'fin de siècle' itself: "the fin de siècle was only an epoch of beginnings and endings if we look for them: the cultural forms and conflicts we find there are inescapably constructed by the double-look of the 1890s and the 1990s, and can only be reconstructed via the discursive practices available to us in the 1990s" (p.4). The editors recoil from Elaine Showalter's (1990) presentist view that the last fin de siècle is being repeated now, but their own account still overstates the interconnections. Many chapters ignore these wider questions and settle down to discuss particular aspects of the last fin de siècle. One of the most interesting contributions is McCracken's (1995), which meets such fundamental questions about the nature of the comparative project of a fin de siècle-based analysis head on.

Doris Lessing (1974) "Afterword to Olive Schreiner *The Story of An African Farm*" in her *A Small Personal Voice* (ed. Paul Schlueter), New York: Alfred Knopf, pp. 97-120. An interestingly written appreciation of Schreiner as a writer that also makes some astute comments about this particular novel. Not surprisingly, Lessing emphasises Schreiner in a South African context and takes seriously the work she produced there.

Phyllis Lewsen (ed, 1960 – 1969) *Selections from the Correspondence of John X. Merriman vol 1,1870-1890; vol 2, 1890-1898; vol 3, 1899-1905; vol 4, 1905-1924* Cape Town: Van Riebeeck Society.

Phyllis Lewsen (1983) "Olive Schreiner's political theories and pamphlets" in (ed) Cherry Clayton *Olive Schreiner* Johannesburg: McGraw-Hill, pp.212-20. Lewsen describes Schreiner as "both a creative and a polemical writer", a dichotomous way of reading her work shared with Richard Rive (1973a). Lewsen's discussion is one of the few specifically concerned with changes over time in Schreiner's writing, and it suggests that her alternation of two styles (the 'plain' and the 'ribbed') became insufficient to express "the vigour and vehemence of her ideas" (p.213), so that her writing moved from the creative and the novel, to the pamphlet and article and the polemical.

Jill Liddington (1984) *Selina Cooper 1964-1946* London: Virago Press.

Constance Lytton (1914) *Prisons and Prisoners* London: William Heinemann.

Anne McClintock (1995) *Imperial Leather: Race, Gender and Sexuality in the Colonial Context* London: Routledge. *Imperial Leather* (says it all, really) is concerned with the "dangerous and contradictory liaison – between imperial and anti-imperial power; money and sexuality; violence and desire; labor and resistance" (p.4). McClintock interestingly recognises that Schreiner's writings were at the edge of radical analyses of imperialism, empire and 'race'. A good read that makes excellent use of Schreiner's own writings and the secondary sources. Discussed in Chapter 4.

Scott McCracken (1995) "Postmodernism, a Chance to reread?" in (eds) Sally Ledger & Scott McCracken *Cultural Politics at the Fin de Siècle* Cambridge: Cambridge University Press, pp.267-89. In discussing Conrad's *Chance*, McCracken discusses whether and to what extent the classifications of modernism and postmodernism are valid as periodising categories; whether the "related crises in the fields of gender, 'race' and class relations are specific to the cultural dominants of the nineteenth century, and must be (but cannot easily be) compared with the postmodernism of the 1990s" (p.274); and whether the complex relation between high and low culture was responsible for this book's narrative disruptions or whether these are instead postmodernist forms. His discussion raises interesting questions that are equally pertinently asked about Schreiner's work.

Scott McCracken (1996) "Stages of sand and blood: the performance of gendered subjectivity in Olive Schreiner's colonial allegories" *Women's Writing* 3, pp.49-73. McCracken uses ideas about performativity drawn from the work of Judith Butler, to look at Schreiner's understanding of colonialism as "one of the constraints that limits the performance of a New Woman subjectivity" (p.2) through a heavily theorised re-reading of various of her allegorical writings. He concludes that, while identity is always a performance, "we need to look carefully at the stage on which the performance takes place" (p.13).

S. Maccoby (1938) *English Radicalism 1855-1886* London: Allen & Unwin.

S. Maccoby (1953) *English Radicalism 1886-1914* London: Allen & Unwin.

Nicki Lee Manos & Meri-Jane Rochelson (eds, 1994) *Transforming Genres: New Approaches to British Fiction of the 1890s* New York: St Martin's Press. David Gryll's review ("The mystery of Holme's ear" *Times Literary Supplement* 16 June 1995 p.14) of this says it all: "The admirable aim of the[se] critical essays… is to restore to 1890s fiction 'a sense of multiplicity, complexity and abundance'… Abandon the perspectives of modernism, adopt more recent critical approaches, and a fresh 1890s emerges. This is stirring stuff, but what in fact emerges is an all-too familiar 1990s… the current compulsive scanning of literature for signs of racism and sexism. Since these evils were ubiquitous in Victorian Britain, it is not too difficult to achieve a high hit-rate. The trick, though, consists in detecting their traces where few have found them before". A hit, a very palpable hit.

Shula Marks & Stanley Trapido (1979) "Lord Milner and the South African state" *History Workshop* 8, 50-80. The foundational text in current historiographical interpretations of the 'scramble' for southern Africa and the origins of the South African War. Schreiner's published and unpublished writings anticipate their analysis in interesting ways.

Shula Marks & Stanley Trapido (1992) "Lord Milner and the South African state reconsidered" in (ed) Michael Twaddle *Imperialism, the State and the Third World* London: British Academic Press, pp. 50–80. Marks and Trapido's reply to critics of their earlier paper, focusing on the centrality of gold.

Shula Marks & Anthony Atmore (eds, 1980) *Economy and Society in Pre-Industrial South Africa* London: Longman.

Shula Marks & Richard Rathbone (eds, 1982) *Industrialisation and Social Change in South Africa* London: Longman.

B.W. Matz (1909) "George Meredith as publisher's reader" *The Fortnightly Review* vol 86, pp.282-98. An interesting account of George Meredith's work as literary adviser to Chapman and Hall. Matz's comments on Schreiner manuscripts is based on Meredith's written reports as well as his own memory, in particular concerning three entries in Meredith's record book. In 1881 'Saints and Sinners' by Ralph Iron is pronounced "'Plot silly. Early part well written'"; on 2 May 1882 his comment on '*The Story of An African Farm*' is "'Return to author for revision'"; and he records its acceptance on 10 August (p.288).

John Maynard (1993) *Victorian Discourses on Sexuality and Religion* New York: Cambridge University Press.

Johannes Meintjes (1965) *Olive Schreiner: Portrait of a South African Woman* Johannesburg: Keartland. An early biographical study which, thirty years on, reads as opinionatedly sexist and amateur in its workmanship (it gets the plot of *Undine* wrong). It treats extracts from Schreiner novels as though they were straightforward accounts of her life. His interpretations are whacky and impossible to tie to any sources of evidence – thus Olive Schreiner was both a heterosexual masochist, and had 'inverted tendencies'. A period piece.

Sara Mills (1994) "Reading as/like a feminist" in (ed) Sara Mills *Gendering the Reader* London: Harvester Wheatsheaf, pp.25-46.

Percy Alport Molteno (1896) *A Federal South Africa* London: Low, Marston.

Gerald Monsman (1991) *Olive Schreiner's Fiction: Landscape and Power* New Brunswick: Rutger University Press. Contains some interesting remarks on Schreiner's use of allegory. Monsman sees Schreiner's position within a colonial society, grappling with internal divisions and separations as well as structural change, as definitional. Schreiner's work is interpreted as a rewriting of the 'master plot' of religion, and as particularly concerned with the topographical nature of her imagery.

Patricia Morris (1983) "Biographical accounts of Olive Schreiner" in (eds) Malvern van Wyk Smith & Don Maclennan *Olive Schreiner and After: Essays on South African Literature in Honour of Guy Butler* Cape Town: David Philip, pp.3-13.

H.W. Nevinson (1923) *Changes and Chances* London: James Nisbet.

Walter Nimocks (1968) *Milner's Young Men: The 'Kindergarden' in Edwardian Imperial Affairs* London: Hodder & Stoughton.

Sylvia Pankhurst (1932) *The Home Front* London: The Cresset Library Reprints.

Ruth Parkin-Gounelas (1991) *Fictions of the Female Self: Charlotte Bronte, Olive Schreiner, Katherine Mansfield* London: Macmillan. Erroneously reads Schreiner's own ideas and views from her novels, particularly the character of Rebekah in *From Man To Man*. Repeats the truism, but referencing no source, that Schreiner worked on the manuscript for over forty years.

Neil Parsons (1998) *King Khama, Emperor Joe and the Great White Queen: Victorian Britain Through African Eyes* Chicago: University of Chicago Press.

Lynne Pearce (1997) *Feminism and the Politics of Reading* London: Arnold.

Richard Peck (1997) *A Morbid Fascination: White Prose and Politics in Apartheid South Africa* Westport, Connecticutt: Greenwood Press.

Karl Pearson (1887) *The Ethic of Freethought* London: Black.

Ian Phimister (1993) "Unscrambling the scramble for southern Africa: The Jameson Raid and the South African War revisited" *South African Historical Journal* 28 pp.203-20. Sensible and very useful review of the major 'positions' taken on the Raid and its relationship to the South African War. Phimister concludes none of these is conclusive, each contain useful advances, and outlines where further research might go. In considering historians' search for the 'real causes' of the Raid and the 'real' relationship between it and the war, however, Phimister doesn't consider that people 'on the ground' might have been motivated by 'unreal' understandings but which nonetheless 'really' led to particular courses of behaviour.

Andrew Porter (1980) *The Origins of the South African War: Joseph Chamberlain and the Diplomacy of Imperialism 1895-9* Manchester: Manchester University Press.

Andrew Porter (1997) "'Cultural imperialism' and Protestant missionary enterprise, 1780-1914" *Journal of Imperial and Commonwealth History* 25, pp. 367–91.

Bernard Porter (1968) *Critics of Empire: British Radical Attitudes to Colonialism in Africa 1895-1914* London: Macmillan.

Lyn Pykett (1992) *The 'Improper' Feminine: The Woman's Sensation Novel and the New Woman Writing* London: Routledge.

Judith Raiskin (1996) *Snow on the Cane Fields: Women's Writing and Creole Subjectivity* Minneapolis: University of Minnesota. Raiskin uses 'creole' as a plastic term to encompass white as well as black, because for her it turns on the colonial experience and linguistic signifiers which exemplifies the creole as outsider. 'Creole subjectivity' is used to discuss the work of Olive Schreiner, Jean Rhys, Michelle Cliff and Zoë Wicomb. Raiskin's two chapters on Schreiner contain often sensible and judicious discussions of work that many commentators ignore or gloss. Oddly, they also contain Raiskin's surprise that Schreiner's thinking was influenced by iffy nineteenth century ideas about 'race' and colonialism.

C.P. Ravilious (1977) "'Saints and Sinners': an unidentified Olive Schreiner manuscript" *Journal of Commonwealth Literature* 12, no 1, pp.1–11. From Matz's (1909) account of George Meredith reading an 1881 manuscript of Schreiner's 'Saints and Sinners' and using Schreiner's brief journal entries, Ravilious argues this could not be an earlier version of *The Story of An African Farm* and there is good circumstantial evidence for it being the manuscript which was later published as *From Man To Man*.

Rykie Van Reenen (ed (1984) *Emily Hobhouse Boer War Letters* Cape Town: Human & Rousseau.

Olive Renier (1984) *Before The Bonfire* Shipstone-on-Stour, Warwickshire: Drinkwater. Olive Renier, previously Corthorn, was the adopted daughter of Schreiner's friend Alice Corthorn. Olive Schreiner is the subject of Chapter 3 and Havelock Ellis of Chapter 4 of Renier's book, and there are also snippets of information about other feminist and socialist friends of Corthorn, including Eleanor Marx, William Morris and Edith Lees. Interesting.

Richard Rive (1973a) "An infinite compassion: a critical comparison of Olive Schreiner's novels" *Contrast* 8:1, pp.25-43. Rive's rather flat-footed approach here is that: "The works of Olive Schreiner may be roughly divided into two sections, her works of imagination and her polemical writings. She seems to have devoted the earlier years of her life to her works of imagination and the latter part to her polemical writings" (p.27).

Richard Rive (1973b) "New light on Olive Schreiner" *Contrast* 8:4, pp.40-7. An interesting discussion of the way Rive's archival work led him to the conclusion Schreiner had completed more work than was published after her death by Cronwright-Schreiner. It deals with the possibility of the 'missing novel' of "New Rush", which Rive concludes was "apparently completed" (p.41). It also points out there were different versions of the end of *From Man to Man* from that imposed by Cronwright-Schreiner; Rive includes within this article the ending Schreiner had written to Karl Pearson in 1886.

Richard Rive (1974) "Introduction to 'Diamond Fields', and an edited version of the manuscript" *English in Africa* 1, pp.1-29. Rive's Introduction (pp.1-12) provides an account, insofar as this can be known, of the history of the fragment "Diamond Fields". His view is that this is a chapter in the manuscript of "New Rush", a novel which he thinks Schreiner completed (her letters describes chapters and episodes within them and a full manuscript seems to have been read by Havelock Ellis and his sister) but was later lost or destroyed. He concludes, hopefully, "The complete manuscript might yet be found" (p.10).

Richard Rive (1975) "Introduction" to Olive Schreiner *The Story of An African Farm* Johannesburg: Donker, pp.7-20. A brief account of the publishing history of *An African Farm* followed by a detailed discussion of its central themes and two 'interpolations' (the allegory of Waldo's stranger, and the story of Blenkins and Sannie), which Rive treats as a distraction from the 'real' plot of the novel.

Richard Rive (ed, 1987) *Olive Schreiner Letters: Volume I 1871-1899* Oxford: Oxford University Press. Rive's "Preface" notes that the recent resurgence of interest in Schreiner has been the product of a revaluation of her life and work which "has depended for its source material on the great volume of her letters which still survive in manuscript form, some of them newly discovered and most only now being explored systematically by researchers" (p. vii). This is undoubtedly in large part due to Rive's own work. Discussed in Chapter 4.

Brian Roberts (1987) *Cecil Rhodes: Flawed Colossus* New York: Norton.

Roland Robinson and John Gallagher with Alice Denny (1981, 2nd edition) *Africa and the Victorians: The Official Mind of Imperialism* London: Macmillan.

Jacqueline Rose (1991) *The Haunting of Sylvia Plath* London: Virago Press.

Robert I. Rotberg with Miles F. Shore (1988) *The Founder: Cecil Rhodes and the Pursuit of Power* New York: Oxford University Press.

Sheila Rowbotham (1977) "Edward Carpenter: Prophet of the New Life" in Sheila Rowbotham & Jeffrey Weeks *Socialism and the New Life: The Personal and Sexual Politics of Edward Carpenter and Havelock Ellis* London: Pluto Press, pp. 25-138. An extremely useful and readable short account of the socialist and freethinking circles Carpenter moved in, as well as key aspects of his own work and life, still not superseded by later work.

Sheila Rowbotham (2000) *Promise of a Dream: Remembering the Sixties* London: Allen Lane the Penguin Press.

Karel Schoeman (1991) *Olive Schreiner: A Woman in South Africa 1855-1881*, Johannesburg: Jonathan Ball Publishers. Originally published in Afrikaans in 1989, this is the most detailed and accurate account of Schreiner's life to when she left South Africa for England in 1881, with a detailed look at what Schreiner was writing at different points in time and an interesting overview of South African literature during Schreiner's lifetime. Its interpretational approach is discussed in Chapter 4.

Karel Schoeman (1992) *Only An Anguish To Live Here: Olive Schreiner and the Anglo-Boer War, 1899-1902* Cape Town: Human & Rousseau. A detailed examination, richly supplemented by photographs, of Schreiner's life and activities over the period of the South African War. Written for a more 'popular' audience than Schoeman 1991. Discussed in the context of Schoeman's wider approach in Chapter 4.

Elaine Showalter (1978) *A Literature of Their Own: British Women Writers from Brontë to Lessing* London: Virago Press, esp pp.182-215. Many of Showalter's remarks herein about Schreiner are dated: she didn't like other women, her female characters "seem monstrous, swollen and destructive" (p.196), while Schreiner herself is described as compulsively neurotic and unproductive as a writer. Probably most embarrassing of all, given Showalter's 1993 collection, is "For years Schreiner published only 'Dreams', sentimental allegories in the most nauseating fin-de-siècle style" (p.197).

Elaine Showalter (1990) *Sexual Anarchy: Gender and Culture at the Fin de Siècle* London: Bloomsbury. A highly idiosyncratic discussion which proposes that the parallels between the last and this present fin de siècle irresistibly point to the existence of common 'crises of ending'; it overstates like mad, but enjoyably so.

Elaine Showalter (ed, 1993) *Daughters of Decadence: Women Writers of the Fin-de-Siècle* London: Virago Press.

Elaine Showalter (ed, 1997) *Scribbling Women* New Brunswick: Rutgers University Press.

Iain Smith (1996) *The Origins of the South African War 1899-1902* London: Addison-Wesley Longman.

S.B. Spies (1977) *Methods of Barbarism? Roberts and Kitchener and Civilians in the Boer Republics January 1900 – May 1902* Kaapstad: Human and Rousseau.

Liz Stanley (1983) "Olive Schreiner: new women, free women, all women" in (ed) Dale Spender *Feminist Theorists* London: The Women's Press, pp.229-43. An introductory account of 'the life and times' of Olive Schreiner, looking at themes and issues across the range of Schreiner's writing, including the particular resonance that childhood, sisterhood and death held for her, and the importance of the South African karoo to her ideas.

Liz Stanley (1992a) *The Auto/Biographical I: The Theory and Practice of Feminist Auto/Biography* Manchester: Manchester University Press. Concerned with developing a 'feminist auto/biography'; this idea displaces referential and foundational claims of writers and researchers, unsettles notions of 'science', problematises the 'expert' claims of research, and questions the power issues most researchers silence or disclaim. Chapter 7 is an in-depth analysis of Cronwright Schreiner's (1924a) *The Life*.

Liz Stanley (1992b) "Romantic friendship? Issues in researching lesbian history and biography" *Women's History Review* 1, 2: pp.189–217

Liz Stanley (2000a) "Is there life in the contact zone? auto/biographical practices and the field of representation in writing past lives" in (eds) Alison Donnell & Pauline Polkey *Representing Lives* London: Macmillan, pp.3-30.

Liz Stanley (2000b) "Encountering the imperial and colonial past through Olive Schreiner's *Trooper Peter Halket* of Mashonaland" *Women's Writing* 7, 2: pp.197-219.

Liz Stanley (2000c) "A 'secret history' of local mourning: the South African War, the Vrouemonument and state commemoration" (in press, *Society in Transition*).

Liz Stanley (2000d) "Mourning becomes…: the spaces between lives lived and lives written" unpublished paper, 4th European Feminist Research Conference, Bologna, Italy, September.

Liz Stanley (2000e) "*For Sociology*, Gouldner's and ours" in (eds) John Eldridge, John MacInnes, Sue Scott, Chris Warhurst and Anne Witz For *Sociology: Legacies and Prospects* Durham, UK: *sociologypress*, pp.56-82.

Liz Stanley (2001a) "Mimesis, metaphor and representation: holding out an Olive branch to the emergent Schreiner canon" *Women's History Review* 10, 1, pp.27-50.

Liz Stanley (2001b) "Holding out an Olive branch: mimesis and alterity in the feminist interpretation of lives" in (ed) Magda Michaelsens *Narrating Selves and Others: Authority and Authorship in Feminist Auto/Biography* The Hague: Martinus Nijhof.

Liz Stanley (2001c) *Electra's Grief: Mourning, Vengeance & Postmemory of the Concentration Camps of the South African War, 1899–1902* manuscript in progress.

Liz Stanley and Sue Wise (2000) "But the empress has no clothes! Some awkward questions about the 'missing revolution' in feminist theory" *Feminist Theory* 1, pp.261-88.

Daiva Stasiulis & Nira Yuval-Davies (eds, 1995) *Unsettling Settler Societies: Articulations of Gender, Race, Ethnicity and Class* London: Sage Publications.

Carolyn Steedman (1995) *Strange Dislocations: Childhood and the Idea of Human Interiority* London: Virago Press.

Richard Stites (1978) *The Women's Liberation Movement in Russia: Feminism, Nihilism and Bolshevism 1860 – 1930* Princeton, New Jersey: Princetown University Press.

Anne Summers (1991) "Correspondents of Havelock Ellis" *History Workshop Journal* 32, pp.167-83. A brief useful guide to the Havelock Ellis collection in the British Library in London, including the papers of Edith Lees (to whom Ellis was married), focusing on Ellis's major correspondents. Olive Schreiner appears briefly.

Keith Terrance Surridge (1998) *Managing the South African War 1899-1902: Politicians v. Generals* Woodbridge, Suffolk: The Royal Historical Society & The Boydell Press. Excellent stuff.

Les Switzer (ed 1997) *South Africa's Alternative Press: Voices of Protest and Resistance, 1880-1960* Cambridge: Cambridge University Press.

Frank W. Sykes (1897) *With Plumer in Matabeleland: an account of the operations of the Matabeleland Relief Force during the rebellion of 1896* Westminster, London: Archibald Constable & Co.

Arthur Symons (1899) *The Symbolist Movement in Literature* London: William Heinemann.

Arthur Symons (1904) *Studies in Prose & Verse* London: J.M. Dent.

Mordechai Tamarkin (1996) *Cecil Rhodes and the Cape Afrikaners: The Imperial Colossus and the Colonial Parish Pump* London: Frank Cass.

Mordechai Tamarkin (1997) "Milner, the Cape Afrikaners, and the outbreak of the South African War" *Journal of Imperial and Commonwealth History* 25, pp.392-414.

Miles Taylor (1991) "Imperium et libertas? Rethinking the radical critique of imperialism during the nineteenth century" *Journal of Imperial and Commonwealth History* 19, pp.1-23.

James Thompson (1880) *The City of Dreadful Night and Other Poems* London: Reeves & Turner.

Leonard Thompson (1960) *The Unification of South Africa, 1902 – 1910* Oxford: Oxford University Press.

Nicola Thompson (1995) *Reviewing Sex: Gender and the Perception of Victorian Novels* Basingstoke: Macmillan.

Mary Beth Tierney-Tello (1996) *Allegories of Transgression and Transformation: Experimental Fiction by Women Writing under Dictatorship* New York: State University of New York Press.

Stanley Trapido (1980) "'The friends of the natives': merchants, peasants and the political and ideological structure of liberalism in the Cape, 1854-1910" in (eds) Shula Marks & Anthony Atmore *Economy and Society in Pre-Industrial South Africa* London: Longman, pp.247-74. Crucial reading on the divisions within liberals 'on the ground' and also the contradictions between the 'grand tradition' of Liberalism and the 'local tradition' in the Cape.

Itala Vivan (ed, 1991) *The Flawed Diamond: Essays on Olive Schreiner* Sydney: Dangaroo Press. A disappointing and superficial collection. The majority of the essays deal with *An African Farm*; *From Man to Man* merits one discussion and the rest of Schreiner's writing is notable mainly for its absence.

Karin Wagner (1994) *Re-reading Nadine Gordimer* Bloomington: Indiana University Press.

Cherryl Walker (1982) *Women and Resistance in South Africa* London: Onyx Press.

Cherryl Walker (ed, 1990) *Women and Gender in South Africa* to 1945 Cape Town: David Philip.

Eric Walker (1937) *W. P. Schreiner: A South African* London: Oxford University Press. A guarded biography of Olive Schreiner's brother Will which gives little away about his political life and almost entirely excises his personal life. There are tantalisingly brief glimpses of his relationship with his sister, in particular concerning the influence that Schreiner's political views and analyses had on him.

Judith Walkowitz (1986) "Science, feminism, and romance: The Men and Women's Club, 1885-1889" *History Workshop Journal* no.21, pp. 37-59. A longer reworked version of this is in Walkowitz's (1992) *City of Dreadful Night*. Both this original article and the later version are usefully compared with Bland's (1990) discussion of the Club.

Judith Walkowitz (1992) *City of Dreadful Delight: Narratives of Sexual Danger in Late-Victorian London* London: Virago Press. Walkowitz's concern is with representations of the city and its sexual dangers in London in the later 1880s. Two chapters deal with W.T. Stead's 'new journalism' of the *Pall Mall Gazette* around the 'Maiden Tribute' articles, while another chapter contains an account of the discussions and representations debated, privately as well as publicly, in the Men and Women's Club. Schreiner features in a 'walk-on' part, through other people's representations of her and her ideas. Much praised in reviews, Walkowitz's study bears the imprint of deconstructionist ideas about representation/history in what may be too great a measure for some readers, too little for others.

Francis Wheen (1999) *Karl Marx* London: Fourth Estate. Riveting reading.

Oscar Wilde (1913/1891) "The Preface" to *The Picture of Dorian Gray* Paris: Ye Olde Paris Booke-Shoppe.

Oscar Wilde (1950) "The decay of lying" and "The critic as artist" in (ed) Hesketh Pearson *The Essays of Oscar Wilde* London: Methuen.

Oscar Wilde (1962) *The Letters of Oscar Wilde* (ed) Rupert Hart-Davis) London: Rupert Hart-Davis.

Cherry Wilhelm (see also Clayton) (1979) "Olive Schreiner, child of Queen Victoria: *Stories, Dreams and Allegories*" *English in Africa* 6 pp. 63-69. A discussion of Schreiner's allegories around two kinds of literature: the imaginative presentation of the real world, and presentations of another world related to the real world by analogy (and in which latter category allegory finds its place). Wilhelm interestingly discusses Schreiner's use of allegory as "extended narrative metaphors for the soul's timeless quest for the truth, but modified by the particular dilemma of the nineteenth-century soul" (p.63), although also indicating her concern to "speak to the burning concerns of her own time" (p.68).

Brian Willan (1984) *Sol Plaatje: South African Nationalist 1876 – 1932* London: Hutchinson.

Virginia Woolf (1979/1925) "Olive Schreiner" in Virginia Woolf *Women and Writing* (Introduced by Michele Barrett) London: The Women's Press, pp. 180-83. Woolf's review of Cronwright Schreiner's *The Letters* suggests that the "jumble and muddle of odds and ends, plans and arrangements, bulletins of health and complaints of landladies" (p. 180) of Schreiner's letters requires the reader to impose some unity on them. For Woolf, this comes through contemplation of the discrepancy between what Schreiner desired and what she actually achieved, concluding that "She remains even now... too uncompromising a figure to be so disposed of" and that "Olive Schreiner was one half of a great writer; a diamond marred by a flaw" (pp. 182-3).

William Worger (1987) *South Africa's City of Diamonds: Mine Workers and Monopoly Capitalism in Kimberley*, 1867-1895 New Haven: Yale University Press.

William Butler Yeats (1955) *Autobiographies* London: Macmillan.

Elisabeth Young Bruehl (1998) *Subject To Biography: Psychoanalysis, Feminism, and Writing Women's Lives* Cambridge, Mass.: Harvard University Press.

Shamoon Zamir (1995) *W.E.B. Du Bois and American Thought, 1888-1903* Chicago: University of Chicago Press.

Index

Name Index